WINE TRAILS
USA & CANADA

INTRODUCTION

We've all experienced it on our travels - whether watching a sunset in California with a glass of chilled Chardonnay or at a barbeque in Texas with a beefy Shiraz - when a local wine could not be more perfectly suited to the moment.

Tasting wine in the place it was made can be a revelation. This book plots a course through 40 of North America's greatest wine regions, with weekend-long itineraries in each. We encounter California's cutting-edge wine scene and the incredible reds being made in Texas' hill country. We venture into the hip urban wineries of Santa Barbara and Portland; travel through Canada's remote Okanagan region; and head out east to explore New York, Virginia, Maryland and more. In each, our expert local writers recommend rewarding wineries to visit and the most memorable wines to taste.

This is a book for casual quaffers; there's no impenetrable language about malolactic fermentation or scoring systems. Instead, we meet some of the continent's most enthusiastic and knowledgeable winemakers and learn about each region's wines in their own words. It is this personal introduction to wine, in its home, that is at the heart of wine-touring's appeal.

CONTENTS

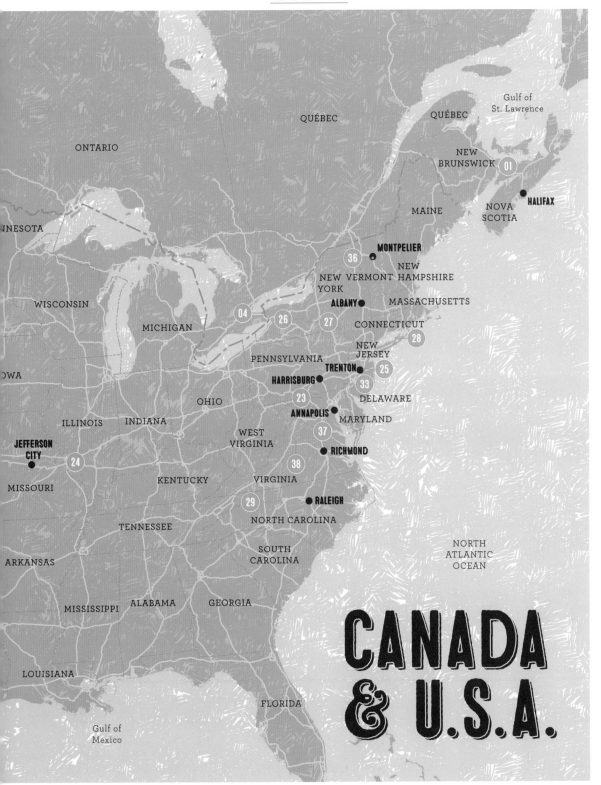

ONTARIO

QUÉBEC

QUÉBEC

Gulf of
St. Lawrence

NEW
BRUNSWICK 01

MINNESOTA

WISCONSIN

MICHIGAN

MAINE

NOVA
SCOTIA

HALIFAX

MONTPELIER

36

NEW VERMONT
YORK

NEW
HAMPSHIRE

ALBANY

MASSACHUSETTS

04

26

27

CONNECTICUT

28

IOWA

PENNSYLVANIA

NEW
JERSEY

TRENTON

25

HARRISBURG

33

OHIO

23

DELAWARE

ILLINOIS

INDIANA

ANNAPOLIS

MARYLAND

JEFFERSON
CITY

24

WEST
VIRGINIA

37

RICHMOND

MISSOURI

KENTUCKY

38

VIRGINIA

29

RALEIGH

TENNESSEE

NORTH CAROLINA

ARKANSAS

SOUTH
CAROLINA

NORTH
ATLANTIC
OCEAN

MISSISSIPPI

ALABAMA

GEORGIA

LOUISIANA

FLORIDA

Gulf of
Mexico

CANADA
& U.S.A.

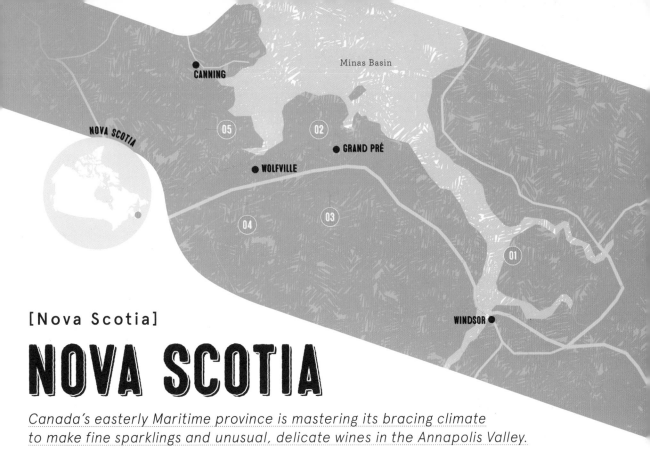

Minas Basin

CANNING

NOVA SCOTIA

05

02

GRAND PRÉ

WOLFVILLE

04

03

01

WINDSOR

[Nova Scotia]

NOVA SCOTIA

Canada's easterly Maritime province is mastering its bracing climate to make fine sparklings and unusual, delicate wines in the Annapolis Valley.

Overflowing farm shops, authentic clapboard settler villages and handwritten pick-your-own fruit billboards signal your arrival in the Annapolis Valley. This is Nova Scotia's bucolic breadbasket, where independent, fair-trade and community-minded enterprises win over both locals and visitors, and fledgling wineries are down-to-earth affairs with no lofty ambitions beyond their organic farming principles.

Though today's wine industry is in its infancy, it was the 17th-century French Acadian settlers who first cultivated grapes here. Nova Scotia's cool climate, enough to send a shiver down the vine tendrils, comes with its challenges for viticulturists – the pulse of the province pounds along with the ocean waves and it's only granted 120 annual days of sunshine compared with about 300 in, say, Australia. Around the Annapolis Valley, vineyards border the tumultuous Bay of Fundy where the highest tides in the world gush in and out each day. The

sea-drenched terroir lends itself to light, zesty or floral whites, acidic reds and sparkling wines.

The local winemakers have had to get inventive to achieve complexity and variety, tearing up the rule books to make way for imaginative techniques, little-known grapes and individual wines. Some have even been engineered for the climate and cuisine: Tidal Bay, the region's signature appellation, is produced to strict criteria and designed to pair with Nova Scotia's local seafood (this is lobster country, by the way). Virtually every winery in the province produces its own version but you'll find it characteristically light, almost crystal clear, with a zing that lashes the mouth like the North Atlantic Ocean.

Nova Scotia is a seasonal destination, so come June to September to ensure all doors are open. The hub of the valley – and a good base for touring – is Wolfville, with its parade of 19th-century, candy-coloured houses, fair-trade coffee shops and big community heart.

GET THERE
Nova Scotia's international airport is in Halifax on the south coast. Hire a car for the 1hr drive to Wolfville in the Annapolis Valley.

① AVONDALE SKY WINERY

See those settler churches gracing every tranquil village in the Annapolis Valley? Your first stop is one of these. Deconsecrated churches that have fallen out of use are being reimagined across Nova Scotia, and the one that houses Avondale Sky was bought for a mere US$1. Owners Stewart and Lorraine fell for the unloved 19th-century structure and decided that rather than see it destroyed, they would use the Bay of Fundy's phenomenal tidal power to relocate the church to their vineyard. It took months to find the right tidal window to transport the building up the river by barge, but it now serves as Avondale Sky's tasting room, illuminated by original stained-glass windows, and the winery has become known as 'the floating church'.

Most of Nova Scotia's signature grapes are hybrid styles that thrive in the province's cool climate. A good one to try here is L'Acadie Blanc, a fuller-bodied grape similar in style to Chardonnay. The name comes from the word Acadia, the historical term for the maritime lands of northeastern North America once ruled by the French, including parts of Nova Scotia.

The winery is a minor detour off the route to Wolfville from Halifax. During the summer months Avondale Sky's D'Vine Morsels restaurant serves lunch, and it's possible to tour the vineyard. *www.avondalesky.com; tel 902-253-2047; 80 Avondale Cross Rd, Newport Landing; 11am–4.30pm daily* ✕

② DOMAINE DE GRAND PRÉ

Just outside Wolfville, the Unesco-inscribed arable plains and marshlands of Grand Pré were toiled over by the Acadians in the 17th century. Archaeological relics, including original dykes and sluices, are considered an exceptional example of how the first European settlers adapted to life on the North American Atlantic coast. You can learn about the legacy of the Grand Pré National Historic Site through information boards inside the winery and at a panoramic lookout point behind the estate, reached by following a nature trail through the vineyards.

The wine estate is arguably the grande dame of the Annapolis Valley, occupying several historic buildings and producing award-winning vintages. Its owners have concentrated mainly on styles of wine that reflect Nova Scotia's clay-rich, acidic soil and oceanic climate – such as Ortega, Riesling and Seyval Blanc – and have even joined forces with Agriculture Canada to work on hardy local varieties. Castel is the heaviest red produced here, but even that could only be considered medium-bodied compared with wines from the US or Australia.

The vineyard also makes ice wines from vidal and muscat

01 The memorial church at Grand Pré National Historical Site

02 The barrel room at Planter's Ridge

03 Pruning the vines at Avondale Sky

04 Flowers and vines at Avondale Sky

grapes, picked by night in the depths of winter and pressed when frozen. Most curious and memorable, though, is its decadent Pomme d'Or cream liqueur – made with apples but exhibiting the viscosity of an ice wine. Make a dinner reservation in advance for the vineyard's fine-dining Le Caveau restaurant. *www.grandprewines.ns.ca; tel 902-542-1753; 11611 Highway 1; 10am–6pm daily* ✖ 💲

03 LUCKETT VINEYARDS

The USP at this Instagram-friendly winery is its bright red phone box – a British design classic that nobody expects to see in a field of vines framed by the looking-glass Bay of Fundy. The owner, Pete Luckett, is a hugely successful British-born, Canadian entrepreneur whom staff call 'the rockstar of retail and wizard of wineries', and his wine shop is stacked like the best-dressed high-street window. Out front, Luckett's canopied terrace bistro is the place to come for a casual lunch with gorgeous views.

Nova Scotian reds are typically quite acidic due to the cool climate, but Luckett's signature Phone Box Red has been cleverly engineered: a blend of four local grapes are partially dried in a heat-controlled environment for fuller flavour, then aged in Hungarian and American oak, to pack a greater punch with tannic notes of raisins and prunes.

If you stay for lunch, order the estate's particularly good, zesty Tidal Bay. This official appellation

The best sipping terrace belongs to Planters Ridge, an understated village winery in a 150-year-old timber barn

wine of Nova Scotia is made for food pairing – especially with local salmon, scallops and lobster. Round off your visit with a photo in front of the phone box, or even a phone call – the line still works and it's free to call anywhere in North America... *www.luckettvineyards.com; tel 902-542-2600; 1293 Grand Pré Rd, Wallbrook; tours 11am & 3pm daily May–Oct* ✖

04 BENJAMIN BRIDGE

For one of the most entertaining winery tours in the valley head to the barnyard hubbub at Benjamin Bridge, where vineyard pigs act as sustainable farmhands and beehives have been erected to encourage natural pollination among the organic vines.

North Americans can't get enough of the Nova 7 sparkling for which the winery is best known. Fizz became Benjamin Bridge's calling card when, as a winery

guide explains, founder 'Gerry took it upon himself to start digging out Champagne caves in the hills behind the vineyard' one year. The local climate is similar to that of the Champagne region and forecasters predict that Nova Scotia is about to enter a peak weather period mirroring that of France fifty years ago, so it seems Gerry's whim was no stab in the dark.

The grapes here are hand-harvested and sparklings are made using the French méthode classique. The signature sell-out Nova 7 is meddled with very little in the cellar, so each vintage has

its own character. With an alcohol volume of only 7%, it makes a light complement to Nova Scotian seafood and summer salads. *www.benjaminbridge.com; tel 902-542-1560; 1966 White Rock Rd, Gaspereau; by appointment* ⑤

05 PLANTERS RIDGE

If Luckett Vineyards is the rockstar, Planters Ridge has to be the gifted average Joe just waiting to be discovered: its quiet cellar door has bags of charm but less of the whizz-bang presentation. And the award for best sipping terrace in the valley (sorry, Luckett) must go to this understated village winery in a 150-year-old timber-framed barn. The best way to get here is by bike, along Port Williams' Starr's Point agritourism loop.

Tropical fruit characterises Planters Ridge's signature white blend, Quintessence, and summer berries come across in its quaffable off-dry rosé made with a blend of Baco Noir and Frontenac Blanc grapes. Sampling done, head to the elevated patio – the perfect place to watch the sun set over the valley's farmlands, glass of wine in hand, as the sky fades to the colour of a blushing grape. Vineyard tours are available by appointment. *www.plantersridge.ca; tel 902-542-2711; 1441 Church St, Port Williams; 10.30am–5.30pm Mon–Sat, noon–5pm Sun* ✖ ⑤

WHERE TO STAY

BLOMIDON INN, WOLFVILLE

This heritage hotel is a statement address in Wolfville, with a grand front lawn and luxurious olde-worlde rooms. There's a highly recommended restaurant, but if you can't be persuaded to go down for dinner simply order your tipple of choice off the wine list. *www.blomidon.ns.ca; tel 800 565 2291; 195 Main St, Wolfville*

PLANTERS' BARRACKS COUNTRY INN

Behind the jelly bean-coloured façade, this boutique country estate offers rooms with period features such as claw-footed tubs. It's in a rustic setting near Port Williams village – ideal for tackling the Starr's Point Loop. *www.plantersbarracks. online; tel 902 697 3303; 1464 Starr's Point Rd, Port Williams*

WHERE TO EAT

THE NOODLE GUY

This artisanal pasta restaurant started life as a stall at the Wolfville Farmers' Market. It's a simple affair, with revolving C$10 dishes chalked up on a board. Jam sessions rock out on Saturday afternoons. *www.thenoodleguy. wordpress.com; 964 Main St, Port Williams; 10am–7pm Mon–Sat*

LE CAVEAU RESTAURANT

Domaine de Grand Pré's restaurant is the pinnacle of fine dining in a valley that focuses mostly on farm-to-table markets and cafes. Chef Jason Lynch champions Nova Scotia on a plate and has won awards for his imaginative use of local ingredients. The restaurant's leafy terrace is a lovely spot on summer nights. *www.grandprewines. ns.ca/restaurant; 11611 Highway 1; 11am–9pm May–Oct, check online for winter opening times*

WHAT TO DO

STARR'S POINT LOOP

This 8km agritourism trail lassoing the village of Port Williams traverses cross-country tracks and field-facing backroads, linking together pick-your-own fruit farms, a cheese-tasting room, antiques barn, innovative small-batch distillery and beloved local Port Pub. It can be explored walking or cycling, but note it's a sweltering hike on sunny summer days as there's precious little shade. *www.starrspointloop. com*

BURNTCOAT HEAD PARK

An hour east of Wolfville, the highest tides in the world have been recorded at this 3-acre park. Up to 1.6 billion tonnes of water surge into the Bay of Fundy's basin each day; when the water drains you can skip for miles. Knowledgeable guides at Burntcoat Head offer tours exploring the area's geological history and tidal pools out on the seabed. At high tide, there are nature trails and a lighthouse museum to visit. *www. burntcoatheadpark.ca*

CELEBRATIONS

NOVA SCOTIA ICEWINE FESTIVAL

Some cellar doors close altogether in winter, but Wolfville's annual ice wine festival in February/March keeps the winemakers' fires blazing. Dessert wines from across the Annapolis Valley are brought to the tasting table, paired with food from local chefs. *www.nsicewinefest.com*

LOBSTER BASH

The king of shellfish is cheap and plentiful along the Bay of Fundy coast. In Digby, a 1.5hr drive from Wolfville, the local lobster is celebrated at the end of June with outdoor concerts and competitions for the best lobster chowder, lobster banding, trap stacking and trap hauling. *www.lobsterbash.ca*

[British Columbia]

NORTHERN OKANAGAN LAKE

The freezing winters of northern Okanagan belie an impressive range of grape varieties grown in vineyards characterised by stunning views and complex soils.

This trail begins not on the ground but in the air, with a 50min flight from Vancouver to Kelowna offering astonishing views of a landscape created by ancient glacial activity. The resulting mountains, snow, endless forests and piercing turquoise lakes are panoramic jaw-droppers, and far-removed from the kind of scenery most associated with wine-growing.

The Okanagan Valley has a complex geology; the glacial movement led to large deposits of silt,

GET THERE
Kelowna is less than an hour's flight from Vancouver. Car hire is available.

sand and gravel on the valley's bed and sides, resulting in a lot of sand-heavy soils in the south and rocky, sparse soils in the north, with assorted differentiations in between, all of which yield refreshingly diverse wines.

With the vineyards lying north of 49°, you might expect the kind of cool temperatures found in Champagne or the Mosel. Many visitors are surprised that vines can be grown here, but despite the icy winters a vast array of grape varieties can succeed, largely thanks to the hot summers. There's another benefit to the northerly location; short growing seasons are compensated for by long sunlight hours, so grapes have no problem reaching maturity. Add in the differentiation between day and night and you have wines that retain great freshness and thus zingy acidity – a signature stamp of the Okanagan.

The wine industry and vines here are young, but growing fast; in 1984 there were 13 wineries in BC, today there are 174 in the Okanagan alone. This means fewer rules with regards to planting (more than 230 grape varieties are sown) and wine styles, and all the more fun for wine fans.

This trail focuses on the Northern Okanagan Valley, from Kelowna down to the cluster of award-winning wineries on the Naramata Bench, and across to the other side: to Summerland and Westbank. These areas are well known for cool climate grape varieties, such as Riesling, Pinot Gris, Chardonnay and Pinot Noir.

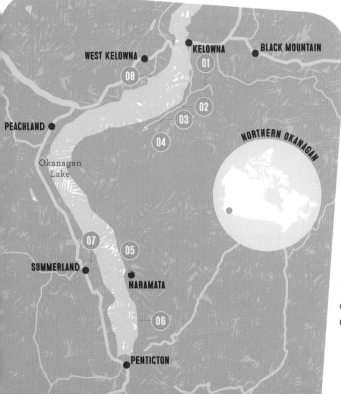

01 Lake views from Bench 1775 winery

02 Summer events at CedarCreek

03 The pyramid at Summerhill

04 Lake fun at Quails' Gate winery

05 The tasting room at Tantalus Vineyards

06 Okanagan lavender fields

01 TANTALUS VINEYARDS

Tantalus has quite a pedigree as the oldest continuously producing vineyard in British Columbia, originally founded in 1927. It's home to some of the oldest plantings of Riesling in BC, from 1978, vines which barely need irrigation, often not at all, and create very intense wines. What's more, some of the vines from this planting are vinified to create a sparkling Riesling which is utterly delicious. Only 200 cases are made so be quick to snap some up. Pinot Noir and Chardonnay are also produced, and there's a rare, crystalline Syrah ice wine. The winery also keeps beehives on the property, as part of a wholehearted commitment to sustainable practice, and sells Tantalus honey.

'We want to achieve a sense of balance in our wines. This includes taking notions from organics and biodynamics; we take everything from our surroundings into account. We keep a 10-acre forest protected by law in the middle of our vineyards, to encourage our ecosystem,' says winemaker David Paterson. *www.tantalus.ca; tel 877-764-0078; 1670 Dehart Rd, Kelowna; 10am–6pm daily* 💲

02 SUMMERHILL PYRAMID WINERY

Summerhill was the first winery in British Columbia to become certified biodynamic, and has been organic since the very beginning. Here, the ethos is as much about taking care of the soils and the environment as it is about making great wines. Flowers, grass and weeds grow in abundance between the vines. Ezra Cipes, son of Stephen Cipes, the current proprietor and founder, says: 'Our vision of perfection does not include clean rows. The vineyard is its own ecosystem.' Gabe, Ezra's brother, creates all of the biodynamic preparations, and you'll find a beautiful little biodynamic garden on site. The focus is on fine sparkling wine, and Stephen has even created a huge pyramid for ageing the wines, a precise 8% replica of the Great Pyramid of Giza. *www.summerhill.bc.ca; tel 250-764-8000; 4870 Chute Lake Rd, Kelowna; 10am–6pm daily* 🍴

03 MARTIN'S LANE WINERY

Built into a steep hillside, this radical six-level gravity-flow winery – where the grapes gently flow from one level down to the next thanks to gravitational force, without the need for pumps or unnecessary handling – is breathtaking on architectural grounds alone, the building mirroring the rough, jagged and

extreme Okanagan landscape. The resulting Pinot Noir and Riesling wines are also rather special, some of the finest (and most expensive) expressions of British Columbia terroir, created by the exceptionally talented winemaker Shane Munn and organic viticulturist Kurt Simcic.

You can't miss the giant bust of Vincent van Gogh, missing ear to the ground, which was unveiled to mark the opening of the winery. 'Project Redhead' by artist Douglas Coupland started with a global search for a van Gogh doppelgänger. Why? It turns out redheads, like Pinot Noir, both the result of genetic mutations, represent just 1.9% of their respective populations. *www.martinlanewinery.com; tel 250-707-2263; 5437 Lakeshore Rd, Kelowna; open by appointment only*

04 CEDARCREEK ESTATE WINERY

With a spectacular vista on to Okanagan Lake, the CedarCreek winery is particularly well known for aromatic grape varieties, predominantly Riesling but also Gewürztraminer and the lesser-known but delicious Ehrenfelser. Of particular note are the Platinum Block 2 and Block 4 Pinot Noirs. They are made in the same way as the Estate Pinot Noirs, but from different soils (sandy versus clay), so you can get an appreciation of how the soil affects the wine.

Yoga classes here in summer are not to be missed and the vineyard terrace restaurant offers fantastic views and farm-to-table fare. *www.cedarcreek.bc.ca; tel 778-738-1027; 5445 Lakeshore Rd, Kelowna; 10am–7pm daily* ✕

05 BELLA SPARKLING WINES

Bella Wines is a beautiful little biodynamically tended farm and winery nestled in a quiet nook next to Okanagan Lake. The winemaking approach here is one of minimal intervention – no additives, only natural yeasts and often zero sulphur. The focus is on two grape varieties, Chardonnay and Gamay, as single-vineyard sparkling wines inspired by the grower Champagne movement. Vinification methods take place to create both *pétillant naturel* (naturally sparkling) and 'traditional method' wine, allowing the occasionally undervalued Gamay grape, in particular, to really shine.

Husband and wife proprietors Jay Drysadle and Wendy Rose named the winery after their original pet bulldog – her successor, little Buddha, even has his own Instagram account (@buddhathefarmdog). 'Our region's like the Wild West, but

our transition period has been so fast. We are getting a grasp...and understanding our sense of place; I love our diversity and micro-regions,' says Jay, adding: 'I think Gamay is really special here in BC, and I wanted to see where this little underdog grape could go.' Bella has an array of antique Champagne coupes and flutes for tasting, so take your pick and enjoy.
www.bellawines.ca; tel 778-996-1829; 4320 Gulch Rd, Naramata; visits by appointment only

06 BENCH 1775 WINERY

Val Tait, previously winemaker at the well-known Mission Hill and Poplar Grove wineries, runs a tight-knit, mainly female team who oversee production of striking Sauvignon Blanc and Syrah as well as some more experimental wines, such as a carbonic 'Malbec Nouveau', and a range of high-quality ice wines.

The estate sits on the popular Naramata Bench, with some of the best views in the Okanagan Valley. Yoga, live music and special dinners take place throughout the summer, and the Bench Patio Bistro serves up seasonal seafood and tasty locally sourced dishes.
www.bench1775.com; tel 250-490-4965; 1775 Naramata Rd, Penticton; 12–5pm Sat, Mon–Fri & Sun by appointment only ✕

07 OKANAGAN CRUSH PAD

Christine Coletta and Steve Lornie built The Okanagan Crush Pad in 2011, currently the only official custom crush pad in the area. In addition to their own Haywire and Narrative organic and natural wines, they provide a base for fledgling wineries, helping them with all aspects of winemaking. The couple quickly gained an international reputation for producing very high-quality organic, minimal intervention and terroir-driven wines, and they also experiment with vessel type; on visiting you'll be able to see egg-shaped concrete fermenters and amphorae in action. Talented duo Matt Dumayne and Jordan Kubek are at the winemaking wheel, and there are skin contact wines (aka orange wines) here to taste, too.
www.okanagancrushpad.com; tel 250-494-4445; 16576 Fosbery Rd, Summerland, BC; 11am–4pm daily (by appointment only Jan–Feb) $

08 QUAILS' GATE WINERY

The Stewart family put down their roots in Canada back in 1908, and purchased this property in 1956. It features the Allison House, a log cabin built in 1873, the first permanent wooden structure on the west side of Lake Okanagan, which now serves as a tasting room. The family planted their first vinifera vines in 1961, making them some of the oldest in the country. Nowadays, the winery focuses on Pinot Noirs, which winemaker Nikki Callaway describes as 'their own creatures', and Chardonnay, as well as some rarities such as a botrytis-affected (noble rot) sweet wine, and rich reds from old Maréchal Foch vines. Nikki has even created a BC Gamay Nouveau, Quails' Gate's answer to Beaujolais Nouveau.

The winery features events throughout the year, from cooking demos to Pinot Clones 101 classes, for those wanting to get their wine geek on, and the Old Vines restaurant offers outstanding farm-to-table creative cuisine.
www.quailsgate.com; tel 250-769-4451; 3303 Boucherie Rd, Kelowna; opening hours vary ✕

WHERE TO STAY

SPARKLING HILL RESORT

A luxurious health and wellness centre in Vernon, in the north of the Okanagan Valley, this hotel offers everything from an aqua meditation room to a salt steam room and even an igloo. Gaze out over panoramic views of Okanagan Lake from the outdoor infinity pool. *www.sparklinghill.com; tel 877-275-1556; 888 Sparkling Place, Vernon*

SANDY BEACH LODGE AND RESORT

On a stunning stretch of beachfront, directly on Okanagan Lake by the Naramata Bench, sits this historic 1940s log lodge. Rooms have private verandas looking out across the lake, and there are also 13 two-bedroom log cottages for intimate, family or group getaways. *sandybeachresort.com; tel 866-496-5765; 4275 Mill Rd, Naramata*

WHERE TO EAT

RAUDZ REGIONAL TABLE

With chef Rod Butters at the helm, this Kelowna hotspot dishes up locally sourced and creative food in its own Canadian style. With a 100% Okanagan wine list, it's a great place to explore the region's wines, too. *www.raudz.com; tel 250-868-8805; 1560 Water Street, Kelowna*

VANILLA POD

Choose the patio on the lake in summer or a spot by the log fire in winter, before tucking into chef Bruno Terroso's innovative sharing plates at this restaurant within Poplar Grove Winery. *thevanillapod.ca; tel 250-493-9463; 425 Middle Bench Rd, North Penticton*

FITZ BISTRO AND SPARKLING BAR

Open during the summer months only, the FITZ Bistro at Fitzpatrick Vineyards offers delicious food following a strictly 'from scratch' policy, all locally sourced. There's also a sparkling wine bar where you can taste the vineyard's own sparkling wine, along with well-known fizz from around the world. *www.fitzwine.com; tel 250-767-2768; 697 Highway 97 S, Peachland*

WHAT TO DO

British Columbia certainly isn't lacking in outstanding natural beauty and wildlife, including 18 volcanoes and multiple mountain ranges, as well as cougars, bears, rattlesnakes, elk and moose. You can opt to explore on two wheels along stretches of the 600km Kettle Valley Railway trail.

OKANAGAN LAVENDER FARM

For a sensory overload, drop in at this beautiful farm, which grows more than 60 types of lavender and an array of 18 aromatic herbs and plants. *www.okanaganlavender. com; tel 250-764-7795; 4380 Takla Rd, Kelowna*

WINE TOURS

If you're in the market for a highly knowledgeable wine tour guide and driver, Matt Wentzell of experiencewinetours.ca will teach you everything there is to know about British Columbia.

CELEBRATIONS

The annual BC Pinot Noir celebration takes place every year in mid-August and provides a great day out. Expect creative canapés and food from top Okanagan chefs, live music and informative masterclasses – as well as, of course, bountiful Pinot Noir to taste from more than 30 wineries. *www.bcpinotnoir.ca*

The map shows numbered locations (01–07) and labels: KALEDEN, Okanogan River, OLALLA, KEREMEOS, CAWSTON, FAIRVIEW, OLIVER, SIMILKAMEEN VALLEY.

[British Columbia]

SOUTHERN OKANAGAN AND THE SIMILKAMEEN VALLEY

From Penticton, the Okanagan Valley stretches south, taking in Skaha Lake and the Golden Mile between Oliver and Osoyoos. West lies the drama of the Similkameen Valley.

Handling a small, mottled rock from his vineyard, Donald Triggs, owner and winemaker of Culmina Family Estate Winery near Oliver to the west of the Okanagan Valley, muses 'How did Mother Nature do that?' This little rock is a store of minerals, deposited millennia ago when glacial lakes receded. These mineral deposits seeped into the soil which today supports a number of grape varieties, such as Cabernet Sauvignon, Merlot, Syrah, Riesling, Semillon and Grüner Veltliner.

The wine-growing regions around Okanagan Lake are the most famous in British Columbia, but equally exciting vineyards are planted to the south, from Skaha Lake to the Okanagan Falls and Osoyoos. Syrah, in particular, flows successfully from the west-facing, sun-soaked strip of sandy-soiled land known as the Black Sage Bench.

This trail leads you west into the Similkameen Valley, one of BC's underexplored wine regions with just 19 licensed wineries, so far. No lakes here – the vineyards are set against a backdrop of mountains, with wild sagebrush growing between the vines and, some argue, perceptible in the wine itself.

On top of the extreme temperatures, a strong wind prevails, helping whoosh away most pests and diseases. This natural deterrent contributes to Similkameen's proud status as Canada's organic farming capital – you'll find orchards, family-run fruit stands and markets – and supports the efforts of many vineyards in using organic, not to mention biodynamic, methods.

It's an exceptional place, where the fluctuating climate conditions allow unlikely combinations of grape varieties, such as Riesling and Cabernet Sauvignon, to succeed at wineries such as Clos du Soleil.

GET THERE
Fly to Kelowna or Penticton from Vancouver in less than an hour. Car hire is available. Hwy 3 runs through the Similkameen Valley to Osoyoos.

① PAINTED ROCK ESTATE WINERY

Husband-and-wife team John and Trish Skinner, with the help of Bordeaux-based consultant Alain Sutre, were convinced they could harness the potential of this gently sloping bench bounded by rocky banks, once the site of a huge apricot orchard. The discovery of 500-year-old pictographs gave the vineyard its name, and the couple set about planning, analysing and planting to fulfil its promise.

The vineyard has used sustainable farming methods since the end of 2010 – weeds and pests are kept at bay without harmful pesticides and larger interlopers, in the form of black bears, are deterred with a solar-powered electric perimeter fence. All the grapes are hand-harvested and processed in the winery on site, a modern and minimalistic structure with curved, reflective surfaces and a wide open terrace overlooking Skaha Lake. Recommended drops include the smoky, herbaceous single varietal Cabernet Franc, and for fans of polished Cabernet blends, the Red Icon is one of the finest of its style. *www.paintedrock.ca; tel 250-493-6809; 400 Smythe Drive, Penticton; 11am–5pm daily and by appointment in winter* ✕ ⑤

② MEYER FAMILY VINEYARDS

Some of the most pure, terroir-driven, minimal intervention, Burgundian-style Pinot Noir and Chardonnay are grown and

crafted by the Meyer Family, as acknowledged by the winery winning 2nd Best Small Winery in the 2017 National Wine Awards. The family focuses on three separate sites, with each wine reflecting its particular expression of soil and climate. Reimer is quickly gaining renown as one of the top single vineyard sites in British Columbia.

In keeping with their small-batch, terroir-focused approach, locally sourced delicacies are available to try alongside the wines in their tasting room. If you can be momentarily tempted away from the grape, there are craft beer and cider choices too.

www.mfvwines.com; tel 250-497-8553; 4287 McLean Creek Rd, Okanagan Falls. 10am–5pm daily and by appointment in winter ✕

03 LE VIEUX PIN

Dedicated to the beautiful old pine tree that stands in the middle of their home vineyard, just outside Oliver down on the Black Sage Bench, Le Vieux Pin is focused on elegant French-style wines. With Frenchwoman Severine Pinte at the helm of the domaine, there are very serious wines being made here, and in particular it is Syrah that really sings, with examples rivalling top Northern Rhône Syrahs. Pinte says, 'I feel like a painter; from the Okanagan we have all the colours on a palette, and I can bring floral, meaty and herbal elements to the wine.'

Food isn't served but you're welcome to bring your own snacks to enjoy in the picnic area while wine-tasting.

www.levieuxpin.ca; tel 250-

498-8388; 5496 Black Sage Rd, Oliver; 11am–5pm daily and by appointment in winter $

04 BURROWING OWL WINERY

Established in the 1990s, Burrowing Owl has become one of the iconic southern Okanagan wineries, seen as a pioneer of Black Sage Bench winemaking. Aside from their trailblazing environmentally responsible credentials, Burrowing Owl's owners, the Wyses, have led the way with their red wines using a combination of French, American and Hungarian oak. Syrah here sees a splash of Viognier, and at The Sonora Room restaurant you can try rare old vintages of Burrowing Owl, many of which are no longer on the market.

The vineyards lie on the dry 'antelope brush ecosystem', evidently prime terrain for grape-growing, but also home to assorted wildlife, including bluebirds, bats, bears, big horned sheep and,

01 The Tasting Room at Painted Rock

02 'Dead Reckoning' by David Robinson at Painted Rock

03 Rural life at Le Vieux Pin

04 Winemaker Severine Pinte at Le Vieux Pin

05 Artful food at Burrowing Owl winery

you've guessed it, the Burrowing Owl. The Wyses are longstanding supporters of the Burrowing Owl Conservation Society of British Columbia which runs a captive breeding programme that has brought back this species from the brink of extinction – not only naming the winery after the bird, but also raising nearly a million dollars for the cause (the $3 tasting fee goes directly to BOCS). *www.burrowingowlwine.ca; tel 877-498-0620; 500 Burrowing Owl Place (off Black Sage Rd), Oliver; 10am–6pm daily Apr–Oct, shorter hours in winter* ✕ ⑤

⑤ CULMINA FAMILY ESTATE WINERY

Culmina is the project of well-known wine industry figure Donald Triggs and his family. Instead of retiring, he poured a lifetime of knowledge into founding this new winery. Fascinating soil mapping has been carried out here and cutting-edge methods are combined with traditional techniques, such as an old-school gentle wooden vertical press, to create the finest wines possible.

The superlative rosé is made from the unusual *saignée* method – it's created by 'bleeding off' a portion of juice from each of Culmina's best Bordeaux varietal vines. The family also makes outstanding wild yeast Grüner Veltliner from a high elevation vineyard named Margaret's Bench, which sits at 595m; a true rarity. *www.culmina.ca; tel 250-498-0789; 4790 Wild Rose St, Oliver; daily Apr–Oct, check website for hours* ⑤

⑥ OROFINO VINEYARDS

Orofino in the Similkameen Valley, west of Osoyoos, is known for its lifted and fresh Riesling, created in homage to fine German Rieslings and fermented naturally in old oak barrels. Orofino are also champions of Gamay and from their Celentano vineyard produce one of the most exciting single-vineyard examples, not just in BC, but worldwide.

An eco-friendly, solar-panelled winery, it's the perfect setting for a lazy picnic among the vines and almond trees. At the annual 1.6 mile dinner, local chefs concoct a feast using only the finest ingredients from artisan producers, all sourced from within that precise 1.6 mile radius of the winery, and paired with Orofino's wines. *www.orofinovineyards.com; tel 250-499-0068; 2152 Barcelo Rd, Cawston. 10am–5pm in summer, seasonal hours apply*

⑦ CLOS DU SOLEIL

On the Upper Bench of the south Similkameen Valley, Clos du Soleil's sheltered location gives it its name ('enclosed vineyard of the sun'). The rocky mountains that border the vineyard form a natural stone wall, which combines with the rich, rough soils and the long hours of sunlight to produce lively, perfumed and floral red and white wines from Bordeaux varieties. Here, winemaker Michael Clark works with minimal intervention, organically and biodynamically, in order to create terroir transparency in the wines. He says, 'My personal belief is that you need a sense of delicacy and elegance to allow the natural expression of a vineyard to shine through.' *www.closdusoleil.ca; tel 250-499-2831; 2568 Upper Bench Rd, Keremeos; 10am–5pm daily, by appointment in winter*

06 Orofino Passion Pit Vineyard

07 Apex Mountain Ski Resort at Penticton

WHERE TO STAY

HESTER CREEK

Watch the sun rise over the rugged landscape from one of the plush villa suites, with snug fireplaces, private patios and soaking tubs, at Hester Creek. Locally sourced breakfast is included.
www.hestercreek.com; tel 866-498-4435; 877 Road 8, Oliver

GOD'S MOUNTAIN ESTATE

This chic Mediterranean-style villa overlooking Skaha Lake even offers a roofless room – indulge in some stargazing at the height of summer. Breakfast is included.
www.godsmountain. com; tel 250-490-4800; 4898 Eastside Rd, Penticton

SPIRIT RIDGE AT NK'MIP RESORT

Looking down onto Osoyoos Lake, this swish resort has two pools and offers water sports down at the lake, plus the Sonora Dunes Golf Course is next door. You can also discover the history of the Osoyoos Indian Band, the First Nations government in BC, and more about local wildlife and ecology at the Nk'Mip Cultural Centre.
spiritridge.hyatt.com; tel 250-495-5445; 1200 Rancher Creek Rd, Osoyoos

WHERE TO EAT

HARKER'S ORGANICS

This little roadside organic store sells produce from a fifth-generation organic family farm, including soup, sandwiches and salads – the ideal pit stop for picking up picnic essentials. There's also a mouthwateringly good selection of ice cream.
harkersorganics.com; 2238 Hwy 3, Cawston

TICKLEBERRY'S

If you haven't had your fill of ice cream, head to Tickleberry's in Okanagan Falls and prepare to be bamboozled by 72 different flavours.
www.tickleberrys.com; tel 250-497-8862; 1207 Main St, Okanagan Falls; 10am–5pm Mar–Apr & Oct–Dec, 10am–7pm May–Jun, 10am–10pm Jul–Sep, closed Jan–Feb

MIRADORO

Celebrated BC chef Jeff Van Geest runs the kitchen at this Tinhorn Creek restaurant. Breathtaking views, creative cuisine with a Mediterranean slant and an outstanding wine list add up to gastro heaven.
www.tinhorn.com; tel 250-498-3742; 537 Tinhorn Creek Rd, Oliver; open daily 11.30am–3pm lunch; tapas 3pm–5.30pm; dinner 5.30pm–9pm

FARMERS MARKET

A vibrant summertime market that celebrates the region's bounty. Your best bet for wholesome picnic provisions.
Lion's Park, Hwy 97; open summer 8am–1pm Sat and 5–8pm Wed

WHAT TO DO

Pack your trainers – the 10km Golden Mile hiking trail gives incredible views from Oliver to Osoyoos, as well as passing ruins from 19th-century gold and silver mines. Access can be gained from Tinhorn Creek winery, where you can also pick up a map. Of course there are also skiing options in winter – Apex Mountain Resort 37km west of Penticton is one of Canada's best small ski resorts.
www.tinhorn.com; www.apexresort.com

CELEBRATIONS

Okanagan Wine Festivals These four seasonal festivals are major events, especially the one in fall. The usual dates are fall (early October), winter (mid-January), spring (early May) and summer (early August). Events at wineries across the valley.
www.thewinefestivals.com

Courtesy of Norman Hardie Winery / Tara McMullen

[Ontario]

ONTARIO

Rooted in cool climates, Ontario's wine region sits between 41 and 44 degrees north, hosting some of Canada's finest wineries, many organic, sustainable and biodynamic.

Benefitting from the moderating effect of the Great Lakes, Ontario's wine regions occupy the southernmost reaches of the province, sharing the same latitude as Burgundy. Without the Lakes, vine-growing would be impossible here. Breezes cool the vineyards during the hot summers and warm the icy air in the depths of winter. At freezing temperatures, even winter-hardy hybrids would be impossible to cultivate without the Lakes.

Latitude, lakes and limestone define Canada's central wine region and its 165 wineries. Though Ontario has fewer wineries than western Canada's British Columbia wine region, more hectares are planted here.

Ontario has three main Designated Viticultural Areas (DVAs): Niagara Peninsula, Prince Edward County and Lake Erie North Shore. The most expansive and famous, Niagara Peninsula, is divided into 10 sub-appellations, mapped out by altitude, soils and, crucially, proximity to the Lakes. That said, the term 'altitude' is taken with a grain of salt: the highest escarpment reaches only 175m, with most of Niagara's landscape formed of gentle rolling hills.

Chardonnay and Pinot Noir excel here, with Chardonnay garnering so much acclaim that Niagara hosts the annual International Cool Climate Chardonnay Celebration every July. Cabernet Franc, Gamay and Riesling also thrive, as does sparkling wine, primarily made in the traditional method. Ontario's climate has also transformed it into the ice-wine capital of the world, producing 80% of the globe's ice wine. While other countries, such as Germany, make authentic (frozen naturally on the vine) Eiswein, Ontario's climate allows for consistent yearly production under stricter quality guidelines.

GET THERE
Niagara's wineries are 120km south then east from Toronto; from Buffalo (USA), it's a 45km drive. Prince Edward County is a 200km drive east of Toronto.

Start your wine tour with the Niagara Peninsula, birthplace of Ontario's modern wine industry. From the thunderous Niagara Falls, it's a short drive to peaceful Saint Catherine's and Niagara-on-the-Lake, where both agritourism and enotourism shine.

01 RAVINE VINEYARD

Ravine is a biodynamically farmed, organic-certified vineyard on historical upper Lowrey Farm, on St David's Bench. The Lowrey family have proudly farmed the 34 acres of this land since 1867. Once past the reconstructed 1802 House of Nations at the front of the property, you'll reach the casual farm-to-table Ravine Winery Restaurant; grab a bite alfresco

If there's one winemaker to have cemented Canada's Chardonnay and Pinot Noir among the best in the world it's Norman Hardie

and enjoy the views over the vines, or join a winery tour and tasting (library tastings are available). If you need to work off lunch, find the outdoor ping-pong table – skilled winemaker Martin Werner is an avid player. He's also, of course, acclaimed for his Cabernet Franc, Merlot and Chardonnay.
www.ravinevineyard.com; tel 905-

262-8463; 1366 York Rd, St David's; 10am–6pm daily ✕ ⑨

02 SOUTHBROOK VINEYARDS

Swing by this LEED Gold-certified winery in the heart of Niagara-on-the-Lake for its striking modern architecture and vineyards views. The green facility, opened in 2008, reflects Southbrook's pioneering biodynamic practices (it was Canada's first Demeter-certified winery), and winemaker Ann Sperling's commitment to making low-intervention, sustainable wines, from ice wine and biodynamic *pétillant-naturels* to skin-contact orange wine, wild ferment Chardonnay and herbal Cabernet Franc.

You'll often see the resident flock of sheep wandering Southbrook's

01 Pizzas at Norman Hardie winery

02 The Patio at Southbrook

03 Sought-after Chardonnay at Pearl Morissette

04 Tending Ravine vineyard

150 acres of vineyards. Book ahead for a food-and-wine pairing tour: Ontario Artisan Cheese or Ice Wine and Cheesecake. Sperling, who also makes wines at her ancestral farm in Okanagan Valley, BC, is one of Canada's most respected winemakers.
www.southbrook.com; tel 905-641-2548; 581 Niagara Stone Rd, Niagara-on-the-Lake; 10am–5pm daily ✕ ⑤

03 PEARL MORISSETTE

François Morissette is Canada's avant-garde naturalist winemaker, turning out uncompromising – and often controversial – wines from his remote, pastoral Niagara vineyards. Trained in Burgundy, Morissette releases small, highly coveted lots of Chardonnay and Pinot Noir, as well as Riesling, Gamay, Cabernet Franc and other delights. His wines are often seen at natural-wine fairs around the world but can be tricky to come by locally as they are snapped up quickly. Tasting through the wines is as much an exercise in philosophy as terroir, with various blends and vessels used to best express site and vintage. In late 2017, Morissette launched The Restaurant at Pearl Morissette, a fixed-menu room serving dishes driven by local, seasonal ingredients and French-inspired technique.
www.pearlmorissette.com; tel 905-562-4376; 3953 Jordan Rd, Jordan; by appointment ✕

04 TAWSE WINERY

Moray Tawse is a Burgundy fan, collector and expert, and it's evident in the remarkable Chardonnay and Pinot Noirs coming out of his Twenty Mile Bench Winery, folded into the Niagara Escarpment. It's also known for its single-vineyard Rieslings. Under the guidance of Burgundian consulting oenologist Pascal Marchand and Niagara-trained chief winemaker Paul Pender, Tawse has expanded his initial 2000 vineyards across neighbouring parcels (they now total 200 acres) and converted them to organic, biodynamic practices. Launched in 2005, the Twenty Mile Bench winery is a six-tier, gravity-flow beauty, with barrel caves carved into the Escarpment.

his pioneering vineyards and winery are quite literally embedded in the area's limestone bedrock. Among locals, the winery is almost as well known for its wood-fired oven and exceptional pizzas, served daily May to autumn.
www.normanhardie.com; tel 613-399-5297; 1152 Greer Rd, Wellington; 11am–6pm daily May–Dec ✖

www.tawsewinery.ca; tel 905-562-9500; 3955 Cherry Ave, Vineland; 10am–6pm daily ⑤

05 MALIVOIRE WINE COMPANY

Malivoire Wine Company is the blockbuster wine-world hit from special-effects director Martin Malivoire (*Resident Evil*, *A Christmas Story*, *Hairspray*). Having done his time in California, Malivoire turned his eyes on the Niagara Escarpment and winemaking became his next scene. This prime spot on the Beamsville Bench has been home to Malivoire's beautiful gravity-flow, Quonset-hut winery since 1998. The 26-hectare, organically farmed vineyard focuses on Pinot Gris, Pinot Noir and Chardonnay, plus a few small-lot gems like Gamay. Winemaker Shiraz Mottiar (yes, he's actually called Shiraz) is a regular face at wine events and mentoring programs, and a vocal leader of sustainable vineyard practices.

www.malivoire.com; tel 905-563-9253; 4260 King St East, Beamsville; 10am–5pm Mon–Fri, 11am–5pm Sat & Sun, extended summer hours ⑤

06 NORMAN HARDIE WINERY

If there's one winemaker who has cemented Canada's Chardonnay and Pinot Noir among the best in the world, it's Norman Hardie. This former Toronto sommelier spent six years apprenticing in top cool-climate cellars around the world before returning to make wines in Ontario's rural Prince Edward County region, where he found his perfect trifecta of climate, clay and calcareous soils. This is extreme winemaking: vintners here must mound over or bury the vines with soils after the harvest to create a protective igloo from the winter freeze. Hardie has earned the acclaim of international critics for his textural, naturalist wines, and

07 HINTERLAND WINE COMPANY

When Jonas Newman and Vicki Samaras decided to begin their family winery in Prince Edward County in 2003, they focused on translating their vines' typically pristine, natural acidity into striking sparkling wines. From the cavernous, converted dairy barn, the winery releases fizz from ancestral to Charmat to traditional method, all sustainably farmed from 15 acres of vineyards. The bubbles don't stop at wine, however; Hinterland also makes a dry and cleansing cherry cider, from local apples and organic cherry juice. In 2015, the owners co-founded County Road Beer Company, a craft brewery located right next door. Every weekend from noon to 4pm, they operate a casual eatery with a menu of seasonal, local foods.
www.hinterlandwine.com; tel 613-399-2903; 1258 Closson Rd RR1, Hillier; 11am–6pm daily ✖ ⑤

WHERE TO STAY

PILLAR & POST

Ontario's only five-star country hotel sits at the heart of the wine scene, with country furnishings, pools surrounded by greenery (and serviced by a patio bar), an indoor spa, and a restaurant wine list that flaunts the hometown pride. *www.vintage-hotels. com; tel 905-468-2123, 48 John St W, Niagara-on-the-Lake*

OLD STONE INN

This Niagara Falls inn provides a welcome retreat through its sumptuous decor and relaxing atmosphere, honouring its 1904 heritage with numerous antiques and period touches, all now suitably modernised. *www.oldstoneinnhotel. com; tel 905-357-1234; 6080 Fallsview Blvd, Niagara Falls*

WHERE TO EAT

From late spring to early autumn, farm-to-table cuisine is ubiquitous in Ontario wine country, and many, if not most, wineries have small restaurants or picnicking options.

TREADWELL

Ontario's stalwart leader in farm-fresh cuisine, with a chic dining room, the top local wine list, and refined fare ranging from wild-mushroom salad to Ontario rainbow trout. *www.treadwellcuisine. com; tel 905-934-9797; 114 Queen St, Niagara-on-the-Lake; 11.30am–2.15pm & 5–9pm Thu-Tue, 11.30am–2.15pm Wed*

BACKHOUSE

From its sleek cocktail list and thoughtful open-fired cuisine to its local wine program, Backhouse would fit perfectly in downtown Toronto – but you'll find it in Niagara-on-the-Lake. *www.backhouse.xyz; tel 289-272-1242; 242 Mary St, Niagara-on-the-Lake; 5–10pm Wed–Fri, 11.30am–2.30pm & 5–10pm Sat & Sun*

JK FARM

One of Canada's most renowned chefs, Jamie Kennedy runs a series of summer farm dinners from a one-room restaurant on his 100-acre farm in Hillier, Prince Edward County; it's an exceptional evening. Expect everything from organic heirloom tomatoes and artisan cheeses to chef JK's famous frites and local porchetta with Ontario cider apples.

Wine pairings feature Ontario's finest offerings, many hard to find. Dinners sell out regularly; the location is unveiled upon booking (essential). *www.jamiekennedy.ca; Hillier*

WHAT TO DO

If you're touring in Niagara, allow half a day to visit the world-famous Niagara Falls. You're in luck: the Canadian side of the falls is much closer, and more dramatic, than its American counterpart. Festivals abound throughout the year in each of Ontario's wine regions, from the summertime International Cool Climate Chardonnay Celebration to winter's Niagara Icewine Festival. For a break from wine, hunt down some of the many local craft breweries; Niagara-on-the-Lake's Silversmith Brewery and Oast House Brewers come highly recommended. Or taste the wares from Dillon's Small Batch Distillers in Beamsville, the region's first craft distillery.

The map shows Vancouver Island and Gulf Islands with the following labels: MAPLE BAY, PORT WASHINGTON, Salt Spring Island, OTTER BAY, North Pender Island, FULFORD HARBOUR, 06, COWICHAN BAY, Portland Island, Moresby Island, VANCOUVER ISLAND, SHAWNIGAN LAKE, MILL BAY, Shawnigan Lake, Saanich Inlet, SIDNEY, James Island, Sidney Island, USA CANADA, SAANICHTON, BRENTWOOD BAY, D'Arcy Island. Numbered markers: 05, 04, 03, 02, 01.

[British Columbia]

VANCOUVER ISLAND

Old-growth Douglas Fir rainforests and crisp Pacific air set the scene in western Canada's Vancouver Island and Gulf Islands, where under-the-radar local wineries are making their mark.

Dangling off Canada's west coast, Vancouver Island is the last landfall before Hawaii or Japan. Items from these Pacific islands wash up on its rugged shores occasionally, carried by the powerful swells that place the west side of Vancouver Island on surfers' bucket lists. The east side is wedged into southern British Columbia, with the foot of Vancouver Island, and BC's provincial capital city, Victoria, dipping beneath the 49th parallel that divides Canada from the USA. Hundreds of islands and inlets lie in the sheltered channel between Vancouver Island and the mainland; a few of the larger islands host year-round residents and their farms, orchards, wineries and breweries.

Vancouver Island spans all terrains, from sandy beaches to rocky shores, marshy lowlands to rolling farmland, and old-growth temperate rainforests to snow-dusted mountains. Stretching 500km southeast to northwest, the Island is bisected by a mountain range,

crossed by undulating rivers and rimmed with countless bays. The mild annual temperatures (Canada's warmest) and modest population (775,000 residents, half of those in Victoria) make visiting year-round easy – and winemaking a flourishing scene.

Vancouver Island is a fertile haven for distillers, brewers, foragers, roasters, cheesemakers, fishers, bakers, chefs, and, of course, vintners. There are more than 30 licensed wineries, focusing on cool-climate grapes that are adaptable to the marine environment. Pinot Gris and Ortega lead in white grapes, while Pinot Noir and Marechal Foch are the main reds. Siegerrebe, Schonburger, Grüner Veltliner, Zweigelt and Cabernet Franc are also familiar finds, along with numerous marine-hardy hybrid grapes that have shown promise. Sparkling wines are a high success rate, with vintners capturing that fresh, clean, natural acidity in bubbles from frizzante to traditional-method fizz.

GET THERE
The BC Ferries terminal and Vancouver Island Airport are north of Victoria. Floatplanes and helicopters fly into Victoria from Vancouver.

Start your wine-touring at the southern end of the island in the beautiful harbour city of Victoria. From its downtown core, it's an easy 40min drive up the Saanich Peninsula to farm/wine country.

01 DEVINE VINEYARDS & DISTILLERY

This sustainably farmed, family-owned winery sits hilltop, with a spectacular panorama of the Pacific Ocean and neighbouring farmlands at its feet. John and Catherine Windsor purchased the rundown farm in 2007, then sought the expertise of neighbour winemaker and distiller Ken Winchester to plant their first vines, including Austrian white Grüner Veltliner (Canada's first commercial Grüner release, Grü-V). Winchester now oversees the estate's organic vineyards, winemaking and distilling. When asked about his goals, Windsor notes: 'We want a true farm winery and distillery, sourcing as much from our farm and the Saanich Peninsula as we can. We've started tapping our maple trees for sap for our whisky, and we're installing hives on the property. Vineyard, Orchard, Field and Hive; that is our philosophy for producing.'

the welcoming farmhouse, where you can taste her traditional dry, English-style ciders. Seasonal new releases and numerous community events keep the local community engaged and supportive, and the beautiful hillside venue is perfect for private events. *www.seacider.ca; tel 250-544-4824; 2487 Mt St Michael Rd, Saanichton; 11am–4pm daily*

03 UNSWORTH VINEYARDS

About 45km (an hour's drive) north over the Malahat Mountain from Victoria, along Hwy 1, you'll find yourself in the heart of the Island wine scene: the Cowichan Valley ('Cowichan' translates as 'The Warm Land'). Since launching Unsworth Vineyards nearly a decade ago, the Unsworth family has bravely walked the edge of this marginal Island climate. Tim and Colleen Turyk, together with their son Chris, have dedicated themselves to producing thoughtful wines from the Cowichan Valley, which have gained wide recognition across Canada and overseas. Sustainable harvesting, modern technology and pioneering use of marine-ready hybrids have made this a leading winery to watch.

And there is ample symbiosis in DeVine's products; the Grüner Veltliner, for example, is also part of the base for the signature Vin Gin, double-distilled from Pinot Gris and Grüner Veltliner before undergoing a third distillation along with a dozen local and wild foraged botanicals. *www.devinevineyards.ca; tel 250-665-6983; 6181B Old West Saanich Rd, Saanichton; 12–5pm Thu–Sun*

02 SEA CIDER FARM & CIDERHOUSE

Sea Cider is one of the cornerstone producers responsible for the Pacific Northwest's artisan cider renaissance over the past decade. When sixth-generation farmer Kristen Needham inherited the family orchard as a teenager in 1986, she wanted nothing to do with farming, instead travelling around Europe and Africa to study environmental management and international development. Upon returning, she replanted the family orchard with traditional English bittersweets and bittersharps, planted a second orchard on her mother's farm, then bought a third orchard where Sea Cider stands. She is now cidermaster of

Chris, sommelier and Culinary Institute of America and WSET Diploma graduate, has much to do with its forward motion. He's the force championing the Cowichan Valley's unique Charme de l'Ile – a Charmat-method fizz, light and fresh, made from Island grapes. The on-site Unsworth Restaurant, featuring produce from local farms, is a must-stop for meals in the area. *www.unsworthvineyards.com; tel 250-929-2292; 2915 Cameron Taggart Rd 1, Mill Bay; tasting room 11am–4pm Sun–Thu, to 5pm Fri & Sat, restaurant 11am–close Wed–Sun* ✗

04 BLUE GROUSE ESTATE WINERY & VINEYARD

Blue Grouse is one of the oldest vineyards on the Island: up to 150 different types of grapes were trialled here by the Ministry of Agriculture in the 1970s. It was reborn and rejuvenated in 2012 under the Brunner family, who constructed an architecturally

remarkable tasting room to welcome guests. The Brunners also planted new vineyards for the first time in 20 years, focusing on Pinot Noir and Pinot Gris. Their diverse portfolio of wines includes the original 1970s plantings of Ortega, Bacchus, Siegerrebe and Black Muscat. As of 2017, you can stay overnight in Grouse House, a two-bedroom 'Bed & Bottle' guesthouse overlooking the vines. *www.bluegrouse.ca; tel 250-743-3834; 2182 Lakeside Rd, Duncan; 11am–5pm daily May–Oct, 11am–5pm Wed–Sun Mar, Apr, Nov & Dec* ✗ⓢ

05 AVERILL CREEK VINEYARD

The Cowinchan Valley climate is what drew Andy Johnston to plant his vineyards here – with the single, ambitious aim of making the best Pinot Noir in Canada. After decades as a medical doctor in the Canadian prairies, Johnston was ready to follow his passion for wine in the late 1990s, and gained experience

working in wineries in Tuscany, Australia, France and New Zealand. Averill Creek's gravity-fed winery is set on the south slope of Mt Prevost and specialises in premium Pinot Noir and Pinot Gris. *www.averillcreek.ca; tel 250-709-9986; 6552 North Rd, Duncan; 11am–5pm daily* ⓢ

06 SEA STAR VINEYARDS

A short ferry ride (or two), to Pender Island is a fine way to visit the Gulf Islands' most impressive winery. Sea Star's 26 acres feature two beautiful vineyards; the upper terraces up to Mount Menzies, while the lower cascades down to the beach. 'To our knowledge, no other vineyard in BC is a beachfront property, and we are proud to be growing and using our own coastal grapes', explains Sea Star winemaker Ian Baker. The winery's vines are supplemented by nearby Clam Bay Farm, keeping sourced grapes to their Island (rather than supplementing their own grapes with others purchased elsewhere). Farming is organic and sustainable, and eager Babydoll Southdown sheep handle grass-control in the vineyards. Sea Star's crisp, lively Ortega is one of BC's best white wines and characteristic of the Wine Islands. *seastarvineyards.ca; tel 250-629-6960; 6621 Harbour Hill Dr, Pender Island; Apr–Nov*

WHERE TO STAY

FAIRMONT EMPRESS

Most of the island's wineries lie within an easy 1hr drive of downtown Victoria. The city's grand-dame landmark commands centre stage of the Inner Harbour, with freshly refitted rooms and restaurants courtesy of an elaborate renovation. Book ahead for the famous afternoon tea if you're craving miniature sandwiches and petit-fours, or sink into sumptuous chaises under giant pop-art portraits of Queen Victoria in the glamorous Q Bar. *www.fairmont.com; tel 250-384-8111; 721 Government St, Victoria*

CRAFT-BREWERY BEDS

For something more low-key, two of Victoria's numerous craft breweries offer accommodation. Swans Hotel & Brewpub has art-filled guestrooms atop a boisterous, welcoming pub, while Spinnakers' three private suites cosy up to Canada's first brewpub, a popular harbourfront restaurant.

swanshotel.com; tel 250-361-3310; 506 Pandora Av, Victoria www.spinnakers.com; tel 250-386-2739; 308 Catherine St, Victoria

WHERE TO EAT

HABIT COFFEE

Victoria's walkable downtown is filled with independent eateries. Don't miss fuelling up with Victoria's best espresso at Habit Coffee; bask in the sun at their Atrium branch. *habitcoffee.com; tel 250-590-5953; 808 Yates St, Victoria; 7am–10pm Mon–Fri, 8am–10pm Sat, 8am–6pm Sun*

AGRIUS RESTAURANT

Brunches concocted from organic, local,

seasonal fare are the draw here. Agrius is also the home of one of Victoria's top bakeries, Fol Epi, if you want to pick up provisions for later. *www.agriusrestaurant. com; tel 778-265-6312; 732 Yates St, Victoria; 9am–2pm Sun–Tue, 9am–2pm & 5–10pm Wed–Sat*

SILK ROAD TEA

This beautiful tea emporium in Chinatown has over 100 types of self-pack loose tea from around the world, and an in-store tasting bar where you can educate and rejuvenate with just-brewed tea. *silkroadteastore.com; tel 250-382-0006; 1624 Government St, Victoria; 10am–5pm daily*

BRASSERIE L'ÉCOLE

Across the street from Silk Road Tea is Victoria's top bistro, nearly 15 years running. It's a slip of a room, but, if the line-up of locals for 5.30pm nightly opening is any indication, this classic, friendly spot is worth the wait. *www.lecole.ca; tel 250-475-6260; 1715 Government St, Victoria; 5.30–10pm Thu–Sat*

WHAT TO DO

When you're visiting the Saanich Peninsula wineries, it's worth taking a small detour to Butchart Gardens, one of the famous gardens of North America and home to elaborate seasonal displays of millions of blooms (*www. butchartgardens.com*).

If you want to get out on the water, or truly appreciate the Island's natural beauty, head for Tofino, on the wild west coast; a 5hr drive northwest from Victoria transports you to old-growth rainforests, kilometres of beaches and some of the planet's best surfing.

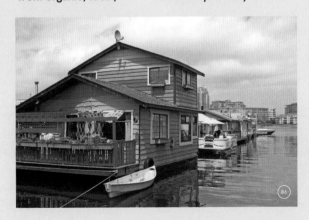

U.S.A.

01

[Arizona]

VERDE VALLEY

The greenest valley in Arizona combines the idyllic wine-growing conditions of the Verde River with the incredible red rocks of Sedona and the rugged escarpment of the Mingus Mountains.

Though Arizona's contemporary wine industry is relatively young, vines were first planted here in the late 1800s. At the time, gold and copper mining made northern Arizona (a high-altitude desert) one of the richest parts of the country. Pioneers believed the craggy landscape could make it a world-renowned wine region akin to parts of northern Spain or Italy – until such dreams were crushed by Prohibition. It wasn't until the 1980s that vineyards began to reappear in the region. Over the last decade, original vines introduced by explorers during the Gold Rush have been rediscovered and are now being cultivated alongside a wealth of Spanish, French and Italian varieties.

While farming in the Verde Valley over the last century has focused on cattle ranching, a local food boom has recently taken hold. Farmers and gardeners now grow a range of produce, both native and introduced, which is making its way to the tables of local restaurants. And this change has brought an increase in local vineyards, too. While Arizona's highest concentration of vineyards still lies in the southeast, the Verde Valley hosts the state's greatest concentration of wineries and tasting rooms.

Arizona has traditionally done well with Rhône varieties including Roussanne, Grenache and Syrah, but, as vineyards have expanded and experimented, Italian and Spanish varieties are appearing. Look out for aromatic white wines made from Malvasia, one of the state's flagship varieties; you'll also discover delicious wines from classic Bordeaux varieties Cabernet Sauvignon and Merlot.

Beyond its wineries, the Verde Valley conceals ancient indigenous settlements and some astonishing landscapes (including Sedona's red rocks), in which to hike.

GET THERE
From Phoenix Airport, it's a 100-mile drive north to Cottonwood or Jerome; head north on I17; take the Verde Valley exit west.

01 JAVELINA LEAP VINEYARD, WINERY & BISTRO

Family-owned Javelina Leap was among Arizona's earliest vineyards and has helped lead the charge in establishing the area's tasting experience, complete with restaurants. A visit to the saloon-like Javelina Leap tasting room shows off some of the most rugged vineyards in the area, over mixed tasting flights of Sauvignon Blanc, Syrah, Merlot, Sangiovese or Tempranillo. This tempting range of wines illustrates how local grape-growers are experimenting with varieties to establish which grows best here.

Food-loving owners Rod and Cynthia Snapp also provide formal pairings and a seasonal tapas menu fuelled by local ingredients to enjoy alongside their wines. Feel free to pop in for a basic tasting or call ahead to schedule an intimate winery tour.
www.javelinaleapwinery.com; tel 298-649-2681; 1565 N Page Springs Rd, Cornville; 11am–6pm daily ✕⑤

02 MERKIN OSTERIA

Merkin Osteria's Italy-inspired, Arizona-ingredients menu features such homegrown delights as pastas made from native heritage grains, sauces concocted from produce grown in the Merkin gardens of the Verde Valley, and meats sourced from local producers. Owner, winemaker and rock star Maynard James Keenan (who swaps touring with bands A Perfect Circle, Puscifer and Tool for winemaking each harvest) is a dedicated supporter of quality Arizona wines. Tipples served in the Osteria are all made and grown by Keenan's own winery, including wines from his Merkin label, with smaller-production experiments also putting in the occasional appearance.
merkinvineyardsosteria.com; tel 928-639-1001; 1001 N Main St, Cottonwood; 11am–9pm daily ✕⑤

03 PILLSBURY WINES

Having landed in Arizona in the late 1990s, New Zealander film-and-wine-maker Sam Pillsbury is responsible for launching some of the state's first contemporary

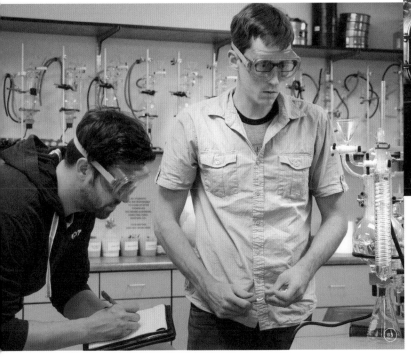

01 Nikki Bagley, Director of
Viticulture, Southwest Wine Center

02 The Southwest Wine Center
at night

03 Enologist Michael Pierce (right)
at the Southwest Wine Center

04 Bottling at the Southwest Wine
Center

The first cooperative winery in northern Arizona, Four-Eight Wineworks has created a boom in smaller Arizona labels

wineries, before then starting his own eponymous label.

Pillsbury's Cottonwood tasting room stars wines grown in Pillsbury vineyards in the southeastern part of the state but poured in the Verde Valley. Tastings include French and Italian varieties, whites and reds, which you can savour under the pines. Pillsbury is one of the world's few producers to work with the rare white variety Symphony, which offers a zesty, aromatic nose that works equally as a dry table or sweet dessert wine. On weekends, expect live music from local musicians. Once you're done swilling, wander Cottonwood's Main St, past restaurants, art galleries and other tasting rooms. *www.pillsburywine.com; tel*

928-595-1001; 1012 N Main St, Cottonwood; 11am–7pm Sun–Thu, to 9pm Fri & Sat $

04 SOUTHWEST WINE CENTER

Arizona is one the USA's few non-west-coast states to offer its own viticulture and enology degree. Northern Arizona's Yavapai College runs a two-year course working with local producers, plus top-notch educators and equipment in its own winery and wine lab. Students farm their own fruit in the school's experimental vineyards and can also source fruit from other wineries in Arizona.

To support the programme, the Southwest Wine Center at Yavapai College delivers tasting flights overlooking one of the

05 Vines at Caduceus
Cellars Vineyard

06 Red Rocks State
Park near Sedona

college vineyards, with a glimpse of the working winery. Each year, students test out their winemaking experiments in the cellar: besides wines made in traditional stainless-steel tanks and oak barrels, there are also varieties aged in clay vessels or fermented in more unusual fashion. All wines are supervised by the Director of Winemaking – so you're guaranteed sound wines while also supporting the region's future wine industry.
southwestwinecenter.org; tel 928-634-6566; 601 W Black Hills Dr, Clarkdale; noon–6pm Thu–Sun $

05 FOUR-EIGHT WINEWORKS

The first cooperative winery in northern Arizona, Four-Eight Wineworks offers drops from a selection of producers who make wine in its cellar. The facility has created a boom in smaller Arizona labels, providing a great first-winery opportunity for graduates of the Southwest Wine Center looking to make their own wine without the capital required to actually establish a winery.

Thanks to the cooperative's diversity of winemakers, tastings are wonderfully varied and you can expect some quite unconventional wines, with shared space and equipment leading to group brainstorming of fresh approaches. You can focus on a single label or fashion your own mixed flight incorporating wines from different producers, which highlights the range of wines crafted in Arizona – everything from lip-puckering Riesling, to fresh, zesty, light-bodied reds. Local beers are also served on tap. Live music on weekends and special events celebrating the release of a new wine are well worth keeping an eye out for.
www.four8wineworks.com; tel 928-649-2007; 907 Main St, Clarkdale; noon–7pm daily $

06 CADUCEUS

Near the top of the hill along Main St in old-town Jerome (a copper-mining town turned bohemian hub), the Caduceus tasting room has become a destination for wine-lovers as much as rock-music fanatics. Caduceus' owner is musician-turned-winemaker Maynard James Keenan, and fans of his rock career often frequent the tasting room hoping to catch a glimpse of the singer; he's also the brains behind Merkin Osteria.

Keenan's premium Caduceus label focuses on small-production, high-end wines from his finest vineyard blocks in both southeastern Arizona and the Verde Valley. Keenan also works to increase vineyard-farming quality and to better understand his own winemaking to raise the bar for Arizona wine.

A tasting at Caduceus will see you sipping a variety of mostly red wines (from Nebbiolo to Tempranillo), perhaps heading home with Arizona-made goods such as the pasta served at Merkin Osteria. Or swing by in the morning when the tasting room morphs into an espresso room.
caduceus.org; tel 928-639-WINE; 158 Main St, Jerome; 11am–6pm Sun–Thu, to 8pm Fri–Sat $

From left: courtesy of Caduceus Cellars / Darren Weiss; © Lonely Planet / Matt Munro

ESSENTIAL INFORMATION

WHERE TO STAY
GRAND HOTEL
Built during Arizona's gold- and copper-mining days, this hotel with a haunted reputation retains much of its historical charm while also being comfortably updated with cosy, unfussy rooms. The downstairs Asylum restaurant is known more for its international wine list than its cuisine. *jeromegrandhotel.net; tel 928-634-8200; 200 Hill St, Jerome*

GHOST CITY INN B&B
Cheery, colourful, individually themed rooms hide within this 1890 Jerome timber boarding house, which has cracking views across Sedona's red rocks and the Verde Valley from its private balconies. *www.ghostcityinn.com; tel 888-634-4678; 541 Main St, Jerome*

WHERE TO EAT
VAQUEROS GRILL & CANTINA
Stop at this old-town Jerome spot for delicious margaritas and beer alongside signature Mexican dishes made with local, seasonal ingredients. The mole sauce is slow-simmered perfection. For a taste of Arizona-Mexican fusion, opt for a Navajo Taco, an Arizona classic with taco stuffings on frybread. *www.vaquerosgrill.org; tel 928-649-9090; 363 Main St, Jerome; 10.30am–8pm Mon–Fri, 8am–9pm Sat & Sun*

WHAT TO DO
RED ROCK STATE PARK, SEDONA
A trip to northern Arizona isn't complete without exploring Sedona's red-rock country, whose flaming-red rock formations are among the world's inimitable landscapes. Walking trails centre on the rocks themselves or the Verde River. During the autumn wet season, a dip in the river is possible, but plan ahead as flashfloods can happen. *azstateparks.com*

MONTEZUMA CASTLE
National Monument, Camp Verde, Arizona

Some of the most fascinating archaeological finds in the USA can be visited in northern Arizona. Montezuma Castle provides a glimpse of a 1000-year-old Sinagua cliff-dwelling settlement. Take a self-

guided tour or arrange time with a tour guide. *www.nps.gov/moca/index.htm*

A DAY TRIP TO FLAGSTAFF
About 50 miles north of Montezuma Castle, Flagstaff makes an excellent day trip from the Verde Valley, driving up the Mogollon Rim, one of the globe's most biodiverse ecosystems. At lower elevations near

Phoenix, the landscape starts with Saguaro cactus forests, then, closer to Sedona, at around 5000ft, juniper forests appear; finally, at the top on the Colorado Plateau, where Flagstaff sits at 7000ft,

lies the largest stand of ponderosa pine in the world. Downtown Flagstaff is graced by buildings dating from the town's founding in the 1800s and populated by restaurants, art galleries, wine bars, and indigenous crafts ranging from woven baskets to handmade silver jewellery. The largest reservation in the US, Navajo Nation, sits just outside Flagstaff. *www.flagstaffarizona.org*

[California]
THE BAY AREA

Can't make it north to wine country? Even in urban California you can still hunt down fine wine tasting thanks to a dynamic mix of urban wineries in San Francisco, Berkeley and Oakland.

People don't think of cities as hot spots for wine tasting, but venture into the San Francisco Bay and you'll find a bevy of urban wineries on both its sides. When Napa and Sonoma started making wine in the 19th century, the vineyards were in wine country, yet most of the grapes were carried by ship into the Oakland and San Francisco harbours. Warehouses along the waterfront served as urban wineries for the growing city population. In the early 20th century, Prohibition changed all that, and urban wineries disappeared. In the last 10 to 15 years, however, they have been reappearing all over the USA – bringing back a little of the Bay's history.

GET THERE
San Francisco and Oakland international airports provide access to these wineries. Travel by BART local trains around the Bay.

If you're staying in the Bay Area and want to do some wine tasting, check out any of these urban wineries. Keep in mind that traffic crossing the Bay Bridge heading west from the eastern Berkeley/Oakland side to San Francisco is notoriously bad in daytime, so you'll want to plan ahead to beat the traffic. For a bit of adventure, you can also take the high-speed Bay Area's Rapid Transit (BART) train under the waves. While on your urban winery tour, you'll encounter plenty of other exciting sites along the way. That's the bonus of an urban winery adventure: it's easy to mix in with a day of shopping, sightseeing and other city-focused activities.

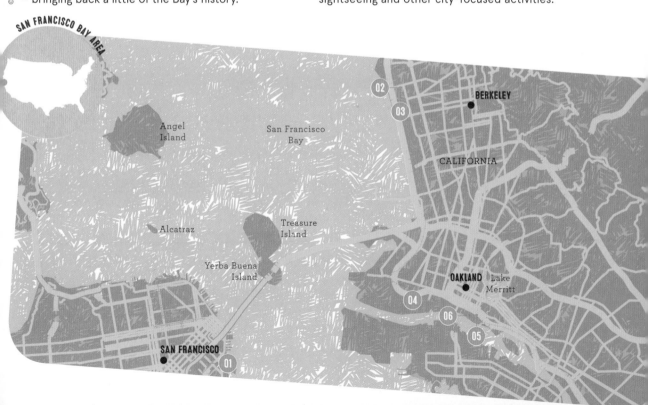

01 BLUXOME STREET WINERY

An urban winery in San Francisco is a rare find – and everyone else thinks it's just as cool as you do. Pop in during the week but be sure to make reservations for the weekend. Once in, you'll enjoy a range of Pinots and ultrafresh whites. Just like the history it pays tribute to, Bluxome Street winery sources grapes from the world-class wine-growing regions to the north, then makes its wines in the city. The focus is on vineyards hugged close to the coast to maintain a sense of crisp, mineral drive inside all that flavour. Keep an eye out for the distinctive Sauvignon Blanc and try the refreshing Chardonnays as well. Culinary offerings focus on low-key tidbits like salumi and cheese platters.

The tasting room sits right inside the urban winery, close to the Bay Bridge, so it's an easy first stop in San Francisco, before then continuing across the bridge to explore more East Bay wineries. *www.bluxomewinery.com; tel 415-543-5353; 53 Bluxome St, San Francisco; 1–8pm daily* ✕ $

02 BROC CELLARS

Broc Cellars is only open to visitors on weekends, but, if you drop in then, you stand a good chance of being greeted by winemaker Chris Brockway himself. In just a decade,

Brockway has pulled off one of the most fashionable wineries in California, making unexpected wines from a vast assortment of varieties: from Rhône blends to fresh Zinfandel and the occasional mineral-driven Chardonnay.

Wines here always come with a great story behind them, as Brockway has a way of finding the most interesting vineyards in northern California. Many of the creative wine labels are hand-drawn and designed by a local artist. During harvest, the tasting room sits inside part of the winery, so you'll get to see plenty of winemaking activity – the perfect opportunity to learn more about unusual styles of winemaking, like fermenting white wines in concrete eggs, or reds in decades-old wooden tanks.
broc-cellars.myshopify.com; tel 510-542-9463; 1300 5th St, Berkeley; 1–5pm Sat & Sun 💲

03 DONKEY & GOAT

Right next door to Broc Cellars sits Donkey & Goat winery. Leaders of the natural-wine movement in the USA, Jared and Tracey Brandt like to make wines with as few additives as possible. They primarily focus on Rhône varieties, both whites and reds, but make some other classics like Chardonnay and Merlot as well. Don't miss their distinctive sparkling wine, with its combination of funk, freshness and bright fruit flavours made from Chardonnay. If you call ahead, they'll set up

Leader of the natural wine movement in the USA, Donkey & Goat likes to make wines with as few additives as possible

01 Lombard St, San Francisco

02 Grape crushing at Donkey & Goat

03 Weekend tasting at Broc Cellars

04 Outside at Donkey & Goat

05 Biking in the Bay Area

a selection of local cheeses alongside the wines. Bocce ball picnics are hosted in summer – a great way to enjoy the house wines and a Berkeley summer with a bunch of other wine enthusiasts.
www.donkeyandgoat.com; tel 510-868-9174; 1340 5th St, Berkeley; 1–6pm Fri–Sun 🍴💲

04 CAMPOVIDA

Campovida grows its grapes at a farm 170km north in Hopland (see The Farm on p62) but makes its own wines available in this Oakland tasting room. The goal is to create a space all about bolstering a sense of community. It's a great spot to cosy up for conversation with friends over a glass of wine and a local-charcuterie plate. It's also

rented out during the week for community events, so you'll need to visit between Thursday and Sunday. You're a long way from the farm itself but the Campovida family manages to share just enough of its passion for the place to make you feel like you've stepped out of the city and into a small-town atmosphere (even if just for a moment). Stop by for a glass or settle in for a tasting flight.

Campovida wines are a varied fresh and flavourful range. Whites include traditional French varieties such as Chardonnay, Pinot Gris and Sauvignon Blanc, along with unusual wines such as northeast Italy's native Tocai Friulano. Among diverse reds, expect Syrah, Zinfandel, Primitivo, Cabernet

Sauvignon and even Nebbiolo. *www.campovida.com; tel 510-550-7273; 95 Linden St, Oakland; 4–9pm Thu & Fri, 1–9pm Sat, 1–6pm Sun* ✕ 💲

05 DASHE CELLARS

The full winery experience, without leaving the city. Winemaker Mike Dashe is one of California's most respected makers of Zinfandel: his Dry Creek Valley Zin is regularly shown in wine classes or tastings as the paradigm of the variety from the region. After learning the ropes at prestigious Californian Zinfandel house Ridge, he established his own label and took a risk by making it in one of the first contemporary urban wineries in Oakland. The gamble paid off:

Dashe Cellars has become an Oakland destination. At the tasting bar you'll be right in the thick of all the winery activity; just across the room you'll see the cellar crew topping barrels and checking the progress of the wine. During harvest, expect a bit of well-organised mayhem as fruit comes in from all over the state to be transformed into the wine you're drinking. Dashe Cellars is one of California's most revered Zinfandel producers, but it's also one of the most affordable. *www.dashecellars.com; tel 510-452-1800; 55 4th St, Oakland; noon–6pm Thu–Sun* 💲

06 URBAN LEGEND CELLARS

Insatiably curious defines the efforts of Marilee and Steve Shaffer and the work they do with Urban Legends winery. Their tasting room is right in the middle of the winery, where the very wines you're tasting were made, and you're guaranteed to be talking with either Marilee or Steve – or both. The couple does everything, from making the wine to managing the tasting room, and sources fruit for wines from all over the state. Options range from light, botanical Albariño and unexpected Italian varieties to zesty Zinfandel, California's classic. When you're done tasting, take a stroll and dine at one of the neighbourhood restaurants. *www.ulcellars.com; tel 510-545-4356; 200 2nd St, Suite 1, Oakland; 3–8pm Thu–Sun* 💲

04

From left: courtesy of Donkey & Goat; Broc Cellars; © Gary Crabbe / Alamy Stock Photos

WHERE TO STAY

REDWOOD HOUSE B&B
For an urban stay with a warm personal touch, seek out this cosy B&B in the heart of the Oakland Hills. It has a peaceful neighbourhood feel, with beautiful views of the Bay, city and surrounding landscapes.
tel 510-530-6840; 39th Selkirk Ave, Oakland

Z HOTEL
It's hard to gain better access to the wealth of activities in Oakland than by staying in bustling Jack London Sq, where you'll have the waterfront, the marina, the business district and shopping right on your doorstep. Z Hotel has a distinct Oakland vibe, with smartly comfortable and contemporary rooms.
www.zhoteljacklondon square.com; tel 510-452-4565; Jack London Sq, 233 Broadway, Oakland

WHERE TO EAT

BARTAVELLE COFFEE & WINE BAR
Serving fresh California ingredients in a tiny little hole-in-the-wall space, the Bartavelle team shows you why avocado toast became

an international craze, and how something as simple as an egg can make everything better. Bartavelle picks its own local produce and combines its menu of morning porridge with excellent coffee, or, later on, prosciutto and Middle Eastern-style tasting plates with an afternoon glass of wine. Step to the left to grab a loaf of bread from Acme Bakery, a Bay Area bread lover's first stop, or to the right for a deep dive into European wine at Kermit Lynch Wine Merchant.
bartavellecafe.com; tel 510-524-2473; 1603 San Pablo Ave, Berkeley; 7am–3pm Mon–Thu, to 5pm Fri & Sat, 8am–3pm Sun

WHAT TO DO

EAST BAY URBAN WINERY BIKE TOURS
One of the fun, unexpected advantages of the recent boom in urban wineries is cycling between them. Spend the day going from tasting to tasting with an organised bicycle tour, or just rent a bicycle and go self-guided. You'll get started at Jack London Sq, within cycling distance of a number of the region's favourite urban wineries.
eastbaywinerybike tours.com; tel 510-285-7884; Jack London Sq, 655 3rd St, Oakland

WHOLE BREW WORLD
If you want to sit back and let someone else do the work, or simply fancy looking beyond wine, join an organised Bay Area beer tour. Whole Brew World works with some of the very best breweries throughout the extended Bay Area to give you a taste of the region's favourite beers. The team assigns a pick-up location upon booking.
wholebrewworld.com; tel 925-725-5029

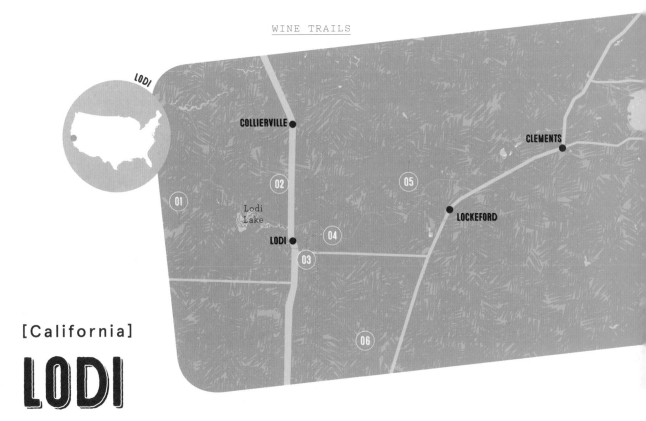

[California]

LODI

On the edges of the Sacramento Delta, between the Sierra Mountains and the San Francisco Bay Area, the swiftly emerging Lodi wine country is blossoming with a family-owned, small-winery scene.

The Sacramento Delta is one of the centres of old-vine Zinfandel. Over several generations, the region's farming families have helped transform the low-lying areas of the Sacramento-San Joaquin River Delta into one of California's most plentiful wine regions. Around the town of Lodi, farming families found success growing a mix of cherries, nuts, orchard fruits and table grapes; wine grapes were planted as just another crop. In the middle of the 20th century, Lodi was one of the country's richest sources of table grapes. But as interest in table wine increased, the value of the region's old vines grew, and newer vineyards went in. Even so, since the fruit used to be sold to bigger winemaking corporations, it's only in the last two decades that family-owned wineries have begun to flourish around Lodi.

Lodi itself sits on a bend in the Mokelumne River, also the name of the region's most central American Viticultural Area (AVA). It's the original home of California's famed Mondavi family (before it made a name for itself in Napa Valley wine) and still carries the rustic charm of a long-standing farming community. Farming needs as well as farming families guide local politics; the annual regional autumn fair, for example, includes prizes for animals and produce, as well as grapes.

The wine-country lifestyle, however, has now begun to change the Lodi landscape. The region's top hotel, Wine & Roses, is known for its wine-themed hospitality and luxury day spa, while the plethora of local tasting rooms ranges from small walk-in warehouse spaces to palatial wineries with gardens and lunch menus.

GET THERE
Lodi is 45 miles south of Sacramento airport, 80 miles northwest of Oakland airport and 100 miles northwest of San Francisco airport.

01 JESSIE'S GROVE

The oldest Zinfandel vines in the USA, as well as some of the most ancient Cinsault vines in the world, find their home at Jessie's Grove. The old building housing the tasting room lingers amid gardens, on the other side of which is the family's historical barn, where you'll catch a glimpse of the region's farming and winemaking past. Founder Jessie Spenker planted the vineyard on land she inherited from her parents, and the current owner Wanda (Jessie's granddaughter) has worked to preserve its history, creating a farm museum from outdated farming equipment.

On Saturday mornings you can usually enjoy a seat next to Wanda on the back patio, where she'll happily share stories about her family's farm history. A short walk around the grounds leads to a timeworn oak grove, the site of an annual music festival and numerous weddings throughout the year. A taste of wines from Jessie's Grove unveils the importance of old vines for both dry table wines and sweet Port-style wines. You could do worse than bringing a picnic lunch to enjoy on the property.
www.jessiesgrovewinery.com; tel 209-368-0880; 1973 W Turner Rd, Lodi; noon–5pm daily $

02 FIELDS FAMILY

Fields Family focuses on small lots of handcrafted wines, both whites and reds, primarily from Rhône varieties. Friends Ryan Sherman and Russ Fields started making wine in their driveway when they ended up with a bunch of grapes one year during harvest. Happy with the result, the duo started producing wine every year – until the quality became so high, and the volume so great, that they began selling it.

Visit the Fields Family tasting room, adjacent to the winery, in the thick of harvest to see the winemaking processes in action. The rest of the year, you can relish flights from across the Fields Family portfolio, which focuses on wines that over-deliver quality for their price range. For whites, the Grenache Blanc is a particular

standout; among the reds, look for their light-bodied Mourvèdre or succulent Syrah. A few recent choice additions include fresh, aromatic Vermentino and old-vine Cinsault, as well as a classic Pinot Noir and a Cabernet Sauvignon. *fieldsfamilywines.com; tel 209-896-6012; 3803 Woodbridge Rd E, Acampo; 11am–5pm daily* $

03 MCCAY CELLARS

Winemaker Michael McCay kickstarted his career working for one of the region's larger wineries, before launching McCay Cellars in 2007, helping to lead Lodi's small-winery boom.

Dedicated to making wines from older vine sites throughout the region, McCay produces single-vineyard Zinfandels and a range of red Rhône varieties. His tasting room and wine club combine his passion for wine with his love for cycling. The Lodi region, with its relatively flat open spaces, is perfect for cyclists, whether you enjoy biking between tasting rooms or genuine endurance rides. McCay Cellars Cycling Club meets monthly for group rides, culminating in an after-ride 'wine-down' with McCay Cellars drops. Otherwise, swing by the tasting room for a single glass or a mixed flight of wines. *www.mccaycellars.com; tel 209-368-9463; 1370 E Turner Rd, Lodi; noon–5pm daily* $

04 ST AMANT

One of Lodi's original boutique-sized, family-owned wineries, sustainably farmed St Amant inspired many of this region's other smaller family wineries. The Spencer family began planting its first vineyard in the Sierra Foothills (now an AVA) in the 1970s. To expand production and understand the vines of another region, Tim Spencer approached some of the most established grape-growers in Lodi, who universally sold their fruit to higher-production wineries and as a result had never tasted wine from their own sites. Tim began making small volumes of Lodi's finest wines, introducing the growers to their own vineyards' tastes; over time, this encouraged many local grape-growing families to start their own wineries.

Tastings at St Amant include the chance to sample wine from some of the oldest vineyards in the region. Dedicated primarily to single-vineyard Zinfandel, St Amant also makes small productions of wine from traditional Port varieties and a little Cabernet Sauvignon. *www.stamantwine.com; tel 209-367-0646; 1 Winemaster Way, Lodi; noon–4pm Thu–Sun or by appointment* 🅢

05 ACQUIESCE

While the history of Lodi wine rests in robust old-vine reds from Zinfandel and other historical mixed-black vineyards, newer producers like Acquiesce have expanded the region's portfolio. Acquiesce owner and winemaker Susan Tipton is devoted to growing and making Rhône white varieties on her family's farm. She and her wines have an ardent fan following and have earned their place among the best of California's Rhône wines; her Grenache Blanc and small-production Picpoul Blanc are particular highlights.

From spring to autumn, you're likely to meet Susan herself pouring the wines in the tasting room, where rotating art displays happen. Her passion is in both food and wine, and each glass is served with a food pairing. Be sure to arrive early though: Acquiesce's wines are relatively small-production and, once they sell out, that's it for the year, meaning the tasting room often closes over winter. *www.acquiescevineyards.com; tel 209-333-6102; 22353 N Tretheway Rd, Acampo; Mar–Dec* 🗙 🅢

06 HARNEY LANE

The Mettler-Lerner family, one of Lodi's founding farming families, has transformed Harney Lane winery into one of the region's destination tasting rooms. You can keep it simple with a mixed-flight tasting at the bar (book ahead for large groups), or schedule a private Grape to Glass tour of the property, which takes in a walk through the vineyards and an educational look at how wine is produced. To enjoy the on-site gardens, opt for bottle service; there are picnic-style cheese and charcuterie platters to wash it all down.

Harney Lane keeps California's signature Zinfandel at the core of its portfolio, of course, but also produces crisp Albariño (perfect for the area's warmer temperatures) and more robust red wines such as Tempranillo or Cabernet Sauvignon. In spring and summer months, keep an eye out for the Zinfandel-based rosé. *www.harneylane.com; tel 209-365-1900; 9010 E Harney Ln, Lodi; noon–5pm daily* 🗙 🅢

ESSENTIAL INFORMATION

WHERE TO STAY
WINE & ROSES
Combine the local wine-country experience with soothing spa sessions at this heart-of-Lodi hotel. Rooms are charmingly stylish, several tucked into the original heritage building. An outdoor pool (ideal for the region's warmer weather), a restaurant, a wine bar and live evening piano are welcome touches. Attached to the hotel is the Lodi Wine & Visitor Centre, which features an intimate look at the region's farming history, especially grape-farming, plus mixed flights from a huge range of Lodi wines. *winerose.com; tel 209-334-6988; 2505 W Turner Rd, Lodi*

HAMPTON INN & SUITES
A pool, spa and fitness centre complement smart, plain rooms at this comfortable, orange-hued Hilton hotel. *hamptoninn3.hilton. com; tel 209-369-2700; 1337 Beckman Rd, Lodi*

WHERE TO EAT
ZIN BISTRO
In keeping with the region's signature wine, Zin Bistro offers casual dining centred on American-style dishes that go well with hearty, red Lodi wines. It's known especially for plates like pork scallopini and slow-cooked lamb, but there are also simpler choices like steak sandwiches. *Tel 209-224-8223; 722 W Lodi Ave, Lodi; 11am–2pm & 5–8.30pm Tue–Sat*

LA CAMPANA TAQUERIA
For authentically good Mexican food at outrageously affordable prices, head to this town-centre taqueria. Tortillas are made fresh; the tacos especially are a standout. *Tel 209-369-2877; 2346 Maggio Cir, Lodi; 5am–6pm Mon–Fri, to 4.30pm Sat*

DANCING FOX
Local grapes inspire the cooking at this winery-brewery-bakery restaurant, whose signature home-baked breads are rooted in Petite Sirah grape cultures. Wood-fired pizzas star on the wide-ranging Mediterranean menu, and brunch is served on Sundays. *www.dancingfoxlodi. com; tel 209-366-2634; 203 School St, Lodi; 11am–9pm Tue–Thu, 11am–10pm Fri & Sat, 9am–3pm Sun*

WHAT TO DO
ISENBERG CRANE RESERVE
Millions of birds migrate between Canada and Alaska in the north and California's Central Valley. In winter, the grasslands outside Lodi become home to thousands of sandhill cranes and American white pelicans, among other species, making this a top spot for birdwatchers. Expand your animal-viewing experience next door at the Micke Grove Park (8am to sunset), home to creatures from around the world; the facility works to save endangered species, and also hosts a Japanese garden. *Woodbridge Rd, Lodi*

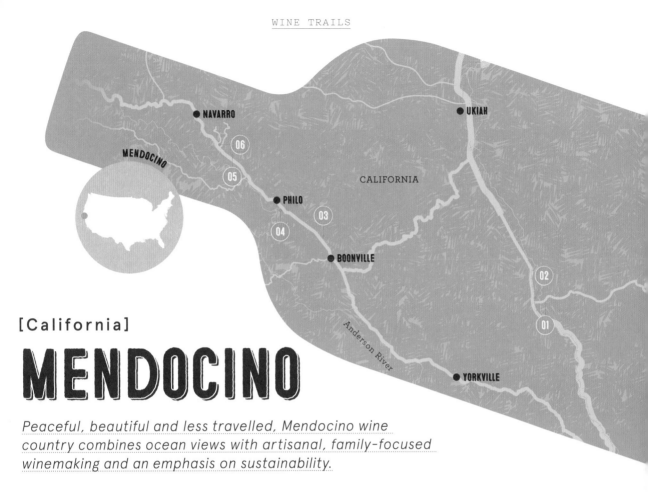

NAVARRO

UKIAH

MENDOCINO

06

05

CALIFORNIA

PHILO

03

04

02

BOONVILLE

01

Anderson River

YORKVILLE

[California]

MENDOCINO

Peaceful, beautiful and less travelled, Mendocino wine country combines ocean views with artisanal, family-focused winemaking and an emphasis on sustainability.

Mendocino sits in the north of California's wine-growing region, with vineyards circling the tiny town of Philo within the famed Anderson Valley AVA. Aromatic varieties like Gewürztraminer have a refreshing wash of acidity in Mendocino, while brightness and fruit purity define the region's Pinot Noir. Cool nights and rugged valleys open to the ocean's revitalising influence mean wines carry depth of flavour with plenty of freshness – and also that you'll need an evening jacket. Even so, temperatures can warm significantly during the day. Wineries further inland are able to ripen more robust wines such as a selection of Italian varieties, though most coastal wines focus on light-bodied styles.

The town of Mendocino, northwest of the Anderson Valley, sits perched over the Pacific Ocean. Here, wines are celebrated alongside fresh seafood often just harvested that morning. At the start of every year, Mendocino enjoys its Crab, Wine & Beer festival, while at the end of every autumn it turns to its Mushroom, Wine & Beer festival. Both foraged-food extravaganzas unite some of the state's top chefs with the region's favourite beverages.

The Mendocino wine area is still relatively remote and the local community more private in comparison to California's other wine-growing destinations. Yet, while this region has been less focused on pushing for the financial benefits of tourism, it also likes a good celebration and you're guaranteed to find it warm-hearted and genuine. Besides the seasonally gathered fruits of the sea and the forest, local restaurants offer specialities like homemade pie for dessert and fresh bread for your sandwiches. At the same time, the area's wines rank among California's best.

GET THERE
Mendocino is 175 miles northwest of San Francisco International Airport, along Hwys 101 and 128.

01 THE FARM AT HOPLAND, CAMPOVIDA

The Farm at Hopland serves as the home property for Mendocino's family-owned Campovida winery, which produces a delightfully varied selection of fresh French-style (Chardonnay, Sauvignon Blanc, Pinot Gris) and unexpected Italian whites, alongside reds ranging from Zinfandel and Nebbiolo to Syrah and Cabernet Sauvignon. Campovida also runs an urban tasting room in Oakland (see p51), but you'll need an appointment to swing by the Farm at Hopland. Visits include a tour of the oak-fringed grounds (which are dotted with original barns dating back to the 1890s) and a food-and-wine pairing session fuelled by ingredients produced on-site.

The Campovida family also especially likes to share food, and often hosts collaboration events with other local wineries and food growers. If booking a farm tour doesn't appeal, drop in at the nearby Piazza de Campovida in Hopland to taste Campovida wines, enjoy the taverna and pizzeria or even stay the night; seven smart suites are available for a private wine-country experience.
www.campovida.com
The Farm at Hopland: tel 707-744-8797; 13601 Old River Rd, Hopland; by appointment ✕ 💲
and Piazza de Campovida: tel 707-744-1977; 13441 S Hwy 101, Hopland

02 GRAZIANO FAMILY OF WINES & SAINT GREGORY

The Grazianos have farmed grapes in the Mendocino region since the early 1900s. Today, some of the same ancient varieties – such as old-vine Carignane and Valdiguie, as well as Moscato – are still cultivated here, though Graziano has also expanded its portfolio as the wine region has grown. Alongside full-bodied wines from Italian varieties under its own label, Graziano also produces a line of French varieties under the label Saint Gregory. Italian immigrants helped establish the early wine industry of northern California, but, after Prohibition, wine-growing shifted to predominantly French varieties. Given the fresher climate in Mendocino, many of the grapes grown here originate in the cooler areas of northern France.

The dedicated Graziano family's members work in both the vineyards and winery. The tasting room is an intimate space that offers mixed flights of both wine labels, as well as tastings of the family's Monte Volpe olive oils.
www.grazianofamilyofwines.com; tel 707-744-8466; 13275 S Hwy 101, Suite 3, Hopland; 10am–5pm daily 💲

03 ELKE VINEYARDS

The Elke family has been growing grapes in Mendocino for over 30 years, establishing some of

01 The tasting room patio at Roederer Estate

02 Sun-blessed vines at Roederer Estate

the area's earliest sparkling-wine vineyards. Today, Elke Vineyards continues to be family-owned, with a focus on Pinot Noir and sparkling wines. A visit to the tasting room here includes a quick

Courtesy of Roederer Estate

history lesson on both the family and wine-growing in this region. Tastings happen in a rustic style, with flights poured at a table made of wine barrels. If you have time, you can find out more about the process of making wine, from vineyard to glass, with a wander through the Elke vines.

As with much of Mendocino's wine industry, the tasting room is only open on weekends; during the week the family is busy farming. Don't be surprised if the family members who grew the grapes are also pouring your wine. For special-release parties and winery events, local chefs prepare food to pair with the family's wines. *www.elkevineyards.com; 707-709-8843; 12351 Hwy 128, Boonville; 11am–5pm Fri-Mon* ✗ ⑤

04 DREW

In the early noughties, Jason and Molly Drew started their eponymous winery dedicated to small-production, handcrafted wines from vineyards of the Mendocino Ridge and Anderson Valley AVAs. With a focus on Pinot Noir and Syrah, Drew wines helped bring attention to the high quality it is possible to extract from the cool, coastal regions of Mendocino. Dew drops are decidedly savoury in character, but also offer fruit purity and great ageing potential.

In the vineyard, the Drews are dedicated to organic farming and sustainable practices. Besides working the estate vineyard, Drew also sources fruit from distinctive sites throughout the region, making single-vineyard expressions of varieties to showcase Mendocino's best. The Drew tasting room is located within The Madrones, a large complex that also hosts accommodation, other Anderson Valley tasting rooms and one of the region's most celebrated restaurants, Stone & Embers. *www.drewwines.com; 707-895-9599; 9000 Hwy 128, Philo; 11am–5pm Thu–Mon* 🟊

05 ROEDERER ESTATE

If you don't know where to look for the Roederer Estate, you're quite likely to miss it. The vineyards and winery are tucked into rolling hills and barely visible from the road. This, of course, means that you can expect a quiet wine-country experience in a pristine spot. While Roederer is considered one of the finest sparkling-wine producers in the world, its Mendocino tasting offering is kept true to the rural wilds of the region – a relaxing, outdoorsy experience focused on the beauty of the forests and hills surrounding the vineyards.

Known for making outstanding Champagne in France, Roederer

03 Winemaker Jason Drew

04 Mendocino's beautiful Pacific coast

Formed in the early noughties, Drew Wines helped bring attention to the high quality it is possible to extract from the cool, coastal regions of Mendocino

expanded its sparkling-wine efforts to the cool climates of northern California in the early 1980s. Plans for the Mendocino property began in 1982, establishing Roederer as one of the very first to make sparkling wine in the Mendocino region. Tastings feature a full range of sparkling wines, including a classic dry white sparkling of

Chardonnay and Pinot Noir and a collection of sparkling rosés. *www.roedererestate.com; 707-895-2288; 4501 Hwy 128, Philo; 11am–5pm daily* 🟊

06 HANDLEY CELLARS

Like most of the top wineries in Mendocino, Handley Cellars is a small-production, family-owned winery. Vineyards, winemaking and even the tasting room itself are run by the Handley family. Though focused on boutique winemaking, the Handleys are recognised for producing wonderfully fresh, top-quality wines at reasonable prices.

Handley Cellars sits on one side of a historical ranch, its original barn and water tower still standing. The property is perfect for patio tastings (which happen to be dog-friendly, too). You'll be sipping right next to the vineyards, and, depending on the time of year, surrounded by blooming lavender or other seasonal flowers. Thanks to the family's passion for travel, you'll also have the chance to explore an unexpected international art collection. Walk-in tastings are welcome, though if you call ahead you can also arrange cheese pairings for your wines, or schedule a private tour of the grounds. *www.handleycellars.com; 800-733-3151; 4151 Hwy 128, Philo; 10am–5pm daily* 🍴🟊

ESSENTIAL
INFORMATION

WHERE TO STAY

HEADLANDS INN BED & BREAKFAST

In the heart of Mendocino town, enjoying coastal views and within easy walking distance of restaurants and art galleries, Headlands provides classic Victorian-home styling with updated comforts. Woodburning fireplaces and spa tubs decorate the rooms, while breakfast features local seasonal favourites. *www.headlandsinn.com; tel 800-354-4431; 10453 Howard St, Mendocino*

VAN DAMME STATE PARK CAMPGROUNDS

Just south of Mendocino, Van Damme State Park offers a beautifully scenic year-round camping experience, with a fine beach and a fern-laden forest, as well as hiking trails and self-guided nature tours. *www.parks.ca.gov; 707-937-0851; 8001 CA1, Little River*

WHERE TO EAT

BOONVILLE GENERAL STORE

Good, honest local food at Boonville General Store includes straightforward classics like omelettes and home-fried potatoes for breakfast, plus soups or sandwiches for lunch. But it's the impressive range of pies that have become the signature offering. *www.boonvillegeneral store.com; tel 707-895-9477; 14077 Hwy 128, Boonville; 8am–3pm daily*

WHAT TO DO

MENDOCINO ARTS CENTER

With its picturesque surroundings, Mendocino is known for its artist community as much as its food-and-wine scene. Local artists can often be spotted outside with a paintbrush, capturing the ocean or vineyard scenery, and the area hosts plenty of art shows and studios. Find out more at the Mendocino Arts Center, which has rotating shows, a local-art shop and an artist-in-residence program. It also provides information on local art festivals, open-studio programs and other gallery experiences. *www.mendocino artcenter.org; tel 707-937-5818; 45200 Little Lake St, Mendocino*

CELEBRATIONS

MUSHROOM, WINE & BEER FESTIVAL

More than 3000 mushroom varieties, including several rare types, grow naturally in Mendocino County, and the end-of-year rains bring them out in full force. Foraging trips and wine- or beer-pairing workshops are the core of this November festival, but you'll also experience live music performances, educational exhibits and a wealth of mushroom-focused dishes. *www.mendocino.com*

CRAB, WINE & BEER FESTIVAL

Mendocino goes crazy for crab season every January. Chefs travel from all over the state, with others even flying in from around the country, to create seafood dishes that are served alongside the region's very best wine and beer. *www.mendocino.com*

③

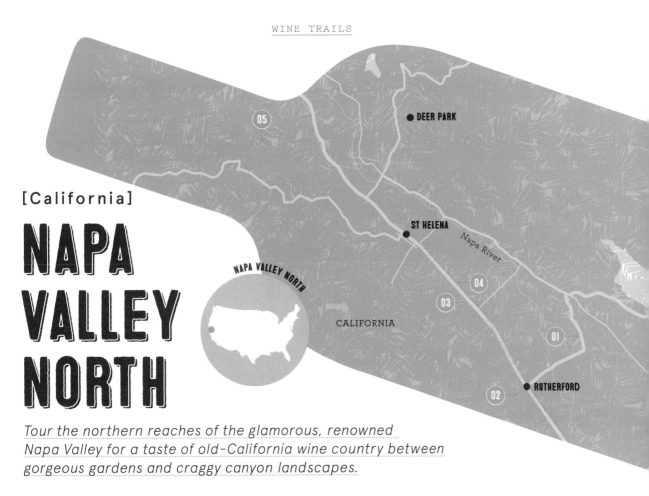

[California]

NAPA VALLEY NORTH

Tour the northern reaches of the glamorous, renowned Napa Valley for a taste of old-California wine country between gorgeous gardens and craggy canyon landscapes.

Home to some of the world's finest and most famed wineries, the northern half of Napa Valley celebrates both the region's rugged past and its luxurious present. Northern Napa Valley is just a 2hr drive north from San Francisco and can even be reached with a quick ferry ride across San Francisco Bay then a short drive. All the way north at Calistoga, you'll find hot springs and some of the state's best spas, while St Helena delivers great restaurants and art galleries. Some of the area's larger wineries build on this creative theme, offering rotating art shows or sculpture gardens to explore. If you'd rather keep things simple, life-on-the-farm experiences or hikes along the river are also possible.

The northern half of Napa Valley basks in warmer temperatures than its southern counterpart, meaning wines from this area are often a bit bolder; as temperatures cool down significantly at night, however, wines also retain their freshness. Cabernet Sauvignon and Merlot are now among the most common varieties here, but not so long ago Zinfandel and Petite Sirah had a greater foothold, and some of these wines can still be sought out today. Reds here tend to be more full-bodied than those from the southern part of the valley.

Northern Napa Valley wineries also make plenty of whites – sometimes with fruit from cooler areas outside Napa – to satiate the curious wine lover. The local Sauvignon Blanc, for example, is rich, infused with stone fruits and complex flavours, rather than being a grassy or gooseberry sample of this variety. Many producers working with Sauvignon Blanc here are also celebrating the inclusion of new oak, which brings additional texture to the wines alongside hints of baking spices and molasses.

GET THERE
Three international airports – San Francisco, Oakland and Sacramento – are all a 2hr drive (60 to 70 miles) from here.

01 FROG'S LEAP

Home to one of Napa's most idyllic farm-and-garden experiences, Frog's Leap is also one of its most affordable wineries, with a keen emphasis on organic, sustainable farming. Owner-winemaker John Williams is considered one of the founders of modern Napa Valley, having moved to the region in the 1970s and launched his winery (now fully solar-powered) in 1981; he can regularly be found at Frog's Leap alongside his 1960s Chevy pick-up truck, and is known for his excellent Merlot, Zinfandel and Sauvignon Blanc.

The Frog's Leap tasting room is one of the valley's most pleasant spots to enjoy well-crafted wines with the power common to northern Napa, while also avoiding the region's often-excessive pricing. Showcasing a flavourful line-up of respected red varieties, alongside a couple of white wines, tastings happen in the midst of the winery gardens. Regular tasting flights provide a solid introduction to the Frog's Leap classics, or you can pay a touch extra to also sample a few of the small-production varieties. Book ahead for tours and tastings. *www.frogsleap.com; tel 707-963-4704; 8815 Conn Creek Rd, Rutherford; 10am–4pm daily* ✕ $

02 INGLENOOK

You'd be hard pressed to find a Napa Valley winery more iconic than Inglenook. Dating from the late 19th century, Inglenook's château is one of the most storied buildings in the northern Napa Valley and was built under Finnish winemaker Gustav Niebaum. The property was purchased in the 1970s by film

01 Misty Napa wine country

02 The view from Stony Hill vineyard

03 Harvest time at Corison

04 A tour at Corison

05 Bottled wine at Stony Hil

Cathy Corison founded her winery back in 1987 and is one of the first women to serve as a head winemaker in the Napa Valley

director Francis Ford Coppola, who has spent the decades since restoring the estate to its original grandeur – with a few upgrades.

Today, visitors can enjoy private tastings, lunch with wine in the bistro, library tastings of older vintages, or simply a sip at the bar. All guests must check in at the front visitor centre. Call ahead to schedule a tour or heritage tasting.

Inglenook wines are classic Napa Valley: finely executed red blends centre on Cabernet Sauvignon and are balanced with other Bordeaux varieties such as Merlot and Cabernet Franc.
www.inglenook.com; tel 707-968-1100; 1991 St Helena Hwy, Rutherford; 10am–5pm daily ✕ ⑤

03 CORISON

One of Napa Valley's most respected and pioneering winemakers, Cathy Corison is a long-term advocate of 100% Cabernet Sauvignon made with both flavour and finesse. She's also among the first women to serve as head winemaker in the valley, having founded Corison back in 1987. Cathy's husband William Martin, meanwhile, is behind the design of the Victorian-inspired winery barn.

Though the Corison label focuses only on Cabernet, Cathy also makes small quantities of Gewürztraminer and rosé to open tastings, which must be booked in advance and come highly recommended. Flights include a refreshing white to accompany a

tour of the winery and old-vine Cabernet vineyard, before you head back inside to visit the single-vineyard Cabernets and an older vintage or two. It's a special tasting experience incorporating some of the region's finest red wines. An in-depth library tasting is also on offer. *www.corison.com; tel 707-963-0826; 987 St Helena Hwy, St Helena; 10am–5pm daily by appointment* ⑤

04 HEITZ

A trip to the Heitz tasting room won't unveil the most lavish aspects of Napa Valley. Instead, its fuss-free, rustic style gives you a glimpse into the region's down-home, farming past. Farmers, often forgotten amid

today's fashionable wine-country lifestyle, are the original founders of Napa Valley and its vineyards.

True to its history, Heitz keeps it simple, without even demanding a fee for tasting wines – unusual in Napa Valley. If you choose to do a walk-in visit, expect to be trying Heitz's more affordable wines. Glasses range from uncommon Grignolino – a grape usually native to Italy, which Heitz produces as both a charming red and a dry rosé – to classics like Zinfandel and less-expensive Cabernet Sauvignons. The wine that made Heitz the world's first cult winery, Martha's Vineyard Cabernet Sauvignon, isn't available to taste by the glass, so you'll have to buy the bottle if you fancy a sip.

www.heitzcellar.com; tel 707-963-3542; 436 St Helena Hwy, St Helena; 11am–4.30pm daily

05 STONY HILL

Tucked into forested mountains northwest of St Helena, Stony Hill is striking in that it focuses on white wines rather than the typical Napa Valley reds. Founded by the McCrea family in the 1940s, this was the first winery in northern California to open after the shutdown of Prohibition, celebrating Chardonnay, Riesling and Gewürztraminer. Today, wines are still made in the exact same way as when Stony Hill launched, even using some of the original barrels. As a result, the wines are fresh and light-bodied, with a focus on aromatics.

06 Historic Stony Hill

07 Farmstead restaurant at Long Meadow Ranch

To round out its portfolio, the business, which remains family owned has also added Cabernet Sauvignon.

Visits to Stony Hill do require an appointment, but they're more than worth the effort for the intimate experience of this historic winery and the personal treatment you'll receive as you taste on the hillside patio of the McCrea family's home. *www.stonyhillvineyard.com; 707-963-2636; 3331 St Helena Hwy, St Helena; 10am–3.30pm daily by appointment* $

WHERE TO STAY
MEADOWOOD
For luxury in a peaceful, private mountain setting, book a suite at the forest-fringed Meadowood estate on the eastern edge of St Helena. Each room has its own deck or terrace, while other perks include a private spa and gym, swimming pools, a nine-hole golf course, croquet lawns and several tennis courts. Meadowood also hosts one of the country's top restaurants, where modern-Californian cooking delivers. If you've missed out on a dinner reservation, cocktails are made to order and the full wine list is also available in the restaurant bar.
www.meadowood.com; tel 866-987-8042; 900 Meadowood Lane, St Helena

UPVALLEY INN & HOT SPRINGS
Providing easy access to the town of Calistoga and northern Napa Valley's major attractions, this boutique spa hotel appeals for the sense of cosy comfort in each of its crisp, contemporary rooms, as well as its geothermal pools, whirlpool and steam room.
upvalleyinn.com; tel 707-942-9400; 1865 Lincoln Ave, Calistoga

WHERE TO EAT
BUSTER'S SOUTHERN BBQ
Don't let the down-to-earth atmosphere fool you: the straightforward food at this locals' favourite is award-winning, and the place been internationally celebrated as destination barbecue. You'll be served your pile of barbecue and beans on a paper plate to eat outside at picnic tables, and there's a good chance you'll sit right beside an area winemaker enjoying a quick bite.
busterssouthernbbq.com; tel 707-942-5605; 1207 Foothill Blvd, Calistoga; 10am–7pm daily

FARMSTEAD, LONG MEADOW RANCH
Long Meadow Ranch prides itself on its gardens, cattle, farmland and wine. At the modern-ranch-style Farmstead Restaurant, the full experience is distilled into a delicious seasonal menu rooted in meats raised on the ranch, produce grown in the gardens and wine from its own vineyards; be sure to order the sliders made with the ranch's own biscuits. The wine list also includes bottles from the extended Napa Valley region, plus a few choice international options. Keep an eye out for live music in summer months, when dining outside is a delight.
www.longmeadowranch.com; tel 707-963-4555; 738 Main St, St Helena; 7am–9.30pm daily

WHAT TO DO
BOTHE-NAPA VALLEY STATE PARK & BALE GRIST MILL HISTORIC STATE PARK
The western side of Napa Valley takes in the most inland coastal redwood forest in North America. A 1990-acre park established in the 1960s, Bothe-Napa Valley State Park offers miles of trails through the redwoods. It's directly beside the Bale Grist Mill Historic State Park, which can be visited for a snapshot of northern California's farming past.
3801 St Helena Highway, Calistoga

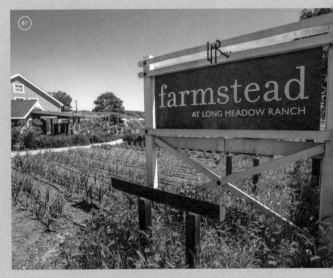

Map labels: 06, OAKVILLE, 05, YOUNTVILLE, Napa River, CALIFORNIA, 04, 03, 01, 02, NAPA

NAPA VALLEY SOUTH

[California]

NAPA VALLEY SOUTH

Cabernet Sauvignon established the world-famous reputation of Napa Valley, but southern tasting rooms near the town of Napa offer delicious diversity beyond this classic wine.

Beyond the northern extents of San Francisco Bay, Napa Valley welcomes wine lovers from around the world as the most well-known, respected and celebrated wine region in the USA. Here you'll find a world of wine experiences: from ultra-exclusive winery visits for the well-connected to fun, friendly wine flights overlooked by farm animals, and urban wineries set to a live-music soundtrack.

Defined by the Napa River (which slices through the middle of the region) and two mountain ranges (the Mayacamas on the west, the Vaca in the east), Napa Valley traces its legendary success back to the 1976 'Judgment of Paris'– when Napa Valley Chardonnay and Cabernet Sauvignon bested what was then considered the finest wine in the world from France in a blind test. All eyes turned to the then-upstart region, ultimately transforming its farming community into one of the globe's most distinguished wine-growing areas.

While Cabernet Sauvignon and Chardonnay still reign as king and queen of the region, today's Napa Valley offers an enormous range of wine types. In comparison to Napa's northern half, southern Napa Valley leans a little more towards cooler-climate varieties, such as Chardonnay, Pinot Noir and even sparkling wine, thanks to the influence of freshening breezes rolling in off Sant Pablo Bay to greet the Carneros AVA.

With its varied accommodations and quality restaurants, the town of Napa makes an excellent base amid beautiful vineyard landscapes. The burgeoning local-food movement means meals and tasting-room snacks are ultra-fresh and creatively served to accompany your wine of choice. Beyond the world-famous wines, Napa Valley offers plenty of hiking, hot-air-balloon rides, bicycle tours and pleasing vineyard views, and there's even a Napa Valley Wine Train for exploring without your own wheels.

GET THERE
Napa town and the southern Napa Valley lie within a 2hr drive (50 to 60 miles) of three airports – San Francisco, Oakland and Sacramento.

❶ THE HESS COLLECTION WINERY

Like many of the world's most renowned wine regions, Napa Valley was originally tended by monks making communion wine. From the 1930s onwards, in the wilds of Mount Veeder, the Christian Brothers built the beautiful stone building that The Hess Collection Winery has now transformed into one of Napa's most accessible luxury wine experiences.

The winery delivers an impressively varied collection of wine styles and quality tiers, from refreshing, light-bodied Albariño to more robust Cabernet Sauvignon, all accompanied by culinary treats that wander from cheese pairings to fresh-from-the-farm lunches.

Tours incorporating, say, a three-course lunch or a discussion about sustainable winemaking can be booked in advance.

Meanwhile, the winery's exceptional contemporary-art collection rotates seasonally, showcasing originals from more than 20 living artists, as well as others recently celebrated. Thanks to owner David Hess and his long-lasting love for art, the gallery generally spans multiple stages of a featured artist's work, and is free to explore. Exhibits have included pieces by the likes of Francis Bacon, Anselm Kiefer and Gerhard Richter, among others. *www.hesscollection.com; tel 707-255-1144, 4411 Redwood Rd, Napa; 10am–5.30pm daily* ✗⑤

Robert Sinskey makes the wines and his wife Maria is the chef. So book ahead for a tasting with a three-course lunch

⑫ OUTLAND – POE, FARELLA, FORLORN HOPE

In the middle of downtown Napa sits one of its newest tasting rooms. With floor-to-ceiling windows, and a contemporary space with a three-dimensional carved wooden map of Napa Valley built into the wall, Outland feels fresh and intriguing. It features three different wineries – Poe, Farella and Forlorn Hope – and thus offers one of the most diverse joint collections of wine varieties and styles in the region.

You can savour a little of all three in a mixed flight, or home in on one particular winery. Farella delivers classic wines from Bordeaux grape varieties (Sauvignon Blanc, Merlot, Cabernet Sauvignon), with

a focus on texture and freshness. Poe specialises in Pinot Noir and Chardonnay from the cooler edges of California's northern coast, while Forlorn Hope shows off how exciting and delicious wines from lesser-known varieties can be. When you're done, head next door for snacks (and more wine?) at neighbourhood wine bar Cadet.
outlandwines.com; tel 707-227-1277; 920 Franklin St, Napa; 1–7pm Wed–Mon or by appointment ⑤

⑬ ASHES & DIAMONDS

A second-generation vintner, Kashy Khaledi describes his Ashes & Diamonds winery as a love letter to the undiscovered Napa Valley of the 1960s. Khaledi has brought together

his passion for contemporary music and film with an admiration for the history of Napa Valley and its world-respected wines.

Working with two celebrated winemakers, Steve Matthiasson, and Diana Snowden Seysses, Ashes & Diamonds offers Bordeaux-inspired wines from both white and red varieties. The wines are made in a refreshing, old-school Napa style that is ready to drink now but built to age for decades. Decidedly modern, with mid-century accents, the tasting room is designed to be welcoming and relaxing, and enables wine tastings to be shaped by its open architecture. Stay a little longer for a seasonal, wood-fired meal alongside your four-wine flight, or book an in-depth winery tour with barrel tasting. Winter workshops range from baking to knitting, and there's also an autumn speaker series.
ashesdiamonds.com; tel 707-666-4777; 4130 Howard Ln, Napa; 11am–7pm daily ✕⑤

⑭ TREFETHEN FAMILY VINEYARDS

Sadly damaged by the 2014 South Napa earthquake, Trefethen's late-19th-century building (originally the McIntyre winery) has now been completely restored to host tastings. The original wooden fermentation tanks still live within, as does much of the old winemaking equipment; today this more of a museum than an active winery, but you'll still catch a glimpse of Napa Valley's early days. Next door stands the modern

Clockwise from top: courtesy of Robert Sinskey / Rob Sinskey; Outland: Robert Sinskey

(05)

winery where Trefethen wine is produced. You can tour the entire facility, history lesson included, or sit beneath the exposed wooden beams of the second floor for a guided flight of Trefethen wines. The winery produces a wide range of regional varieties from Chardonnay to Sauvignon Blanc and Riesling to Pinot Noir or Cabernet Sauvignon. *www.trefethen.com; tel 866-895-7696; 1160 Oak Knoll Ave, Napa; 10am–4.30pm daily* ⑤

05 ROBERT SINSKEY VINEYARDS

Robert Sinskey Vineyards welcomes walk-in visitors, but its real highlights are a booked-ahead tour of the gardens, winery and caves, or a library tasting accompanied by a three-course lunch. Founder Robert Sinskey makes the wines and his wife, chef

01 Oven time at Ashes & Diamonds

02 The tasting room at Robert Sinskey

03 Fresh food at Robert Sinskey

04 The Outland group of wineries

Maria, does the cooking, so visits here are a family affair. Maria guides you through to their gardens to showcase the food that follows with your private tasting. If time won't allow for the full experience, you can still taste the Robert Sinskey wines amid beautiful surroundings in the winery garden, or at the rustic bar inside the stonewalled tasting room.

The Sinskeys are among Napa's favourite first-generation winemakers, having launched their vineyard in the late 1980s and made a name for themselves with their celebrated Pinot Noir. They also craft a collection of aromatic

whites, and, if you ask nicely, you might even get to taste their limited-production Merlot. *www.robertsinskey.com; tel 707-944-9090; 6320 Silverado Trail, Napa; 10am–4pm daily* ✕⑤

06 ROBERT MONDAVI WINERY

Napa Valley's global reputation is in part thanks to the work of influential winemaker Robert Mondavi, who championed its quality at home and abroad. In the architecturally remarkable winery, which he founded in 1966, Mondavi brought together his taste for good wine with his love of food, music and art, creating what we know today as the Napa Valley lifestyle.

This notion continues to shape the tasting-room experience at Robert Mondavi Winery, where sculptures from renowned artists are scattered throughout the property and live concerts can be enjoyed in the winery gardens in warmer months. Walk-in visits are welcome if you'd like a casual tasting, but you can also schedule a guided tour, a delve into older vintages or a cheese, chocolate or charcuterie pairing. The winery produces an enormous range of wine varieties and styles (including Fumé Blanc), so it's the perfect spot to please every taster. *www.robertmondaviwinery.com; tel 888-766-6328; 7801 St Helena Hwy, Oakville; 10am–5pm daily* ✕⑤

WHERE TO STAY
BEAZLEY HOUSE
Still owned and operated by its founders, Beazley House became the region's first B&B 30 years ago and is something of a Napa Valley institution. Striking the balance between elegant and comfortable, it offers seasonal regional breakfasts, and is walking distance to everything in downtown Napa. *www.beazleyhouse.com; tel 707-257-1649; 1910 1st St, Napa*

THE COTTAGES OF NAPA VALLEY
Homey, comfy individual cabins are the order of the day here. Wood fireplaces for winter and private outdoor lounges year-round make the Cottages ideal for a cosy, relaxing retreat that's also convenient for everything you want to enjoy in the southern Napa Valley. *www.napacottages. com; tel 707-252-7810; 1012 Darms Ln, Napa*

WHERE TO EAT
AD HOC
Thomas Keller made a name for himself opening Michelin-star restaurants in Yountville and New York. His famed French Laundry is still considered one of the best – and hardest to get – dining experiences in Napa Valley. For a more casual, still delicious taste of the Thomas Keller culinary approach (impeccable service included), Ad Hoc serves finely executed comfort food in a fun, easygoing atmosphere. The menu changes daily and is kept to the point with just a few dishes and an expertly chosen wine list. Be sure to try the signature fried chicken. *www.thomaskeller.com;*
tel 707-944-2487; 6475 Washington St, Yountville

HERITAGE EATS
The last place you'd expect to find in a strip mall, Heritage Eats has become a Napa locals' favourite. Offering food served fast-casual, the eclectic menu spans everything from Vietnamese sandwiches to stir-fry bowls and seasonal wraps. Ingredients are all sourced locally. *www.heritageeats.com; tel 707-226-3287; 3824 Bel Aire Plaza, Napa; 11am–8.30pm daily*

MIMINASHI
Inspired by Japanese Izakaya cuisine, Miminashi has captured a cult following for its blend of Japanese recipes and California ingredients, and its custom-made cocktails featuring some of the world's finest spirits. The wine list extends beyond Napa Valley, so ask your server for help picking the perfect pairing for your spicy pork ramen or grilled-chicken skewers. *miminashi.com; tel 707-254-9464; 821 Coombs St, Napa; 11.30am–2.30pm & 5–10pm Mon–Fri, 5.30–11pm Sat, 5–9.30pm Sun*

WHAT TO DO
OXBOW MARKET
Don't miss this mixed-use open market in downtown Napa. It's packed with walk-up eateries, outdoor stores and shops carrying locally made goods, fresh Napa Valley produce and everything you need to round out your home bartending experience. Check the schedule for the farmers' market, which changes seasonally. *oxbowpublicmarket. com; 610 1st St, Napa; 9am–9pm*

NORTHERN SANTA BARBARA

Discover venerable vineyards, celebrated winemakers and charming small-town tasting rooms as you travel from Los Olivos in the Santa Ynez Valley to Orcutt, just outside the Santa Maria Valley.

Santa Barbara County is awash with landscapes of undulating hills adorned with ancient oaks and row upon row of vines. Temperatures climb as you head inland, moving east from the ocean-cooled Lompoc area near the Pacific to Los Olivos and Ballard Canyon, two of the four sub-appellations within the Santa Ynez Valley AVA (the others are Santa Rita Hills and Happy Canyon of Santa Barbara). These diverse micro-climates lead to a delightfully wide variety of grapes, with Rhône wines shining in the Santa Ynez Valley. Meanwhile, the county's northernmost AVA, the wind-lashed Santa Maria Valley, is especially strong on Pinot Noir and Chardonnay. Drive through the heart of Santa Barbara County along Hwy 101, from Los Olivos to Orcutt via Los Alamos, and you'll uncover some of this vino-loving region's finest tasting rooms.

GET THERE
Los Olivos is a 130-mile, 2.5hr drive northwest from Los Angeles.

Get started in the small town centre of Los Olivos, where historical homes have been converted into winery tasting rooms, plus the odd restaurant, gallery and shop. Spin north through vineyard-dotted countryside to the one-horse town of Los Alamos, whose distinctive temperate climate and fine, varied wines hold the promise of a potential future AVA. Key stops here along Main St include a clutch of tasting rooms and art galleries, and one of the county's most popular restaurants, Flatbread. Travelling north again you'll reach Orcutt, just south of the city of Santa Maria. This town has recently reimagined itself as an artisanal, boutique-style Santa Barbara enclave, home to a wealth of small local-family businesses – including a slew of enticing tasting rooms perfect for wine aficionados looking for family-owned, handcrafted drops from the immediate area.

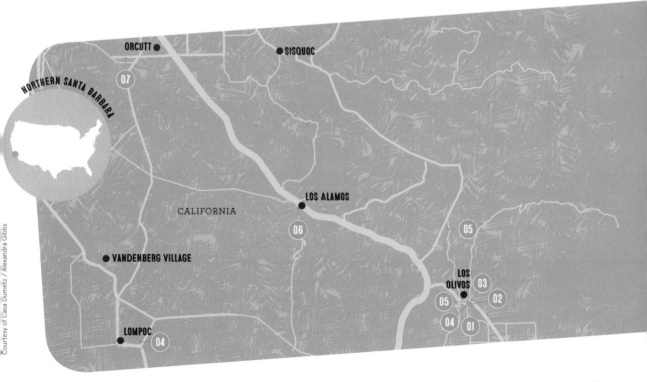

Courtesy of Casa Dumetz / Alexandra Gibbs

01 LARNER

The Larners' vineyard stands on the family ranch in the Ballard Canyon area of Santa Barbara's Santa Ynez Valley AVA, a region known for its Rhône varieties – from Grenache Blanc to Syrah and Mourvèdre. The Larners sell fruit to some of the most celebrated wineries in this region, but they also save a small portion for making their own award-winning wines. Winemaker Michael Larner produced wine in both Italy and France before returning to Santa Barbara County to lead the family winery.

Generous flavour fires the label's medium- to full-bodied reds, though it's certainly also worth asking about the ultra-small-production Malvasia Bianca – a beautiful, crisp aromatic white made in tribute to the family's love for Italian wine. The tasting room in Los Olivos is charming and uncluttered, with artistic flair; Michael's wife Christina uses grape pigments for painting and her work often graces the walls.
www.larnerwine.com; tel 805-688-8148; 2900 Grand Ave, Los Olivos; 11am–5pm daily $

02 DRAGONETTE CELLARS

Three friends are behind leading Los Olivos winery Dragonette

01 Sonja Magdevski of Casa Dumetz

02 Tasting at Andrew Murray Vineyards

03 Andrew Murray Vineyards

04 John, Steve and Brandon of Dragonette

05 Winemaker Clarissa Nagy

06 The Alamo motel

showing off their family members. The theme continues in the den-like Los Olivos tasting room, with its warm woods and leathers, designed for small groups, private tastings or patio seating.

Saarloos & Sons focuses primarily on Rhône varieties – wines from Grenache, Syrah and Mourvèdre grapes grown on either of the family vineyards. It also develops small lots of other varieties. Wines are only available through the tasting room itself, so you'll have to drop by for a taste, guided by devoted, knowledgeable staff. *saarloosandsons.com; tel 805-688-1200; 2971 Grand Ave, Los Olivos; 11am–4.30pm daily* Ⓢ

04 STOLPMAN VINEYARDS

Stolpman Vineyards was among the first of the wine producers to plant in Santa Barbara County's Ballard Canyon and has provided fruit for some of the finest local Rhône producers. In the 1990s, Stolpman launched its family-owned label based on grapes from its own estate vineyards. Wines here – which you can sample at the Los Olivos tasting room – are chiefly Rhône varietals; Syrah is the flagship for reds, while the white Roussanne is a big hit. Over time, however, the Stolpman Vineyards portfolio has broadened to welcome a handful of more unusual finds, such as Trousseau, one of the latest additions. On the premium side, you will encounter Italian-inspired Sangiovese.

A little further west, the Stolpman

Cellars. Brothers John and Steve Dragonette, along with Brandon Sparks-Gillis, founded the winery after falling in love with wine working together in Los Angeles. The threesome moved north to Santa Barbara County to try their hand at the craft with a few small-production wines; the project quickly developed into one of the area's foremost wineries.

Dragonette Cellars produces small lots of single-vineyard Pinot Noir, as well as Sauvignon Blanc and Syrah. This mixture of varieties allows it to maintain a clear stylistic focus while getting to know notably diverse parts of the Santa Ynez

Valley, from the cool reaches of the Santa Rita Hills for Pinot, to the warmer midlands for Syrah and the hotter inland areas for Sauvignon Blanc. Wine tastings at the tasting room in Los Olivos span the portfolio, including small-lot wines you won't find anywhere else. Book ahead for a reserve tasting. *dragonettecellars.com; tel 805-693-0077; 2445 Alamo Pintado Ave, Los Olivos; 11am–5pm daily* Ⓢ

03 SAARLOOS & SONS

One of the long-standing farming families of Ballard Canyon, the Saarloos celebrate generations of ancestors with creative wines often

winery in Lompoc runs weekend tastings and prebooked vineyard hikes through the twirling vines. www.stolpmanvineyards.com Tasting Room: tel 805-688-0400; 2434 Alamo Pintado Ave, Los Olivos; 11am–5pm daily Winery: tel 805-736-5000; 1700 Industrial Way, Unit B, Lompoc; noon–5pm Fri–Sun ⑤

⑤ ANDREW MURRAY VINEYARDS

Pop into the oak-panelled Los Olivos-based tasting room of this family-owned winery to sip your way through its sustainably produced, Rhône-focused drops. Alternatively, seek out a more in-depth experience at the Foxen Canyon Winery & Visitor Center Tasting Room, just north of town, where you can also picnic under the oaks. The newly remodelled space offers educational tastings, plus chocolate- and cheese-pairing options; factor in a little extra time for a private winery tour, though you'll need to book in advance. andrewmurrayvineyards.com

Los Olivos Tasting Room: tel 805-686-9604; 2901 Grand Ave, Los Olivos; 11am–5pm daily Foxen Canyon Winery & Visitor Center Tasting Room: tel 805-686-9604; 5249 Foxen Canyon Rd, Los Olivos; 10.30am–5.30pm daily ✕⑤

⑥ CASA DUMETZ

A love for Grenache launched Casa Dumetz wines in 2004. Winemaker Sonja Magdevski devotes her attention to vineyards in the central stretch of the Santa Ynez and Los Alamos portions of Santa Barbara County, constantly exploring how the soils and microclimates of different vineyards affect the variety's expression.

Try a single-vineyard Grenache tasting, or hunker down with a glass of rosé in the country-feel tasting room, with its handpainted wooden seating, old photos and sketches on the walls. Magdevski knows her handcrafted beers as well; check out the selection and grab a bite to eat next door at Babi's Beer Emporium. Speaker series takes

place at the winery on Fridays, and Saturdays host music programmes. casadumetzwines.com; tel 805-344-1900; 388 Bell St, Los Alamos; noon–7pm Thu, 11am–7pm Fri & Sat, 11am–6pm Sun ✕⑤

⑦ CNAGY

Over the last few years, the Orcutt area has soared in popularity, with an influx of small-winery tasting rooms. cNagy was one of the original wineries to move its tasting room here, bringing with it a sense of community wine spirit.

Clarissa Nagy launched her own small-production, single-vineyard project cNagy with just a few wines in 2005, and has been one of Santa Barbara County's most celebrated winemakers for decades. The collection revolves primarily around just four wines: two Burgundy varieties (Pinot Noir and Pinot Blanc) and two Rhône varieties (Viognier and Syrah). Each wine is a single-vineyard expression from a site Nagy has worked with and admires, combining savoury freshness, lovely aromatics and enjoyable length offered through the particular character of its specific variety. Nagy also crafts a rosé of Pinot Noir in the spring and summer months. nagywines.com; tel 805-286-7228; 145 S Gray St, Suite 103, Orcutt; 1–5pm Wed, Thu, Sat & Sun, to 8pm Fri ⑤

From left: courtesy of cNagy; © David Litschel / Alamy Stock Photo

WHERE TO STAY

FESS PARKER WINE COUNTRY INN

A luxury wine-country experience awaits at this pick within walking distance of Los Olivos' village centre and its tasting rooms. Spacious rooms are done up with modern-ranch styling, high ceilings and plenty of natural light. Refined ranch cuisine is the draw at The Bear & Star downstairs, and there's also an on-site wine shop. *www.fessparkerinn.com; tel 800-446-2455; 2860 Grand Ave, Los Olivos*

ALAMO MOTEL

Every room is different at this freshly updated, long-standing motel, opposite Casa Dumetz. Country-boutique flair runs through the crisp, wood-floored rooms, some of which have freestanding claw-foot tubs. Right in front sits a Municipal Winemakers tasting room. *www.rememberthe alamomotel.com; tel 805-344-2852; 425 Bell St, Los Alamos*

WHERE TO EAT

FLATBREAD

With a menu centred on its wood-fired oven, Flatbread has long been both a destination restaurant and local favourite. It's all about casual dining with interesting, world-wandering flavours, and a list list of local wines and beers. *fulloflifefoods.com; tel 805-344-4400; 225 Bell St, Los Alamos; 4.30–9pm Thu, 4.30–10pm Fri, 1–3pm & 4.30–10pm Sat, 1–3pm & 4–8pm Sun*

FAR WESTERN TAVERN

Dating back to before this region was part of the USA, Santa Maria BBQ is a style of dry-rubbed, wood-fire grilling entirely unique to the Santa Maria Valley, which is one of the USA's most diverse agricultural growing regions. Far Western Tavern combines a wealth of home-grown produce with a menu built around Santa Maria BBQ for a local culinary experience you won't find anywhere else. *www.farwesterntavern. com; tel 805-937-2211; 300 E Clark Ave, Orcutt; 11am–9pm Tue–Fri, 10am–9pm Sat, 10am–8pm Sun*

WHAT TO DO

HI-WAY DRIVE-IN THEATRE

One of the last-standing drive-in theatres in the country, screening two movies a night – so tune the radio to the designated station and enjoy your popcorn in the privacy of your own car. *www.playingtoday.com/ cinema/hi-way-drive-in/; 3170 Santa Maria Way, Santa Maria*

BOOMERS FUN PARK

Go kart racing, miniature golfing, indoor-arcade exploring, and splashing around a miniature water park – Santa Maria's Boomers Fun Park offers all kinds of indoor and outdoor activities. Admission is technically free; once here, you have the option of buying a full pass to access any part of the park for the day, or partial tickets to mix and match activities. *www.boomersparks. com; tel 805-928-4942; 2250 N Preisker Ln, Santa Maria; 11am–8pm Mon–Thu, 11am–11pm Fri, 10am–11pm Sat, 10am–8pm Sun*

[California]

PASO ROBLES

For a taste of the Wild West in wine country, pull on your cowboy boots and seek out Rhône blends and ranch-style wineries along California's Central Coast.

Halfway between San Francisco (to the north) and Los Angeles (to the south), the increasingly popular wine-growing region of Paso Robles rolls out a happy-medium wine-country experience. Tucked against the California Coast Ranges, the Paso Robles AVA lies a 30-minute drive east of Pacific beaches, yet also a 30-minute drive west from the desert. All that open sun and desert heat means the vines aren't struggling for ripeness and, when it comes to wine, Paso Robles is known for producing drops bursting with flavour. Venture west into the mountains, though, and nights can get chilly, so here you'll delight in wines with a little more restraint. Though Pinot Noir is a rare find in Paso Robles, a few western-range producers make respectable examples of it. But you're more likely to come across peppery Rhône reds, especially Syrah and Grenache, as well as succulent Rhône whites like Roussanne or Viognier. Further east, winemakers are also growing impressive Cabernet Sauvignon and Merlot.

The Paso Robles area has its roots in cattle-ranching history and today still carries a sense of the Wild West. Downtown Paso Robles centres on a plaza, much like many of California's other historical towns. A cluster of restaurants and tasting rooms circle the plaza, around which you'll find attractive boutique hotels to retreat to. Thanks to the region's incredibly varied topography, outdoor activities abound, from mountain biking, horse riding and golfing to days out on the lake or sun-soaking by the ocean.

GET THERE
San Luis Obispo Regional Airport is 35 miles south of Paso Robles town, or you can drive from LA (200 miles) or San Francisco (200 miles).

① TURLEY WINE CELLARS

Known for its full-bodied Zinfandels, Turley Wine Cellars has brought old-vine vineyards into the spotlight across California. It also specialises in other varieties native to California's past, such as Petite Sirah, Syrah and mixed-Rhône field blends. Expect to try single-vineyard expressions of heritage vines from California's Central Coast and northern regions, with sampling options ranging from four-wine Zinfandel Tastings to Focused Tastings with a wine educator.

Walking tours of the undulating green vineyard unveil why the team is so passionate about preserving old vines. Each of Turley's vines develops its own character with age, while the wines show just how old vines bring greater depth of flavour and concentration.

Turley's wines made from its vineyards in California's Sierra Foothills, Napa Valley and Sonoma Country are also highlights. *www.turleywinecellars.com; tel 805-434-1030; 2900 Vineyard Dr, Templeton; 10am–5pm daily* ✕ ⑤

② DEOVLET WINES

Thanks to the warm desert temperatures that dominate this region, Paso Robles wines are particularly full-bodied. But Deovlet Wines does something different: sourcing its fruit entirely from the cool-climate vineyards of Santa Barbara County to the south. Soak up the Wild-West feel of old-town Templeton while enjoying finely built Pinot Noir and Chardonnay in the Deovlet tasting room.

Ryan Deovlet, a California boy at heart, enjoys the best of both worlds, by making his wines in San Luis Obispo with Santa Barbara County grapes, and pouring his wines in Paso Robles. In the last couple of years, he has added a traditional-method sparkling white to his portfolio – it's hard to beat his crisp sparkling Chardonnay on a hot Paso Robles afternoon. *www.deovletwines.com; tel 805-712-8817; 3750 CA46, Paso Robles; 11am–5pm daily* ⑤

③ GIORNATA WINERY

You'll need a booking to savour the Italian-inspired creations of Giornata Winery, whose rows of looping vines weave across rolling hills. Brian and Stephanie Terrizi focus on wines made from Italian grape varieties grown on California's Central Coast. Stephanie farms several local vineyards and has helped introduce varieties previously unknown to the area, while Brian turns his long-standing

love of Italian wines to the cellar to produce tipples from the grapes farmed by his wife. Together, they've expanded their bootstrap operation into one of the most respected husband-and-wife wine businesses along the Central Coast.

The Terrizis were also among the first wineries to establish themselves in Paso Robles' Tin City, a collection of small urban wineries, homegrown eateries and artist collectives. *www.giornatawine.com; tel 805-434-3075; 470 Marquita Ave, Suite A, Paso Robles; by appointment* Ⓢ

04 CLOS SOLÈNE WINERY

Winemaker Guillaume Fabre began his career in France but fell for the vibrancy and rich growing conditions of California's Central Coast, dedicating his winery to his wife Solène. The pair farm a Rhône vineyard huddled into the mountains on the western side of Paso Robles, and also source fruit from across the region to deliver full-bodied reds carried by a long finish. In the tradition of France's southern Rhône, most Clos Solène wines are a blend, with one variety – such as Grenache or Syrah – as the foundation.

www.clossolene.com; tel 805-239-7769; 2040 Niderer Rd, Paso Robles; 10am–4.30pm daily Ⓢ

05 TABLAS CREEK VINEYARD & WINERY

Known as the godfather of California's Rhône wines, Tablas Creek has done more than any other winery to make French varieties available in the USA. Founded by a partnership between the USA's Haas family and the Perrins' famed Beaucastel of Châteauneuf-du-Pape in the southern Rhône, it brings impressive pedigree to the wilds of Paso Robles, basing wines entirely on its own estate vineyards.

Rhône varieties grow tucked into the folds and cool pockets of the Coast Ranges on the western side of Paso Robles, enjoying an ideal balance of ripening daytime sun and long chilly nights. As a result, the wines offer wonderful restraint, each carried by a long, refreshing finish. The tasting-room team happily show how vines are planted and discuss the importance of the many Rhône varieties Tablas Creek has imported from France; with time, you can take a personalised walking tour.

The winery also works hard to encourage sustainable wine production in the region. In hot Paso Robles, Tablas Creek's reusable water bottles, for

wines; the collection runs from Pinot Noir and Chardonnay to Zinfandel and Cabernet, plus Rhône wines like Picpoul Blanc and Syrah.

In the contemporary ranch-style tasting room, you can choose from an array of sampling sessions. Alternatively, book in advance for an educational reserve tasting including a mix of Adelaida's older vintages and smallest-production wines. The Hilltop Tasting, meanwhile, sees you in a private picnic area with sprawling vineyard views. *www.adelaida.com; tel 800-676-1232; 5805 Adelaida Rd, Paso Robles; 10am–5pm daily* 💲

08 ANCIENT PEAKS

You could just drop in for a glass or two at Ancient Peaks' Santa Margarita tasting room or schedule a tour of the entire ranch along with your tasting. But for something a little different, jump right into Ancient Peaks' on-site zip-line course: you'll be soaring right over the sweeping vineyards.

Ancient Peaks produces a healthy range of wines at a quality that far outshines its reasonable pricing; fine Cabernet Sauvignon, beautifully crisp Sauvignon Blanc and deliciously balanced Merlot are standouts. *www.ancientpeaks.com; tel 805-365-7045; 22720 El Camino Real, Santa Margarita; 11am–5.30pm daily* 🍴💲

example, have reduced its waste by several hundred thousand plastic bottles a year. *tablascreek.com; tel 805-237-1231; 9339 Adelaida Rd, Paso Robles; 10am–5pm daily* 💲

06 HALTER RANCH

A venerable property from the late 1800s, Halter Ranch has retained its remote mountain feel while upgrading with modern comforts. Far more than just a winery, it's now a multi-use ranch with livestock, vineyards, preserved natural wildlands, and its original Victorian-style home. The focus here is on savoury, spiced Rhône wines with a balance of restraint and depth of flavour.

The winery-and-cave tour includes tastings and an in-depth look at how Halter Ranch wines are made, and you can also add on a barrel tasting experience. If you want to really get to know the ranch, book an excursion tour: you'll hop in the jeep for a ride around the property's mountainous landscape, and glean an insight into the work behind the team's numerous sustainability awards for reducing water and electricity usage. *www.halterranch.com; tel 888-367-9977; 8910 Adelaida Rd, Paso Robles; 11am–5pm daily* 💲

07 ADELAIDA VINEYARD & WINERY

Established in the early 1980s, Adelaida has become one of Paso Robles' destination wineries, with some of the region's tallest hilltops looming in the midst of its ranch property. As one of the few local spots cool enough to grow resplendent Pinot Noir, Adelaida produces an impressive range of

WHERE TO STAY

SUMMERWOOD WINERY & INN

Recognised for its innovative design, the Inn offers an intimate, luxurious stay in a real-deal winery in the wilds of Paso Robles' wine country. Freshly made breakfasts are included, and you can reserve a private wine experience with the winemaker, tasting small-production wines unavailable anywhere else. *www.summerwoodwine. com; 2130 Arbor Dr, Paso Robles*

CARRIAGE VINEYARDS BED & BREAKFAST

Paso Robles' horse-ranch history meets its more recent wine-country influence in a personal overnight experience on a running vineyard ranch. Rooms are comfortable and private, and you'll roll out of bed to breakfasts of fresh local produce. Don't be put off by the working-ranch atmosphere: it's a great way to fully appreciate local life.

www.carriagevineyards. com; tel 805-227-6807; 4337 South El Pomar, Templeton

WHERE TO EAT

ARTISAN

California founded the farm-to-fork movement and Paso Robles is no exception. At Artisan, expect all locally sourced ingredients, from produce and meats to dessert. The wine list features a collection of Paso Robles wines you won't find anywhere else, and local winemakers frequent the restaurant. *artisanpasorobles.com; tel 805-237-8084; 843 12th St, Paso Robles; 11.30am–2.30pm &*

4.30–9pm Mon–Sat, 10am–2pm & 5.30–9pm Sun

THOMAS HILL ORGANICS

With emphasis on organic local ingredients, the menu here is fresh and seasonal, while the wine list celebrates wines from the extended area. In keeping with Paso Robles' usually warm temperatures, there's an outdoor patio to dine on. *www.thomashillorganics. com; tel 805-226-5888; 1313 Park St, Paso Robles; 11am–3pm & 5–9pm*

WHAT TO DO

HEARST CASTLE

Hearst Castle was

built in the 1940s by the eccentric William Randolf Hearst, who made his fortune in newspapers. At the time, San Simeon was utterly remote, and guests had to be brought to the top of the mountain by carriage or horseback to enjoy the luxury of 165 rooms, gold-lined pools and acres of gardens. Hearst also had an exotic-animal sanctuary: his herd of zebra were let loose after his death and still roam the surrounding hills! *75 Hearst Castle Rd, San Simeon, CA93452; 8am–4pm daily*

RAVINE WATER PARK

Summers in Paso Robles can be very hot. If you find yourself here without a pool, check out the Ravine Water Park for its wave pool, water slides, winding river, and private cabana rental. A great option for families. *ravinewaterpark.com; tel 805-237-8500; 2301 Airport Rd, Paso Robles*

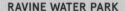

Courtesy of Talley Vineyards

[California]
SAN LUIS OBISPO

From pastoral hills to dramatic panoramas of the Pacific Ocean, enjoy some of the most diverse landscapes in California – with a dynamic wine scene to match.

Beginning north of Santa Barbara's Santa Maria Valley, San Luis Obispo wine country takes in some of California's most diverse terrain, at an extraordinary intersection of desert and ocean. Cold night-time temperatures and the persistent cooling influence of the Pacific Ocean mean wines here are savoury with resplendent acidity. As you head north along the coast, the land begins to climb. Coastal forests reach all the way to the beaches, providing astonishing views of mountains to the east and the untamed ocean to the west. Climb north into the mountains instead and you'll note how temperatures slowly increase. As a result, the San Luis Obispo region produces cool-climate Pinot Noir and Chardonnay, as well as richer Rhône varieties like Grenache and

Syrah, and even a few wines crafted from unexpected Spanish varieties. This is a cycle-friendly area, so biking between wineries is a delight.

It's hard to find a more ideal region to enjoy the Californian landscape than this. When you're done wine tasting, take a stroll on white sands to the tidal pools and morros (ocean rock formations) sprinkled along the many lovely local beaches; you can even camp shoreside in some spots. Urban life awaits in the city of San Luis Obispo, where bohemian coffee shops, live music and an affordable gastronomic scene come courtesy of the local university. There's plenty of regional history to explore, too: venture into the mountains to travel along the old Mission trails, and uncover the past of this former Spanish settlement.

GET THERE
Fly into San Luis Obispo airport, or drive an hour (about 95 miles) northwest from Santa Barbara along Hwy 101.

① PRESQU'ILE

The founders of the palatial Presqu'ile winery have a dramatic story. Their multi-generational family home was destroyed during Hurricane Katrina; without a place for the extended family to return to for holidays, they went in search of a new place to build their future. Son Matt Murphy visited the Santa Maria Valley and fell in love with the region and its wines. Sitting on the edge of Santa Barbara and San Luis Obispo counties, Presqu'ile produces wine from both regions. What they share is the profoundly cooling influence of the Pacific Ocean, and the effect is a combination of savoury flavors with freshness in both Pinot Noir and Chardonnay. Expect sweeping views of the valley and ocean from the tasting room, where you can opt for a seat at the bar or arrange a more formal tasting with charcuterie. In warm months, the team hosts a series of concerts.

www.presquilewine.com; tel 805-937-8110; 5391 Presquile Dr, Santa Maria; 11am–5pm daily ✕ 🟢

② QUPE & VERDAD

Bob Lindquist is recognised as one of the founders of both California's Rhône wine tradition and winemaking on its Central Coast. Qupe celebrates his love for Rhône wines and has inspired a generation of winemakers since the early 1980s, with Lindquist sharing his knowledge to support newer winemakers' projects. Verdad – launched by Bob and his wife, Louisa Sawyer-Lindquist – focuses on their passion for Spanish wines and biodynamic farming, celebrating flavourful examples of Albariño, Tempranillo and Graciano.

Both Verdad and Qupe wines are made with grapes sourced from Santa Barbara County and San Luis Obispo vineyards. They find sites that gain enough daytime heat to ripen these more robust varieties, while still retaining the cooling ocean influence for a snappy spine of crisp acidity. While the urban tasting room in the town of Arroyo Grande is fairly nondescript, it stocks Qupe and Verdad together

01 Loading grapes at Talley farm

02 The tasting room interior at Presqu'ile

03 The tasting room exterior at Presqu'ile

04 Winemaker Eric Johnson at Talley

05 The vineyard view at Talley

06 The Madonna Inn at San Luis Obispo

– the perfect opportunity to investigate a mixed flight of both French Rhône and Spanish varieties in one pleasant afternoon. *www.qupe.com, www.verdadwine. com; tel 805-270-4900; 134-A W Branch St, Arroyo Grande; noon–5pm daily* $

⓪③ TALLEY

The Talley family was among the first to develop Pinot Noir and Chardonnay in San Luis Obispo's Arroyo Grande region. Today, this winery is considered not just a tasting room but a destination in its own right. Designed to showcase the Talleys' range of estate-grown, single-vineyard wines, the property serves fine cuisine alongside outdoor tastings on its working farm and vineyard, where you'll probably spot the family horses in the distance beyond the vines that produced the wine you're sipping. Multi-course meals feature seafood from the nearby coast, locally sourced meats, and a range of seasonal produce.

Walk-in tastings include current-release wines from Talley, and there's a pretty picnic area; for an in-depth private tasting or large-group visits, reserve ahead. The private El Rincón Adobe Tasting happens in the salmon-pink 1860s house that graces all Talley bottles, and includes a fascinating side-by-side look at wines from different vineyards – an excellent opportunity for serious wine lovers to explore the idea of site expression while

with plenty of sunshine during the daylight hours.
www.chamisalvineyards.com; tel 805-541-9463; 7525 Orcutt Rd, San Luis Obispo; 10am–5pm daily 🍴💲

05 CENTER OF EFFORT

Focused on the quality wine experience, Center of Effort is dedicated to making Pinot Noir and Chardonnay from Arroyo Grande-area vineyards. It's an exceptional project: the goal is to offer crafted wines elevated to an artistic level. The winery produces just one Pinot Noir and one Chardonnay from every vintage; what goes into the bottle is what the team believes to be the best expression of the variety from that vintage.

Winemaker Nathan Carlson has been involved in wine from this region for more than 12 years. He returned to the San Luis Obispo to produce premium wines after first making Pinot Noir and Chardonnay from several of California's other celebrated wine regions. While Carlson has been praised for his in-depth technical know-how in winemaking, he brings together this experience with something more like intuition to deliver Center of Effort's distinctive wines.

You'll need a reservation to visit. *www.centerofeffortwine.com; tel 805-782-9463; 2195 Corbett Canyon Rd, Arroyo Grande; by appointment* 💲

also getting to know the Talley approach and history.
www.talleyvineyards.com; tel 805-489-0446; 3031 Lopez Dr, Arroyo Grande; 10.30am–4.30pm daily 💲

04 CHAMISAL

Though within easy drive of the ocean, Chamisal's vineyards sit just inside a band of hills, protected from the coldest ocean influence that tends to chill the rest of this region. So outdoor tastings in the gardens are a delight here and, if you call ahead, you can organise a picnic lunch with your wines. To add an educational component to your winery experience, schedule a tour and private tasting. The Chamisal team will take you on a leisurely drive through the vineyards (so you can see exactly where the wines you're about to taste originate) and explain the intricacies of this region's perfect growing environment for Pinot Noir and Chardonnay.

The Chamisal Tasting incorporates the winery's flagship selection, or you can splash out to taste the premier wines. The tasting space has a picnic spot with views of the vineyard and the Santa Lucia foothills; you'll be surrounded by seasonal plants and blossoms,

WHERE TO STAY

SYCAMORE MINERAL SPRINGS

Combine proximity to the ocean with a relaxing mineral soak in the hillsides of Avila Valley. Located on 100 wooded acres, Sycamore immerses you in tranquility – with suites graced by four-poster beds – yet it's also a quick drive to city life in San Luis Obispo or to Avila Beach for a beach walk. *www.sycamoresprings. com; tel 805-595-7302; 1215 Avila Beach Dr, Avila Beach*

MADONNA INN

Suites at the Madonna are designed with whimsical flair, while the dining room feels a little like celebrating Valentine's Day every day, with its golden chandeliers and love signets dominating the red-hued décor. The look is certainly extravagant, but rooms are comfortable and the location is handy for both beaches and mountain escapes. *www.madonnainn.com;*
tel 805-543-3000; 100 Madonna Rd, San Luis Obispo

WHERE TO EAT

FROMAGERIE SOPHIA

Packed with speciality cheeses from around the world, Fromagerie Sophia has become a destination cheese shop for the Central Coast. You can buy cheeses as gifts (or for yourself, of course), or stop in for a cheese plate embellished with charcuterie, pâté and other local treats – eat in or takeaway.
www.fromageriesophie. com; tel 805-503-0805; 1129 Garden St, San Luis Obispo; 10am–6pm Mon– Sat, noon–5pm Sun

CAFÉ ROMA

A truly local experience, this urban restaurant celebrates the Italian history of the San Luis Obispo region with a classic American-Italian menu of pizzas, pastas and more robust dishes such as veal marsala or Barolo-braised short ribs. *www.caferomaslo.com; tel 805-541-6800; 1020 Railroad Ave, San Luis*
Obispo; 11.30am–2pm & 5–9pm Mon–Fri, 5–9pm Sat

WHAT TO DO

MORRO STRAND STATE BEACH

With over three miles of beach, Morro Strand is ideal for lazing away an afternoon along the Pacific Ocean. You can purchase firewood for late-afternoon bonfires along the shore, and there's a campground for overnight stays. It's two miles south of Cayucos on Hwy 1. *www.parks.ca.gov*

FARMERS' MARKET: DOWNTOWN SAN LUIS OBISPO

Every Thursday evening (weather permitting), the population of San Luis Obispo converges on Higuera St between Nipomo and Osos for a farmers' market. The market bursts with produce from local growers, as well as crafts by local artists and an array of food trucks. There's also live music. *downtownslo.com/ farmers-market*

06

CALIFORNIA

SANTA BARBARA

● SANTA BARBARA

PACIFIC OCEAN

01 · 04 · 05 · 02 · 03 · 06

[California]

SANTA BARBARA FUNK ZONE & THE PRESIDIO

Jump on to Santa Barbara's urban wine trail to explore boutiques, breweries and tasting rooms in converted warehouses within easy reach of the ocean.

Between Santa Barbara's beach and Hwy 101, an eclectic collection of converted warehouses and old buildings has morphed into a favourite new part of town: the Funk Zone. Over a decade, this disused area of the city became first an artist hangout, then, over time, home to surf shops, breweries, local restaurants and a tempting selection of wine-tasting rooms. Many of the Funk Zone's earliest business owners have launched creative life-work spaces, and it's the local residents that help guarantee this popular spot's authentic Santa Barbara beach vibe.

A few minutes' walk east, the Presidio is another formerly rundown area now reimagined as a destination Santa Barbara neighbourhood. Boutiques, cafes and tasting rooms have set up shop amid distinctive Spanish Colonial Revival architecture.

For wine-lovers, the Funk Zone and Presidio are laced with opportunities for sampling the famously diverse local wines of Santa Barbara County. Get started with one of the region's sparkling wines or the county's signature grape Pinot Noir, then explore its other flagship style with Rhône varieties like Syrah and Grenache. Santa Barbara County wines range from light- to full-bodied and whites to reds, but there is always a confident acidity to them; the county's proximity to the Pacific Ocean ensures freshness across varieties. The ocean's cooling effect enables this region to enjoy the longest growing season in the state, which guarantees plenty of flavour even for light-bodied wines. If you'd like to venture beyond wines, celebrated local breweries and distilleries also offer tastings within the Funk Zone and Presidio.

GET THERE
Fly into Santa Barbara Airport, or drive 100 miles (just over two hours) northwest up the California coast from Los Angeles.

01 WHITCRAFT WINERY

Founded by Chris and Kathleen Whitcraft in the 1980s, Whitcraft is considered an outstanding yet under-the-radar winery for Pinot Noir, Chardonnay and Syrah. Second-generation winemaker Drake Whitcraft now leads the winemaking, having learned both craft and history from his father. He's continued in the family tradition, producing wine alongside the Pacific in Santa Barbara while sourcing fruit from some of the best wineries in the Santa Ynez Valley just over the hill and the Santa Maria Valley further north.

Occasionally, Whitcraft also offers special small-production wines from unexpected varieties and regions, like an Italian red LaGrein grown in Paso Robles or a Pinot Noir cultivated in Mendocino to the north. A tasting at Whitcraft is not only a look into the family's impressive wine list but also a deep dive into the region's winemaking history. You can catch a glimpse of the family-owned urban winery itself, as it's connected to the tasting room. This is a rustic operation, but one with exceptional wines and a team full of charm and talent. *whitcraftwinery.com; tel 805-730-1680; 36 A S Calle Cesar Chavez St, Santa Barbara; noon–4pm Fri–Mon or by appointment* ⑤

02 KUNIN WINES

One of the original tasting rooms to move into the Funk Zone, Kunin Wines is a Santa Barbara go-to for Rhône-style wines, and takes

full advantage of its beachside location. The team set up next to a surf shop and transformed beach-house styling into an easygoing wine-tasting room.

Founding winemaker Seth Kunin has had a profound influence on the USA's food and wine community, and his wines were the first to show the beauty of Santa Barbara's Rhône varieties. Kunin's flagship wine, the Pape Star, is a classic red Rhône blend of the style known as Châteauneuf-du-Pape. More recently he's added a white blend, and he also makes Viognier as both a dry table wine or dessert sticky. To learn more about individual Rhône varieties, taste your way through Kunin's single-variety bottlings. For reds check out Syrah or single-vineyard Carignan. Kunin occasionally releases a non-Rhône variety like Sauvignon Blanc or

Chenin Blanc, but what all his wines have in common is a savoury, fresh quality, at a competitive price. *www.kuninwines.com; tel 805-963-9633; 28 Anacapa St, Santa Barbara; 11am–7pm daily* ⑤

03 MUNICIPAL WINEMAKERS

Styled with what feel like upcycled yard-sale finds, Municipal Winemakers is one of the Funk Zone's hippest tasting rooms. Amateur oil paintings line the walls and seating is a mix of repurposed cinema chairs, beach seats and picnic tables. Owner-winemaker Dave Potter founded Municipal Winemakers to be about joy and the spirit of sharing. Wines are designed to be affordable and delicious. Highlighting this playfulness, he's named his wine club Club Awesome. Potter only makes small-production wines, primarily Rhône varieties, so your

only chance to sample them is right here in the tasting room. What's available changes with the season and as wines sell out, but there's usually a good choice of white blends, seasonal rosés, Grenache or Syrah. You might uncover the occasional Pinot Noir as well, and, if you don't spot them on the shelves, be sure to ask about Potter's other, even smaller production wines from his Potek label. Art and food events add to the lively scene.
www.municipalwinemakers.com; tel 805-931-6864; 22 Anacapa St, Santa Barbara; 11am–8pm Sun–Wed, to 11pm Thu–Sat $

04 THE VALLEY PROJECT

To really understand the growing conditions and wine styles of Santa Barbara County, The Valley Project is an essential Funk Zone stop. The loft-style tasting room includes a wall-sized chalkboard map of the entire county, highlighting the key features that influence local wine-growing, such as its mountains, ocean and fog zones. Vineyards that provide fruit for the project are also marked on the map.

Sit down at the bar to sample a portfolio of wines that show off the full assortment of light- to full-bodied wines native to this region. Begin, perhaps, with Pinot Noir and Chardonnay from the cooler coastal areas, then move on to Grenache and Syrah from the balanced mid-zones. Finally, savour a full range of Bordeaux varieties, including Sauvignon Blanc, Merlot and Cabernet Sauvignon, from the warmer inland areas. Founders Seth Kunin and Magan Eng describe the project as a love letter to Santa Barbara County, and the wines carry that joyful seriousness with plenty of flavour and freshness.
www.avasantabarbara.com; tel 805-453-6768; 116 E. Yanonali St, Santa Barbara; noon–7pm daily $

05 RIVERBENCH

True to its name, the Riverbench vineyard sits on the northern edge of Santa Barbara County along a gravel-ridden bench of alluvial stones set down over centuries by the Santa Maria River. It's one of the region's founding vineyards, responsible for enlightening wine devotees on the great quality the Santa Maria Valley could offer for Burgundian varieties. It produces a crisp range of sparkling wines and dry table wines – both made from Chardonnay and Pinot Noir grown in the cool reaches of the Santa Maria Valley. The spacious urban Riverbench tasting room, in the Funk Zone, is all tall ceilings, weathered-wood walls and photographs showing off the big skies and open scenery of the Santa Maria vineyard. You can taste at the bar, or enjoy cushioned, leather seating. *www.riverbench.com; tel 805-324-4100; 137 Anacapa St, Suite C, Santa Barbara; 11am–6pm daily* 💲

06 AU BON CLIMAT & CLENDENEN FAMILY VINEYARD

Founded in the early 1980s by Jim Clendenen, Au Bon Climat has been internationally celebrated for its Pinot Noir and Chardonnay. It was one of the first vineyards to bring such acclaim to wines from Santa Barbara County – but Clendenen's influence doesn't stop there. Many of the region's finest young winemakers found their break making wine at Au Bon Climat, learning alongside Clendenen while also starting their own label.

His tasting room in the Presidio offers a classic experience amid rich woods and leather seating with a wine-library feel. Current releases are the focus, though there's also the occasional anniversary release from previous vintages. Clendenen's small-production label, Clendenen Family Vineyards, made with fruit from his home vineyard, is also available, featuring wines that take on more of an Italian focus, alongside some French varieties. The label includes some of the finest Nebbiolo in the state as well as more unusual wines like Mondeuse rosé, Tocai Friulano or single-vineyard Aligote. And don't miss the Clendenen Family Chardonnay, which brings the rich winemaking experience of his Au Bon Climat label to his family's own vineyard. *www.aubonclimat.com; tel 805-963-7999; 813 Anacapa St, Santa Barbara; noon–6pm Mon–Fri* 💲

04

01 Santa Barbara style

02 Seth Kunin pouring at The Valley Project

03 The Valley Project's interior

04 The interior at Municipal Winemakers

05 El Presidio De Santa Barbara State Historic Park

WHERE TO STAY

HOTEL INDIGO

Only a block from the Pacific Ocean, in the Funk Zone, Hotel Indigo has charming, colourful rooms with full windows to enjoy Santa Barbara's natural beauty and light. The Waterfront Shuttle stops nearby. *www.indigosanta barbara.com; tel 805-966-6586; 121 State St, Santa Barbara*

INN OF THE SPANISH GARDEN

In-room massages, a palm-shaded pool and subtly luxurious chambers with balcony or terrace, around a central courtyard, are the draw at this Spanish Colonial-style inn. Art by one of the owners adorns the property. *www.spanishgardeninn. com; tel 805-564-4700; 915 Garden St, Santa Barbara*

WHERE TO EAT

THE LARK

California cuisine is defined by local, seasonal ingredients, and The Lark is one of the Central Coast's prime restaurants for true SoCal cuisine. Designed as a shared-

meal experience, fresh, flavour-packed dishes (cheese boards, farm-fresh veg, grilled tuna) are served family-style, in some cases at the communal table, accompanied by regional wine, beer and spirits. Book ahead! *www.thelarksb.com; tel 805-284-0370; 131 Anacapa St, Santa Barbara; 5-10pm Tue-Sun*

LES MARCHANDS

Les Marchands combines a European-inspired restaurant and wine bar with a bistro-style menu, delivering some of the hippest wines from Santa Barbara County alongside many of the European originals that inspired their winemakers.

www.lesmarchandswine. com; tel 805-284-0380; 131 Anacapa St, Suite B, Santa Barbara; 11am-9pm Sun-Thu, to 10pm Fri & Sat

WHAT TO DO

SALT

With a goodie-stocked space on one of Santa Barbara's main shopping streets, Salt allows you to decompress in the heart of the city – with the unusual twist of subterranean salt caves. Book 45-minute in-cave relaxation sessions or a range of treatments from Swedish-style massages to sound and vibration healing sessions. *www.saltcavesb.com; tel 805-963-7258; 740 State St; 10am-7pm Mon-Sat, noon-7pm Sun*

EL PRESIDIO HISTORIC STATE PARK

Before California became part of the USA, Santa Barbara was the home of one of the major Spanish garrisons in what was then known as the Alta California coast. This site protects the last remaining military buildings from that era; visit on a self-guided walking tour and swing by ongoing archaeological excavations during designated hours. *www.parks.ca.gov; 123 East Canon Perdido, Santa Barbara*

SANTA BARBARA BOTANIC GARDEN

A beautiful five-mile walking path leads through a Japanese tea garden and a grove of coastal redwoods at Santa Barbara Botanic Garden. Historical landmarks here include the Mission Dam & Aqueduct, built in the early 1800s. *www.sbbg.org; tel 805-682-4726; 1212 Mission Canyon Rd, Santa Barbara; 9am-6pm Mar-Oct, to 5pm Nov-Feb*

CALIFORNIA

04
CUPERTINO
SAN JOSE
LA HONDA
PALO ALTO HILLS
05
SARATOGA
03
LOS GATOS
GLENWOOD
BONNY DOON
SCOTTS VALLEY
DAVENPORT
02
RIO DEL MAR
SANTA CRUZ MOUNTAINS
SANTA CRUZ
Monterey Bay
01

[California]

SANTA CRUZ MOUNTAINS

Defined by its high elevation, the Santa Cruz Mountains AVA encompasses vineyards surrounded by forests of coastal redwoods and others gazing out on the San Francisco Bay Area.

The Santa Cruz Mountains wine-growing region was one of the first in California to be officially recognised for its elevation. Situated above the morning-fog line, vineyards here huddle against steep slopes deep in forests of coastal redwoods. At the uppermost elevations, they're perched on mountaintops, opening up astounding views of the surrounding landscapes. Wineries in the north part of this region lie only an hour's drive southeast from San Francisco, while the AVA's namesake city, Santa Cruz, is around a 1.5hr drive.

Thanks to the area's mountainous landscape, temperatures vary significantly between vineyards, engendering an enjoyably wide range of wine styles: the Santa Cruz Mountains create top-notch Pinot Noir just as readily as first-rate Cabernet Sauvignon, while also acting as one of California's major homes of Rhône wines. But there's a host of more experimental varieties dotted around too; you'll find people celebrating obscure Portuguese grapes alongside some more recognisable Italian varieties.

The region as a whole is spread out and, with its rugged terrain, can take time to travel around, so do plan ahead. If you want to simplify your travels, cross the Coastal Mountains and head straight to Santa Cruz, where you can focus on in-town tasting combined with time on the beach; you might not find the vineyard views, but you'll be able to maximise your tasting experiences. Otherwise, make for the wineries themselves and stay in the heart of the AVA at one of its mountain resorts, amid coastal redwood forests that feel plucked from an ancient era.

GET THERE
Santa Cruz is easily reached from San Francisco and San Jose airports, 65 miles northwest and 35 miles north respectively.

01 SANTA CRUZ MOUNTAIN VINEYARD & QUINTA CRUZ

Head into the Surf City Vintners complex in west Santa Cruz to seek out this urban warehouse winery, in the thick of one of the most food-centric parts of this California beach town. Santa Cruz Mountain Vineyard has a deep-rooted history in this region, having produced some of its earliest celebrated examples of both Pinot Noir and Cabernet Sauvignon.

If you'd like to taste beyond the expected classics, hunt down the tasting room's older vintages.

The Quinta Cruz label focuses on unusual Portuguese varieties grown in the Santa Cruz Mountains, and you'll also uncover wines made from Castelão or Sinzão from other wineries in the state. Alternatively, dig into the blend of Toriga Nacional and Toriga Franca for a dry version of the varieties traditionally used to make Portuguese signature sweet wine. The extended warehouse complex hosts several other regional tasting rooms, a stash of breweries, a much-loved bakery and every local's favourite charcuterie stop.

www.santacruzmountainvineyard. com; tel 831-426-6209; 334-A Ingalls St, Santa Cruz; noon–5pm daily

02 BONNY DOON

Bonny Doon founder and winemaker Randall Grahm is one of the USA's most famous vintners. His innovative thinking and marketing mastery brought attention to the American Rhône movement, to accurate ingredient labelling on wine bottles, and to the value of the screw cap in ensuring consistency and age-ability in wine bottles without cork taint.

If you want to keep it simple, head straight to Santa Cruz where you can combine in-town tasting with time on the beach

Ø1 The annual Day of the Doon event at Bonny Doon

Ø2 The Bonny Doon tasting room

Ø3 Big Basin Winery

Ø4 Santa Cruz surf opposite Bonny Doon

Ø5 Above the clouds at Ridge Vineyards Monte Bello

Ø6 Coastal redwoods at Santa Cruz

Today, he continues to forge ahead in his approach while staying true to Bonny Doon's origins.

Grahm's love for Rhône wines sits at the centre of any experience in the Bonny Doon tasting room, perched on a hill in the little village of Davenport, just across Hwy 1 from the Pacific Ocean. His spiced, red-fruit-driven Grenache is among the most affordable and delicious in California, while his classic Rhône blend, Le Cigare Volant, pays tribute to the balance, complexity and earthy accents celebrated by the famed Rhône region of

Châteauneuf-du-Pape. Ocean views and a glimpse of the winery's history round out your tasting. Walk-in tastings are welcome (unless you're with a large group), though if you're keen for a winery or vineyard tour you'll want to book at least a month in advance. Hours vary from season to season, so it's best to call ahead. *www.bonnydoonvineyard.com; tel 831-471-8031; 450 CA-1, Davenport; 11am–5pm daily* 💲

Ø3 BIG BASIN VINEYARDS

One of the great pleasures of wine-tasting along the California coast

is the chance to combine it with marveling at the coastal redwoods. Utterly unique to this region, they're among the most majestic trees in the world. Big Basin Vineyards hosts two tasting room locations, both close to the coastal redwoods. Visiting the mountaintop tasting room next to the winery in Boulder Creek demands steady nerves: you tackle a curvy road through these genuinely jaw-dropping trees, and the views, tranquility and, of course, wines make the trip absolutely worth it. You'll sit outside in the forest

picnic-style, hosted by impressively knowledgeable winery staff, fantastic hiking trails threading through the surrounding mountains.

If you can't reach the remote mountains of Santa Cruz, head instead to the Big Basin tasting room in the old village area of Saratoga. At either location, you'll have the opportunity to enjoy a flight of mixed French varieties. Big Basin is known for its talent with both varieties of Burgundy – Chardonnay and Pinot Noir – and Rhône reds – Grenache and Syrah especially.
www.bigbasinvineyards.com
Vineyard Tasting Room: tel 831-621-8028; 830 Memory Ln, Boulder Creek; noon–5pm Sat & Sun
Saratoga Tasting Room: tel 408-564-7346; 14598 Big Basin Way, Saratoga; noon–5pm Sun, Mon & Thu, to 7pm Fri & Sat $

04 THOMAS FOGARTY VINEYARDS & WINERY

Only an hour's drive south from San Francisco, Thomas Fogarty specialises in single-vineyard Pinot and Chardonnay grown on its estate on one of the ridgelines of the Santa Cruz Mountains. It was among the first to plant along the elevated Skyline Blvd, an area now internationally recognised for its superb growing conditions. The tasting room certainly takes advantage of its location: horizon-reaching views of San Francisco Bay accompany your wines.

Besides its famous Burgundian varieties, Thomas Fogarty produces an intriguing collection of other wines. The latest project, Lexington estate, features wines from Bordeaux varieties grown in a warmer section of the local mountains. The winery is still owned and led by the Fogarty family, often spotted on-site working with the tasting-room staff. Thomas Fogarty Sr is a retired cardiovascular surgeon and Stanford professor who invented the life-saving balloon catheter; he used the money from his patent to launch his eponymous winery. Today, son Tommy leads the winery alongside winemaker Nathan Kandler and, together, they've turned it into one of the region's destination wineries.
www.fogartywinery.com; tel
650-851-6777; 19501 Skyline Blvd, Redwood City; 11am–5pm daily $

05 RIDGE MONTE BELLO

The story of Ridge Vineyards Monte Bello began in the 1880s when a Bay Area doctor, Osea Perrone, bought land on a ridgetop south of the city and planted vines on it. He released his first vintage, naming the winery Monte Bello, in the 1890s. Planted at 2600ft, it remains one of the highest-elevation vineyards on the California coast; the tasting room is graced by views across the valley below. A little uphill walk away lie some of the vineyard's oldest vines, with vistas of the surrounding pine forest.

The vineyard fell into obscurity during Prohibition, until the adjacent property was purchased in the 1940s by a set of four friends who started making wine. Over time Perrone's original vineyard was also unearthed and the two locations combined into Ridge winery. The foursome eventually hired Paul Draper, one of California's most respected and influential winemakers. His work at the Ridge Monte Bello site created the Monte Bello Bordeaux blend – widely considered one of the world's finest wines. You can also taste some of the winery's celebrated Zinfandels.
www.ridgewine.co; tel 408-867-3233; 17100 Montebello Rd, Cupertino; 11am–4pm Sat & Sun, by appointment Mon–Fri $

From: left: courtesy of Ridge Monte Bello; © Shutterstock / kurdistan

WHERE TO STAY

HOTEL LOS GATOS

The town of Los Gatos sits snuggled into the eastern side of the Santa Cruz Mountains, within easy driving distance of the Bay Area and still only a half-hour from the ocean via a winding mountain road. This Mediterranean-style villa with pools, gym and spa makes an intimate retreat in the heart of town. *hotellosgatos.com; tel 408-335-1700; 210 E Main St, Los Gatos*

CHAMINADE

Santa Cruz's Chaminade resort stands on a hilltop on the eastern side of town, offering blissful ocean views, forest hiking trails, an on-site spa and dining options that range from casual restaurant to luxury meals. Rooms have a private feel and forest or resort panoramas. *www.chaminade.com; tel 800-283-6569; Chaminade Ln, Santa Cruz*

WHERE TO EAT

KELLY'S FRENCH BAKERY

Just around the corner from the Santa Cruz Mountains Vineyards & Winery tasting room, Kelly's French Bakery is a long-standing local favourite. It's famous for turning out some of the best brownies and pastries in the state, but you can also enjoy lunch and a glass of wine. *Tel 831-423-9059; 402 Ingalls St, Santa Cruz; 7am–7pm daily*

WHALE CITY BAKERY, BAR & GRILL

If you find yourself hungry near the ocean, pop into Whale City Bakery for reliably good breakfasts of scrambles and avocado toast, or such heartier mains as burgers, crab cakes or the house favourite calamari. It's along the highway from Santa Cruz to Davenport, an easy walk to both the Bonny Doon tasting room and the ocean. *whalecitybakery.com; tel 831-423-9009; 490 Hwy 1, Davenport; 6.30am–8pm daily*

WHAT TO DO

MOUNT HERMON ADVENTURES

For the ultimate view of the coastal redwoods, try a zip-line adventure through the forest canopy or a team-building ropes course. This adventure site is seven miles north of Santa Cruz, with mountain hiking trails nearby. *mounthermon adventures.com; tel 831-430-4357; 17 Conference Dr, Felton; 9am–5pm Mon–Thu*

ROARING CAMP RAILROAD

Early in the 20th century, the beachside town of Santa Cruz was one of the resort communities for families living in the urban Bay Area, but highways weren't yet built. Vacationers instead took a train trip through the Coast Range to the beach, and this small-gauge rail line still exists in part, opening up an intimate view of the local forest. *www.roaringcamp.com; tel 831-335-4484; 5401 Graham Hill Rd, Felton*

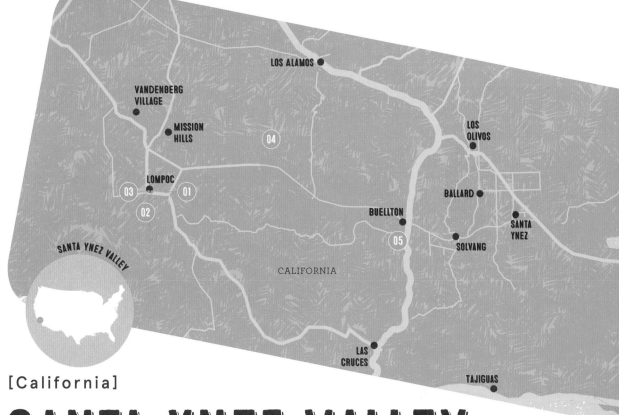

[California]

SANTA YNEZ VALLEY

This drive from Lompoc to Buellton begins in a buzzing converted industrial quarter of tasting rooms and concludes at one of the region's signature estates.

To the wider world, Santa Barbara is possibly best known as a playground for the well-heeled of Los Angeles, 100 miles to the southeast. Its wine country was also the setting for the misadventures of Miles and Jack in the 2004 film *Sideways*, as they sip their way through their mid-life crises. For oenophiles, though, this beautiful stretch of coastline — the so-called 'American Riviera' — jutting into the Pacific 100 miles north of Los Angeles is notable for other reasons. Along the west coast of the US, Santa Barbara county is the only well-established winegrowing region fully exposed to the fogs and cool weather of the Pacific. Consequently, it has the longest growing season in California, with sunny days but cool temperatures. The results include some of the best Pinot Noir in California,

but there are wines across all varieties with lots of flavour concentration and fresh acidity. Vineyards planted closest to the ocean tend to offer lighter-bodied wines, while the warmer temperatures found inland create bolder, fuller-bodied reds and whites.

Highway 101 crosses the full length of the county, north to south, so it's easy to pay a visit to the region. The beach-loving community of Santa Barbara itself, faces south so you can expect warmer temperatures there than in the town of Lompoc in the more exposed north. East of Lompoc, temperatures rise as you progress away from the coast and into the desert hills — locals like to say temperatures go up 1°F per mile. So, while travelling Santa Barbara wine country, pack with layers. You'll want a mix of clothes for warm weather as well as chilly moments.

GET THERE
Fly into Santa Barbara airport, then drive 30 minutes, or if you start in LA, drive along the coast three hours, to start the tour in Lompoc.

01 PALMINA

For over 20 years Palmina has focused on crafting food-friendly wines from Italian varieties grown in Santa Barbara county. 'The intention with Palmina is to share the perspective of Italian culture through the wines,' says owner Steve Clifton, 'with a little California lifestyle and personality thrown in.' New releases are offered alongside a recipe developed in the Palmina kitchen (pair grilled pork chops with fennel and radicchio with Palmina Nebbiolo Rocca, for instance; wine club events include Clifton's cooking as well). Tasting room options include aromatic and refreshing Malvasia, charming and delicious Dolcetto, or serious and beautiful Nebbiolo, as well as a range of other distinctly Italian varieties, and single-vineyard options from throughout the region. The tasting room sits alongside the winery, which has been fitted into a converted warehouse space for a friendly, urban feel. Walk-ins are welcome but call ahead for larger groups. *www.palminawines.com; tel 1805-735-2030; 1520 E Chestnut Court, Lompoc; 11am–5pm Thu–Sun & by appointment* ✕ $

02 LONGORIA

It's hard to find a winemaker that has had more influence on the development of the Santa Barbara County wine region than Rick Longoria. Arriving in the region's early days in the 1970s, Longoria helped found some of the area's

most important wineries, while also advising on vineyards throughout the region. At the forefront of Longoria's own winemaking is his Fe Ciega Pinot Noir, the wine he makes from his own vineyard. In all Longoria's wines, the goal is to create a wine that delivers in its youth but is built to age. 'In the beginning the wine has youthful tenacity but as they mature, they become more complex and bigger than their skeleton.' Expect an array of other single-vineyard Pinots and Chardonnays

from the famed Sta Rita Hills. Longoria has a love for the wines of Spain as well so he's included a few Spanish varieties such as Albariño and especially Tempranillo. Next to the winery is the tasting room, in a historic former clubhouse building for business leaders of the last century (charcuterie and nibbles are available).
www.longoriawine.com; tel 1-866-RLWines; 415 E Chestnut Ave, Lompoc; 11am–4.30pm daily

03 BREWER-CLIFTON

Winemaker Greg Brewer has spent his entire winemaking career in the world-famous Sta Rita Hills and helped create the official AVA. His single-vineyard Pinot Noir and Chardonnay showcase the sun-ripened flavors of California sun with the savoury accents and mouthwatering acidity redolent of farming along the coast. The winery is built into a converted warehouse space in the centre of Lompoc; the tasting room sits in the winery building, with a minimalist aesthetic, modern and urban, and a knowledgeable staff. Schedule in advance for a private tasting in the barrel room complete with a look at older vintages from the portfolio. If you enjoy Chardonnay, be sure to ask if any of Brewer's wines from his small production Diatom label are also available.
www.brewerclifton.com; tel 1805-735-9184; 329 N F St, Lompoc; 11am–4pm weekends & by appointment $

04 MELVILLE

The Melville family was among the first to develop vineyards and full-estate winemaking in their corner of the Sta Rita Hills. Along with other founding winemakers they helped define the conditions of this famed region. The winery sits along Hwy 246 between Buellton and Lompoc in the heart of the Sta Rita Hills AVA surrounded by some of the Melville vineyards and the region's rolling desert hills. In the accompanying tasting room — a relaxed adobe-style affair — explore their Chardonnay, Pinot Noir, and Syrah. Enjoy a flight of wines at the bar, or, weather permitting, a bottle on the outdoor patio and lawn. For larger groups or for a 90-minute vineyard tour along with your tasting, call ahead (only a few tours spaces are available on the weekends). *melvillewinery.com; tel 1-805-735-7030; 5185 E Hwy 246, Lompoc; 11am–4pm daily, till 5pm Fri, Sat* $

05 ALMA ROSA

Founder Richard Sanford planted the Alma Rosa vineyards deep in the Sta Rita Hills at the start of the 1970s. In doing so, he established the very first vineyard there, effectively launching what today is recognised as one of California's pre-eminent Pinot Noir regions. At the tasting room just inside the town of Buellton, try a flight from across the Alma Rosa portfolio of Pinots and Chardonnays in a converted-warehouse complete with repurposed furnishings, accents of rock from the area and a large olive tree from the winery estate as centerpiece (tastings at the Alma Rosa estate are available by appointment). Afterwards, head next door to Industrial Eats (see opposite), a local favourite. Don't be surprised if there are winemakers at every other table. *www.almarosawinery.com; tel 1-805-688-9090; 181 C Industrial Way, Buellton; 12pm–5.30pm Mon–Fri, 11.30am to 5.30pm Fri–Sun* $

WHERE TO STAY

PEA SOUP ANDERSEN'S INN

A relaxed roadway style inn, Pea Soup Andersen's is a regional classic. If you've ever done a road trip across California, you've probably seen the billboards advertising its adjoining restaurant - it does offer more than split-pea soup... The hotel is simple, comfortable and central. From here it's easy to get anywhere in the county. *www.peasoupandersens. com; tel 1800-732-7687; 51 East Hwy 246, Buellton*

SANTA YNEZ VALLEY MARRIOTT

The newly redesigned Marriott in the centre of Buellton is clean, and urban in design, and offers access to the wineries and surrounding landscape in Santa Ynez Valley (the building has also been certified sustainable). Rooms are spacious and comfortable. You'll also find a fitness centre and pool onsite, and the hotel is pet friendly.

www.marriott.com; 555 McMurray Rd, Buellton

WHERE TO EAT

INDUSTRIAL EATS

The Industrial Eats Restaurant & Butcher Shop offers a menu of wood-fire pizzas, seasonal salads, and a selection of daily specials. Beer and local wines are served on tap. Food is available via walk-up counter service to eat on site, or take away deli-style. *www.industrialeats.com; tel 1805-688-8807; 181 Industrial Way, Buellton*

THE HITCHING POST II

Made famous by the movie *Sideways*, The Hitching Post is a long-standing restaurant serving up steakhouse-style cuisine, local wines and a range of classic cocktails. Expect Western-style décor with mood lighting and friendly service. *www.hitchingpost2.com; tel 1805-688-0676; 406 E Hwy 246, Buellton*

WHAT TO DO

FIRESTONE WALKER BREWING COMPANY

Curious about beer? At the Firestone Walker Brewing Company in Buellton you can do a barrel tasting, but there is also a self-guided tour through the brewery. *www.firestonebeer.com; tel 1805-697-4777; 620 McMurray Rd, Buellton*

OSTRICHLAND

Curious about giant flightless birds? Feed them at Ostrichland or take a self-guided tour to learn more about these striking animals. There is an educational gift shop offering insights about both ostriches and emus. *www.ostrichlandusa.com; tel 1-805-686-9696; 610 E Hwy 246, Solvang*

LA PURISIMA GOLF COURSE

If you want to fit in a round during your visit to wine country, the La Purisima Golf Course hosts 18 holes and sits on the eastern side of Lompoc. It is a public green so available for out of town guests looking for some tee time. *www.thegolfnexus.com; tel 1805-735-8395; 3455 State Hwy 246, Lompoc*

01

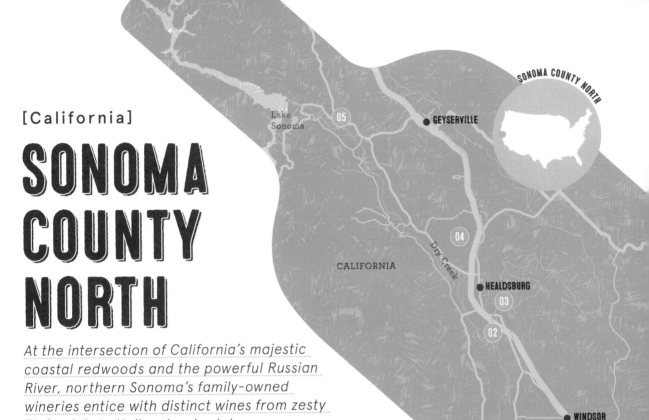

[California]

SONOMA COUNTY NORTH

At the intersection of California's majestic coastal redwoods and the powerful Russian River, northern Sonoma's family-owned wineries entice with distinct wines from zesty Zinfandels to Italian-inspired drops.

One of California's most geographically diverse counties, Sonoma is also one of its most vibrant wine areas. The Coast Ranges hug the Pacific Ocean on the western side of Sonoma County, protecting it from the cold ocean currents rushing along the coast from the north. On the far eastern side, the Mayacamas Mountains carve the county line between Sonoma and Napa. In the middle, the Russian River Valley creates a series of rippling hills and flood plains. And it's the notable change in temperature and conditions, between coastal and inland reaches, that enables such diversity in northern Sonoma's wines.

Home to 17 different wine-growing regions, or AVAs, Sonoma County grows everything from full-bodied Zinfandel to structural Bordeaux blends, spicy Rhône varieties, elegant Pinot Noir and refreshing, crisp whites. The region enjoys warm daytime temperatures ample enough for producing robust reds, with still fairly cool nights, and this combination leads to wines with plenty of flavour and bright, refreshing acidity. From May to October, river tours by canoe or kayak are possible, or you can rent bicycles to pedal between the vineyards of northern Sonoma's AVAs.

Among these are warmer inland AVAs such as Dry Creek Valley, known for its spicy Zinfandel; and Alexander Valley, celebrated for its full-bodied Cabernet Sauvignon. You'll also uncover wines from the famed neighbouring Russian River Valley and the Pacific-fringing Sonoma Coast, both with award-winning Pinot Noir. Many local tasting rooms fall within the urban centres, so you can easily taste wines from tricky-to-access parts of the county.

The charming town of Healdsburg sits on the shores of the Russian River on Sonoma's north edge. Set around a plaza, it hosts tasting rooms, art galleries, farm-to-table restaurants and shops selling local goods; it makes a wonderful base for wine touring.

GET THERE
Healdsburg is 80 miles north from San Francisco International Airport, across the Golden Gate Bridge and along Hwy 101.

Courtesy of Idlewild

① TWO SHEPHERDS

The newest wineries in California cluster in urban centres, delivering top-notch wines in the middle of the city. Family-owned Two Shepherds highlights such an experience, opening its Windsor warehouse winery and tasting room for walk-ins on weekends and by appointment during the week. Winemaker William Allen launched Two Shepherds to express his passion for Rhône varieties, focusing on ultrafresh wines resplendent with acidity, in whites, rosés and reds. Expect to see either Allen or his partner Karen Daenen pouring the wines: they do practically everything for the bootstrap operation themselves. You'll also likely catch a glimpse of their two dogs, sometimes featured on wine labels. The space isn't fancy, but the team makes up for it with personal charm.

twoshepherds.com; tel 415-613-5731; 7763 Bell Rd, Windsor; 12–5pm Sat & Sun or by appointment ⑤

② HIRSCH

It takes a helicopter or a two-hour drive to get far enough into the mountains of the Sonoma coast to reach the Hirsch vineyards. Thankfully, to make its wines more accessible, Hirsch has launched a tasting room in downtown Healdsburg, though you'll want an appointment to guarantee a spot. The communal tasting experience sees wines poured around a large table, accompanied by food pairings sourced from neighbourhood restaurants. Known for its collection of estate Pinot Noirs, Hirsch also makes a delicious Chardonnay.

Founder David Hirsch — whose biodynamic, organic methods have inspired other California winemakers — was among the first to plant in the wilds of Sonoma's Coast Ranges, in the early 1980s. Today, he still leads

01 Idlewild's grape press

02 Food and wine served at Idlewild

03 Sample Sonoma Pinot Noir at Hirsch

04 Misty mountains at Hirsch

05 Treading grapes at Idlewild

06 Dry Creek town in Sonoma

farming on the family homestead, while his daughter Jasmine Hirsch runs the business. She's often travelling the world sharing the story of Sonoma Pinot, but you may also catch her in the tasting room serving the family wines. The Hirsch family has been so influential when it comes to Pinot Noir in Sonoma County that other celebrated local wineries bottle their own wines from the Hirsch vineyards.
www.hirschvineyards.com; tel 707-847-3600; 51 Front St, Healdsburg; by appointment ✖ Ⓢ

⓪③ IDLEWILD

Though today's Sonoma County is primarily known for its Pinot Noir and Zinfandel, it was 19th-century Italian immigrants who established a robust wine industry across the region. Idlewild winemaker Sam Bilbro fuses this rich local history with his own personal love for Piedmont in Italy to make some of the most affordable yet delectable wines in the region. Focused on Italian varieties, Bilbro's wines include a crisp Cortese, delicious Dolcetto and Barbera, and an impressive Nebbiolo for the serious Italian-wine lover.

Just around the corner from Healdsburg's plaza, the Idlewild tasting room provides a relaxed flight through these Italian-based wines. You'll often bump into Bilbro himself here sharing stories; he's a second-generation Sonoma winemaker. This is a friendly, slightly rustic tasting room, refreshingly designed to set you at ease, without that often-prevalent push to sell wine. You'll want to take some home with you though, as these wines are exceptional value. There's live music on weekends.
www.idlewildwines.com; tel 707-385-9410; 132 Plaza St, Healdsburg; noon–7pm daily Ⓢ

⓪④ RIDGE LYTTON SPRINGS

Though we now know its origins reach back to an obscure variety in Croatia, Zinfandel found its fame in northern California. In the 1970s, Ridge helped elevate it from jug-wine to fine-wine status. By producing both region-specific and

single-vineyard examples, Ridge proved just how site-expressive this variety can be. Ridge is also known for its Monte Bello Bordeaux blend, considered one of the finest wines in the world. Though the Monte Bello wine is made at Ridge's other winery, it's also poured at Lytton Springs. The Monte Bello winery in Santa Cruz – 140 miles south of Lytton Springs – shepherds the vines that go into Monte Bello, while Ridge's rich Zinfandel heritage can be found at Lytton Springs. Here, century-old vines front the tasting room, within which you can sample wines made directly from them.

For an insight into how Ridge promoted Zinfandel, go for a Zinfandel tasting flight led by knowledgeable staff, which takes in a range of wines from different sites, all united in that their old vines are part of California grape-growing history.
www.ridgewine.com; tel 408-867-3233; 650 Lytton Springs Rd, Healdsburg; 12–4pm daily $

05 PRESTON FARM & WINERY

Arrive for just a glass, stay for the afternoon. Though the Dry Creek Valley AVA is one of the most densely planted in Sonoma County, Preston – more mixed-use farm than tasting room – provides an intimate, low-key experience. The Preston family has maintained the property's rustic country feel, simply updating its original farmhouse (where wine tastings happen) and barn with a few modern conveniences. Produce from the on-site gardens and farm animals is sold in the farm store, while picnic tables and bocce courts invite you to relax outdoors over your glass of wine. Be sure to try the Preston olive oil and freshly baked sourdough bread too.

Lou and Susan Preston, who founded the farm and vineyard in the 1970s, have led the charge for sustainable farming in Sonoma County from the beginning. They live on site and can often be found tending the gardens and chickens. If you're visiting in autumn, check out the pick-your-own-pumpkin patch designed for families. Holiday activities for families run throughout the year.
prestonfarmandwinery.com; tel 707-433-3372; 9282 W Dry Creek Rd, Healdsburg; 11am–4.30pm daily ✕ $

WHERE TO STAY

BEST WESTERN DRY CREEK INN

Reliably comfortable, the Dry Creek Inn revolves around the charms of wine-country life, such as outdoor patios with wood fireplaces set against red-tile architecture with a Tuscan feel. Rooms are cosily contemporary, while the Villa Toscana has its own balcony and soaking tub. Other perks include a spa, a steam room and double pools. *www.drycreekinn.com; tel 707-605-0880; 198 Dry Creek Rd, Healdsburg*

HOTEL HEALDSBURG

One of northern Sonoma's most fashionable, fresh hotels, with contemporary styling, spa treatments featuring local ingredients, and an excellent location in the heart of downtown Healdsburg. *hotelhealdsburg. com; tel 707-431- 2800; 25 Matheson St, Healdsburg*

WHERE TO EAT

LOS PLEBES

Many locals consider Los Plebes the best taco truck along California's northern coastline and those in the know drive several hours to sate their taco cravings. Tortillas are made fresh while you wait; try the steak tacos with sautéed onions. Service is fast but expect a line. *Geyserville Taco Truck, Hwy 101, east side of Lytton Springs/ Geyserville exit; 10am– 5pm daily*

SPOONBAR

Northern California is all about the farm-to-table, seasonal-ingredients experience – even when it comes to cocktails. Grab a stool at Spoonbar to see how terrific cocktails crafted with fresh ingredients and top-notch spirits can be. Or pair your liquid mix with a surf-and-turf-style meal; seafood and meats are all locally sourced. *spoonbar.com; tel 707- 433-7222; 219 Healdsburg Ave, Healdsburg; 5–9pm Sun–Thu, late Fri & Sat*

WILLI'S SEAFOOD & RAW BAR

Sampling Sonoma's local seafood is a must. Some of the best oysters in North America appear in the raw bar at Willi's. The restaurant is both locally loved and a destination for tourists, known as much for its Sonoma-seafood selection as its globetrotting cocktails. *www.starkrestaurants.com; tel 707-433-9191; 403 Healdsburg Ave, Healdsburg; 11.30am– 9.30pm Sun–Thu, to 10pm Fri & Sat*

WHAT TO DO

RIVER'S EDGE KAYAK AND CANOE TOURS

Explore the scenery of Sonoma County with an afternoon on the river. Trips range from leisurely paddles to challenging backcountry stretches for more experienced paddlers and can be solo tours or large-group day trips. Waterborne adventures are also the best way to get up close with Sonoma's birds. *riversedgekayakand canoe.com; tel 707-433- 7247; 1 Healdsburg Ave, Healdsburg*

SONOMA COUNTY SOUTHEAST

GLEN ELLEN 04
Lake Suttonfield

03

CALIFORNIA

SONOMA
01
02

05

SAN ANTONIO

[California]

SONOMA COUNTY SOUTHEAST

Undulating hills, soaring mountains and the cooling influence of San Pablo Bay collide with a wine-meets-farm-country feel in southeastern Sonoma County to roll out Chardonnay, Pinot Noir and Cabernet Sauvignon.

Perched on the northern side of San Pablo Bay, just over the Mayacamas Mountains from Napa Valley, the southeastern section of Sonoma County is California wine country with a more easygoing atmosphere. Less developed than neighbouring Napa, while still suitably luxurious, and less urban than northern Sonoma, the town of Sonoma appeals with its back-to-the-farm-style wine tasting, glimpse of California history and views of low-lying hills, beyond which lie forested mountains.

When California became a state in the mid-19th century, General Vallejo made Sonoma town his headquarters (local historical landmarks include his home), bringing the first grape vines into the region; he even supplied the early vineyards established next door in celebrated Napa Valley. Take a self-guided tour of the town-centre plaza and check

out the monument to the Bear Flag Revolt, which occurred here in Sonoma town and helped make California part of the USA.

When it comes to winemaking, southeastern Sonoma County provides a pleasing fusion of warm daytime temperatures and cool nights. It's this daily shift that gives the local wines great flavour and freshness. You'll find plenty of Pinot Noir throughout this region, but, if you venture into more protected areas, you'll meet producers able to ripen Cabernet Sauvignon as well. A smattering of intriguing, aromatic whites, spiced Rhône reds, and one of California's most classic Chardonnays round out the package. If you'd like to expand your wine explorations, the town of Napa, with its wine riches, is only a 20min, 14-mile drive east (see from p66 for our Napa wine trails).

GET THERE
From San Francisco International Airport, it's approximately a 60-mile drive north to Sonoma town.

① SCRIBE

With views of San Francisco Bay, Scribe offers two distinctive tasting experiences on one property, just east of Sonoma town. Head to the original tasting room tucked into a repurposed cabin for wines served alongside plates of local charcuterie. Alternatively, book in for the more involved lunch experience at the recently opened hacienda. Either way you'll enjoy your wines outdoors and vineyardside, and you'll want to reserve your tasting in advance.

Scribe has quickly become one of the most popular destination wineries in Sonoma County thanks to the fashionable farm vibe created by the 30-something owners, the Mariani brothers. Fresh Riesling, summertime rosés and flavourful reds shine among their wines.
scribewinery.com; tel 707-939-1858; 2100 Denmark St, Sonoma; 11am–4.30pm Thu–Mon by appointment ✕ ⓢ

② GUNDLACH BUNDSCHU

Affectionately referred to locally as GunBun, Gundlach Bundschu has been part of the fabric of Sonoma wine for generations. The farm was founded in the 1850s, and today's tasting room and grounds still retain equipment and decor from the original era. Expect a laid-back, welcoming environment, with multiple tasting spaces ranging from stand-up bar to outdoor seating. Call ahead to reserve a tour of the GunBun wine caves, with a taste of wines still ageing in barrel before being bottled, plus a walk around the vineyards. You can even reserve a two-hour tour of the entire property in an Austrian army vehicle. Check out the aromatic whites and medium-bodied reds, especially the Cabernet Sauvignon or the Bordeaux-inspired Mountain Cuvée. In summer, the winery hosts an open-air concert series.
www.gunbun.com; tel 707-938-5277; 2000 Denmark St, Sonoma; 11am–5.30pm daily ✕ ⓢ

03 HANZELL

The oldest continuously producing Pinot Noir and Chardonnay vines in California can be found at Hanzell – reserve an in-depth tour and tasting and you'll have the one-off chance to sample them. Tours also include a look at the world's first stainless-steel temperature-controlled tanks; considering that this technology now serves as the backbone of winemaking all over the globe, that's no small feat. You'll then venture out for a drive around Hanzell's Moon Mountain vineyards.

Founded in the 1950s, Hanzell has held on to its historical feel by conserving its original winery and older vine plantings, though outdoor art and sculptures from natural materials also lie dotted around the property. Surrounded by forests, with panoramas of San Francisco Bay, this is one of the prettiest spots in Sonoma County to taste wine.
hanzell.com; tel 707-996-3860; 18569 Lomita Ave, Sonoma; 10am–3pm daily by appointment 💲

04 LAUREL GLEN

Laurel Glen has been growing Cabernet Sauvignon in the volcanic soils of Sonoma Mountain for so long its vines are now recognised as a certified selection of the variety. Originally planted in the 1960s, the Laurel Glen vines adapted outstandingly to the site, developing their own characteristics. With a savoury flavour of forest and herbs, Laurel Glen Cabernet offers mountain energy in an elegant frame.

Led by owner Bettina Sichel, visits to the tasting room tie together local expertise, friendly atmosphere and charming environs; displays include a combination of Laurel Glen history and winemaking insight. Tastings can be designed to include only current-release wines, or, for a marginally higher price, some older vintages smartly paired with chocolates custom-made to complement the exact wine that you're sipping. If you get to meet Sichel herself – she's often in the tasting room as well – you're in for a treat. She has helped to lead some of the finest wineries in California and her passion for Laurel Glen is evident.
www.laurelglen.com; tel 707-933-9877; 969 Carquinez Ave, Glen Ellen; 11am–4pm daily 🍴💲

Courtesy of Gundlach Bundschu (2)

05 **KELLER ESTATE**

Designated in late 2017, Sonoma County's newest recognised grape-growing region is the Petaluma Gap AVA. Defined by the influence of the persistent wind that blows through the region thanks to the proximity of the Pacific Ocean, the Petaluma Gap turns out Pinot Noir, Chardonnay and Syrah with resplendent acidity; the wind helps maintain the freshness by cooling the fruit during warm periods.

Family-owned Keller Estate was among the first to plant in the Petaluma Gap, helping lead the charge in establishing the AVA as its own distinct wine region.

You'll need to make a reservation to visit during winter months; in the warmer part of the year, you can just drop in on weekends, though scheduling in advance is still recommended. Visits include a private tour with wines and a venture out to the overlook to enjoy them with full vineyard views. It's a great chance to test out wines characteristic of southeastern Sonoma, but also to learn about California's freshest celebrated growing region. *www.kellerestate.com; tel 707-765-2117; 5875 Lakeville Hwy, Petaluma; 11am–4pm Sat & Sun approx May–Oct or by appointment* 💲

Courtesy of Sonoma Scribe / Leo Patrone (2); © Getty Images / S. Greg Panosian

01 Outdoor eating at Scribe

02 & 03 Gundlach Bundschu and family

04 & 05 Interior at Scribe and Andrew & Adam Mariani

06 City Hall at Sonoma

WHERE TO STAY

COTTAGE INN AND SPA

Right in the heart of Sonoma town, within walking distance of the plaza's shops, the Cottage Inn and Spa focuses on easygoing comfort. Suites are all old-school charm with contemporary smartness; go for one with a private hot tub or, if you fancy a self-catering setup, reserve a suite with kitchen. Within easy reach of the region's wineries, this is a particularly excellent option if you're visiting from spring to autumn, when the weekly farmers' market takes place nearby.
cottageinnand spa.com; tel 707-996-0719; 310 First St, Sonoma

INN AT SONOMA

Just two blocks south of Sonoma Plaza, this glammed-up inn offers plush, crisp rooms featuring rich-red fabrics, floral-patterned furnishings, and fireplaces for cosy wintertime stays, with plenty of space to relax. You can drive to all the best wineries, or even hop across to neighbouring Napa.
www.innatsonoma.com; tel 707-939-1340; 630 Broadway, Sonoma

WHERE TO EAT

EL MOLINO CENTRAL

Rustling up home-cooked Mexican classics with seasonal flare, El Molino Central is a locals' favourite, and a homey, comfortable spot especially designed for nice weather. If you want to picnic, grab a takeaway plate, or pick up a bag of the delicious tamales.
www.elmolinocentral. com; tel 707-939-1010; 11 Central Ave, Sonoma; 9am–9pm daily

FREMONT DINER

Roll up to Fremont Diner for a dose of country-style comfort food, perhaps biscuits and gravy or a plate of fried chicken. Outdoor seating in the warmer months is often accompanied by roaming chickens. On cooler days, cosy up in the old-school country-diner interior.
www.thefremontdiner. com; tel 707-938-7370; 2698 Fremont Dr, Sonoma; 8am–3pm Mon–Wed, to 9pm Thu–Sun

THE GIRL AND THE FIG

A Sonoma town classic, The Girl and the Fig was one of this region's first celebrated restaurants. The seasonal Californian menu (featuring local cheeses and charcuterie) accompanies a robust list of Rhône-variety Californian wines, including Grenache Blanc, Viognier and Syrah. There's also an antique bar serving delicious aperitifs inspired by French cocktails.
www.thegirlandthefig. com; tel 707-938-3634, 110 West Spain St, Sonoma; 11.30am–10pm Mon–Thu, 11am–10pm Fri, 8am–11pm Sat, 10am–10pm Sun

WHAT TO DO

SONOMA PLAZA

The Plaza at the heart of Sonoma town serves as an enormous park with two playgrounds, multiple duck ponds, a performing stage, and a weekly farmers' market in warmer months. State laws allow outdoor drinking for those who are old enough, so it's also a popular spot for picnicking with a bottle of local wine.

[California]

SONOMA COUNTY WEST

Venture into western Sonoma for afternoon walks through millennium-old coastal redwoods and a collection of flavourful wines grown in the cool maritime influence of the Pacific Ocean.

Tucking into forests of coastal redwoods, the western reaches of Sonoma County still carry more of a locals' vibe than an upmarket wine-country feel. This area is a charismatic blend of hippie values, oyster picnics, redwood hiking trails, towns set deep in the woodland or against ocean backdrops, and wines made ultra-fresh by the cooling Pacific Ocean. If you know to look for them carefully, wineries and tasting rooms can be found woven into the landscape all over west Sonoma, from its rolling hills cut through by rivers to its coastal reaches, where cliffs plunge straight into the ocean and houses perch just above the waves.

Though the Coast Range protects Sonoma County from the most severe weather blowing in off the Pacific, a low spot in the mountain chain enables fog and cold nighttime temperatures to seep in. These cool nights serve the vineyards well: wines here tend to be fresh and vibrant. You're more likely to meet a medium-bodied red wine that's perfect for a meal, rather than a robust, full-bodied red. There are also crisp whites to pair with the region's ocean-fresh seafood. The best-known wines here are made from Pinot Noir, but you'll also encounter Chardonnay, Syrah and some light-bodied Zinfandels. Producers here tend to be independent thinkers: unexpected varieties and wine styles are thrown into the mix, too – anything from medium-bodied wines from one of California's historical accidents, Valdiguie (which arrived in the area masquerading as another variety entirely) to savoury, wild-hearted sparklings.

From Sonoma West's wine lands, or the region's most convenient base Sebastopol, it's easy to reach nearby Bodega and Tomales Bays for fishing expeditions and oyster lunches. If you're in the mood for a more luxurious trip, stay at Bodega Bay Lodge, or hit one of the state's most challenging golf courses, Links at Bodega Harbour.

GET THERE
Sebastopol is 70 miles north of San Francisco Airport on Hwy 101. 'West county' begins at Sebastopol and includes everything west to the Pacific.

01 WIND GAP

A few years ago, Sebastopol reclaimed its ancient town-centre apple and grain warehouses and converted them into what is now known as the Barlow – a fantastic mixed-use space of boutiques, restaurants, distilleries, breweries and wineries. The Wind Gap tasting room sits at the front of the actual Wind Gap winery, combining reclaimed timbers, weathered metals and leather to create a western-made-modern feel. Pull up a stool to sip your way through California's cold coastal vineyards, from intense Syrah and zesty Pinot Noir to energetic Chardonnay. Winemaker Pax Mahle sources fruit from sites pressed close to the ocean, as far south as the Santa Cruz Mountains and north up to Mendocino. Expect freshness and a pleasing range of flavours. *www.windgapwines.com; tel 707-331-1393; 6780 McKinley St 170, Sebastopol; 11am–6pm Sun–Thu, to 8pm Fri & Sat* 💲

02 HANNA WINERY

Dr Elias Hanna grew up in a farming family, then went on to become a famous heart surgeon. With his success, he decided to find a new way to reconnect with his family's farming heritage and founded what has become one of Sonoma's iconic wineries. Today, his daughter Christine Hanna leads Hanna Winery, maintaining the high-quality, impressively drinkable wines for which the family is known. Their Sauvignon Blanc is a flagship wine, perfect for enjoying on the patio of the Russian River Valley tasting room. Or pick from a range of other Burgundian and Bordeaux varieties, each made with a resplendent acidity that makes Hanna a go-to brand for many. While there is a tasting fee, it's waived with the purchase of two bottles. You're welcome to bring along a picnic lunch, too. In the northern part of Sonoma County, just northeast of Healdsburg, lies Hanna's more palatial tasting room, with beautiful vineyard views and a rotating art show. *www.hannawinery.com;*

Dr Elias Hanna, a famous heart surgeon, reconnected with his family's farming heritage by founding one of Sonoma's iconic wineries

Hanna Russian River Valley: tel 707-575-3371; 5353 Occidental Rd, Santa Rosa; 10am–4pm daily Hanna Alexander Valley: tel 707-431-4310; 9280 Hwy 128, Healdsburg; 10am–4pm daily $

03 EMERITUS VINEYARDS

Emeritus Vineyards creator Brice Cutrer Jones has founded some of the most influential wineries in Sonoma County, and headed up the petition that made one of its biggest AVAs, the Sonoma Coast, officially recognised. In 1999, he turned his focus chiefly to Emeritus Vineyards, to deliver handcrafted Pinot Noir from the exceptional growing regions of Sonoma County. Revolving around vineyards close to the coast, Emeritus offers distinctive single-vineyard Pinot Noir with backbone. In the tasting room, you'll learn all about how well this variety expresses the particular character of its site. Though all Emeritus vineyards sit on the far western side of Sonoma County, each has its own elevation, soil and growing conditions – and these differences show in the glass. While Emeritus wines come from multiple locales along Sonoma's Coast, the tasting room is a true reflection of the Russian River Valley. Appointments are not required, except for tours, larger groups, personalised experiences and, if you fancy, a picnic lunch to accompany your tasting.

www.emeritusvineyards.com; tel 707-823-9463; 2500 Gravenstein Hwy N, Sebastopol; 11am–4pm Mon–Thu, 10.30am–4pm Fri–Sun ✕⊗⑤

⑭ DUTTON ESTATE

It's hard to find a more signature experience of Sonoma's Russian River Valley AVA than a visit to Dutton Estate. Joe and Tracy Dutton both come from families that have lived in Sonoma County for generations, and their work clearly embodies the heritage of their farming region. Today, Joe is co-owner of the Dutton Ranch founded by his parents in the Green Valley sub-zone of the Russian River Valley, and the couple's children are also part of the winery.

Dutton Estate wines centre primarily on the varieties the region is famous for: Chardonnay and Pinot Noir. The tasting room, on the edge of the vineyard, offers a full range of experiences, from straightforward tastings across the winery portfolio to pairing menus starring seasonal, California-style cuisine crafted by the winery chef. With reservations, you can enjoy a farm-to-table tasting, a personalised wine-and-food experience guided by your own wine educator. But for an intimate look at how wines here are made, book a combined tour and tasting; you'll visit the vineyards where the grapes are grown, explore the winery itself, learn about the winemaking process and uncover the Dutton family history, before settling into a tailored wine-and-food pairing session.
www.duttonestate.com; tel 707-829-9463; 8757 Green Valley Rd, Sebastopol; 10am–4.30pm daily ✕⊗⑤

⑮ PORTER CREEK

A little cabin hidden away on a hillside vineyard encircled by forest, Porter Creek feels refreshingly laid-back and authentic, and far enough out of the way to combine a sense of adventure with privacy. Still a family-run winery, it was established in the mid-1970s by George Davis. Second-generation winemaker Alex not only produces the wines and manages the vineyards, but also handles every aspect of the business, and you may spot him pouring your wines in the tasting room. Porter Creek wines offer wonderful tension brought by the cool nighttime temperatures of the area. The focus is on reds: look for Pinot Noir and a mix of the region's favourite varieties, like Zinfandel, Carignan and Syrah.
www.portercreekvineyards.com; tel 707-433-6321; 8735 Westside Rd, Healdsburg; 10.30am–4.30pm daily ⑤

WHERE TO STAY

BODEGA BAY LODGE
For a room overlooking the Pacific Ocean, head 15 miles southwest into Bodega Bay, where Bodega Bay Lodge has crisp, neutral-hued rooms with private balconies. From here, it's a quick jump to the area's best fishing, local golf courses and regional wineries. *bodegabaylodge.com; tel 707-875-3525; 103 Coast Hwy One, Bodega Bay*

SEBASTOPOL INN
Sebastopol Inn offers cheerful, brightly coloured, balcony-equipped rooms, within a few steps of the town centre. Easily arranged local activities include zip-lining through the coastal redwoods, canoe or kayak tours of the Russian River, and hot-

air-balloon rides over Sonoma County. *www.sebastopolinn. com; tel 800-653-1082; 6751 Sebastopol Ave, Sebastopol*

WHERE TO EAT

RAMEN GAIJIN
For a cosy meal accompanied by Japanese whiskeys and local beers on tap, hunt down Ramen Gaijin in downtown Sebastopol. As the name suggests, fantastic ramen bowls in multiple styles dominate the menu, though there's a selection of other

noodle dishes, too. *ramengaijin.com; tel 707-827-3609; 6948 Sebastopol Ave, Sebastopol; 12.30–2.30pm & 5.30–10pm Tue–Sat*

ZAZU KITCHEN & FARM
Known for its home-cured meats and farm-fresh foods, Zazu Kitchen & Farm is all about California comfort food. Offering both lunch and dinner, Zazu also showcases locally made wines. *zazukitchen.com; tel 707-523-4814; The Barlow, 6770 McKinley St 150, Sebastopol; 5–9pm Mon–Wed, 11.30am–11pm Fri & Sat, 9am–9pm Sun*

HOG ISLAND MARSHALL OYSTER FARM
Find your way to Tomales Bay for a picnic by the water and grab raw or BBQ oysters with a selection of local cheeses and charcuterie. Or book a Shuck-Your-Own Picnic table, which allows you to bring your own food and prepare your own oysters (bought on-site, of course).

Reservations definitely recommended. *hogislandoysters.com; tel 415-663-9218; 20215 Shoreline Hwy, Marshall; 9am–5pm daily*

WHAT TO DO

ARMSTRONG REDWOODS STATE NATURAL RESERVE
Journey back in time with a walk through the coastal redwoods just outside the town of Guerneville, 15 miles northwest of Sebastopol. Armstrong Redwoods State Natural Reserve includes some of the oldest – and tallest – trees on the planet, many of which have been given their own names. The park's eponymous tree, the Colonel Armstrong tree, has been dated at over 1400 years old, and numerous others in the reserve approach 1000 years of age. Picnic areas, self-guided nature trails and tree-hugging platforms are dotted around. Campgrounds lie outside the reserve (you can't camp within it). *www.parks.ca.gov; 17000 Armstrong Woods Rd, Guerneville*

[Colorado]
GRAND VALLEY

With some of the highest-elevation vineyards in the world, Colorado wineries offer soul-stirring vistas of mountains and the Colorado River, plus a refreshing twist on traditional wine styles.

Colorado has long been known for its fantastic skiing, alpine hiking and a flourishing craft-brew culture. But the Centennial state is also home to an eclectic community of grape-growers and winemakers – a passionate, curious bunch who produce iconoclastic wine styles brimming with personality that comes from alkaline soils and thin mountain air. This unique terroir rewards patience and perseverance, and Colorado's winemakers have both in spades. On a visit, you'll be greeted with generous hospitality and an infectious enthusiasm for what's possible in a place that remains a well-kept secret in the wine world.

Colorado winemaking is still a new frontier. While it has roots in the 1800s, as late as 1990, only five wineries were in operation. Now, more than 100 wineries lie scattered across the state – from the front range (Boulder/Denver) to the state's four-corner town of Cortez near the grand Mesa Verde. However, the largest concentration of vineyards can be found hugging the Rocky Mountains'

western slopes around Grand Junction, where the low humidity and intense ultraviolet rays of the high desert make it possible to grow a wide range of grapes despite a shortened season.

The Grand Valley AVA is home to the highest concentration of vineyards in Colorado. Many of them sit at around 4500ft, soaking up the sunshine that radiates off the valley's chalky Book Cliffs. It's unlikely you'd find these exact growing conditions anywhere else in the world, and, perhaps surprisingly, Bordeaux, Rhône and Italian varieties all thrive here, despite a short, challenging season in comparison to other regions that champion these classic longer-growing varieties.

About an hour's drive (75 miles) southeast, the Delta region in the West Elks AVA offers an extremely different microclimate, home to Pinot Noir, Riesling, Pinot Grigio and Pinot Meunier that manage to grow at 7000ft. Dovetailing these two areas makes an ideal weekend getaway for a broad perspective on what is going on in Colorado's wine scene.

GET THERE
A 230-mile drive west from Denver to the Grand Valley will have you passing the Continental Divide. Alternatively, fly into Grand Junction's airport (GJT).

01 TWO RIVERS

In 1999, Bob Witham and his wife Billie opened Colorado's 44th winery, with a vision of making high-quality wine in their home state. Bob and Billie live amid their vines, off the beaten path in the Redlands area at the mouth of the Colorado National Monument, attracting visitors from all corners of the world. French wines inspire them, as is made clear in their variety of choice (Cabernet Sauvignon, Merlot, Chardonnay, Syrah) – and also by the property's countryside château-styled buildings. Stay the night at Two Rivers' Wine Country Inn. *tworiverswinery.com; tel 970-255-1471; 2087 Broadway, Grand Junction; 10am–5pm Mon–Sat, 12pm–5pm Sun*

02 RED FOX CELLARS

'Respectful but unbound by tradition' is the proud motto Red Fox uses to blaze trails in Colorado's wine industry. Not only does this winery play with Italian varieties like Nebbiolo, Dolcetto and Teroldego, it also experiments with ageing traditional grapes in spirit-seasoned barrels from local distilleries. A smooth, long-lasting Bourbon-barrel-aged Merlot is Red Fox's bestseller; in 2017, the winery took home a silver medal at the Governor's Cup for its tequila-barrel-aged Chardonnay (with surprisingly chipper lime-like notes and bright acidity). Founders Sherry and Scott are inspired by Colorado's craft-beer movement and don't see why the wine industry can't have a little more fun, too.

Their 'urban barn' in the heart of Palisade is a relaxed, social space with a rustic feel. In addition to signature wines, it offers wines and cider on tap and creative wine cocktails. Tours by appointment. *www.redfoxcellars.com; tel 970-464-1099; 695 36 Rd C, Palisade, CO 81526; 11am–5pm Fri & Sat, 11am–4pm Sun–Tues*

03 PLUM CREEK

It began in 1976 with just a few friends playing with Colorado grapes. But, by 1984, Doug Philips and Erik Brewner had become the 10th bonded and oldest existing winery in Colorado. Doug and his wife Susan moved to Palisade, focusing on high-quality winemaking using only Colorado fruit.

Thick wooden beams set the

Stone Cottage Cellars prides itself on having the highest Merlot vineyard in the world, at 6200ft

tone for Plum Creek's warm, welcoming winery, while local art and sculpture bring depth to its landscape. Each vintage dictates the team's focus in the cellar, but the Old World guides stylistic choices, with Cabernet, Merlot and Chardonnay leading Plum Creek's award-winning wines. Galen Wallace has managed vineyards here since 1990, while Corey Moresworth leads the winemaking with endless ideas for how to keep Plum Creek at the forefront of Colorado's wine tradition. Drop in for tastings or book tours ahead.

www.plumcreekwinery.com; tel 970-464-7586; 3708 G Rd, Palisade; 10am–5pm daily $

04 COLTERRIS

Set among vineyards, orchards, lavender and rose gardens, Colterris has created quite the stir in recent years. Scott and Theresa High's Col-Terris, 'of the Colorado land', is built on high aspirations, with a talented team of experienced vineyard-focused winemakers and 100% estate fruit.

The couple lived for a time in Tuscany, Umbria and Bordeaux and investigated land in Mendoza, eastern Washington and Sonoma. But, in the end, the challenging singular climate and geography of Colorado presented unbeatable appeal. Scott explains how, with Colterris sitting at over 4700ft, 'the intense sunlight gives unique character to these wines; thick skins give way to distinctive flavour and incredibly deep colour.'

The Highs have two talented winemakers in charge, Bo Felton and Justin Jannusch, under whose watch Colterris prides itself on being a Bordeaux-style winery. In summer, visit the separate Colterris at the Overlook tasting room for riveting panoramic views of the Colorado River, Grand Valley and majestic Book Cliffs. Private tours can be booked ahead, or just drop by for tastings.

www.colterris.com; tel 970-464-1150; Colterris Winery Tasting Room: 3907 North River Rd, Palisade; 10am–5pm daily Colterris at the Overlook Tasting Room: 3548 E 1/2 Rd, Palisade; 10am–5pm daily Jun–Oct $

05 WHITEWATER HILL

Whitewater Hill owners John Behrs and Nancy Janes were drawn to Colorado's dramatic daily temperature change – sometimes as much as 30 degrees' day-to-night difference in the fruit-maturation months of August and September. They turned from engineering to winemaking in this unique terroir, which sits on ancient marine limestone in a high desert. The thick grape skins that develop in defense of this climate provide a character unlike any other. Nancy describes her red wines as taking on cloves and nutmeg, and even whites have a haunting spice.

Whitewater Hill is also one of the few Colorado wineries to make ice wine: Riesling is only picked frozen so this delectable treat isn't always available – if you're in luck, don't miss it! www.whitewaterhill.com; tel 970-434-6868; 220 32 Rd, Grand Junction; 10am–5.45pm daily $

[Delta/Paonia]

06 STONE COTTAGE CELLARS

Seventy miles southeast of Grand Junction, the northern Fork/Delta/Paonia wine country is higher than the Grand Valley AVA – averaging 6500ft to 7000ft. Stone Cottage's owner Brent Hellickson explains that 'growing grapes at this elevation is hard and different to anywhere else; wineries here are more intimately attached to the mountains.'

His vineyards sit upon a south-sloping mesa – good for aspect and draining off cool weather. The family farm rests on clay-based rocky soils with a sublayer of calcium marl, basalt boulders and volcanic material, allowing vineyard roots to draw mineral character into the wines; this Old World expression makes Chardonnay a favourite. Wine acidity here is higher than elsewhere in the state, producing other subtle, light styles: Stone Cottage specialises in Alsatian varieties like Gewürztraminer and Pinot Gris.

The winery, which radiates an old-Colorado Western charm, also prides itself on having the highest Merlot vineyard in the world (6200ft). Looking out from the winery, the West Elk Mountains stare back in the distance. Tours are available by appointment. www.stonecottagecellars.com; tel 970-527-3444; 41716 Reds Rd, Paonia; 11am–6pm daily

07 JACK RABBIT HILL

It isn't every day someone moves from California to Colorado to make wine, but that's what Lance Hanson did in 2001. He had no script when founding Jack Rabbit Hill – just a desire to understand this marginal, high, dry climate and its unusual challenges, and grow grapes in the most sustainable, ecologically thoughtful way possible. He converted to biodynamic farming in 2006 – Jack Rabbit Hill is Colorado's only Demeter-certified winery.

These wines are some of Colorado's most Old World-style drops. Hanson's love for Loire Valley, Burgundy and Beaujolais wines speaks to his surprisingly elegant, soft-spoken expressions born of Pinot Noir, Riesling and even Pinot Meunier, a red grape often seen in Champagne that imbues deep colour and a morello-cherry kirsch-like flavour to a blend. There's award-winning cider on offer, too.

Only 18 of 72 acres are under vine here; the rest is pasture, ponds, sage and livestock. And, at this high-in-the-sky winery, you'll soak up 360-degree views of the grand mesa to the west and the eye of the Black Canyon of Gunnison National Park. www.jackrabbithill.com; tel 970-361-4249; 26567 North Rd, Hotchkiss; by appointment $

WHERE TO STAY
WINE COUNTRY INN AT TWO RIVERS
Sleep among the vines at this château-like pick, where rooms are plush yet charming, and the Champagne Suite has an oversized bath and a four-poster bed draped in warm-toned fabrics. *tworiverswinery.com; tel 970-255-1471; 2087 Broadway, Grand Junction 81507*

HIGH LONESOME RANCH
For those seeking a remote, five-star experience in homestead cabins or even safari tents, with excellent cuisine. *www.thehighlonesome ranch.com; tel 970-283-9420; 275 County Rd 222, DeBeque*

BROSS HOTEL
Retreat to a slower pace in Paonia, where this snug B&B is known for its hospitality, charming frontier ambience and fruit-named rooms. *www.paonia-inn.com; tel 970-527-6776; 312 Onarga Ave, Paonia*

WHERE TO EAT
TACOPARTY
For a fun, casual scene, don't miss Tacoparty, where fresh local ingredients fuel the Mexican menu and there's deliciously creative gelato – a must during sweetcorn season. *www.tacopartygj.com; tel 970-314-9736; S 5th St, Grand Junction; 11am-3pm & 5-9 pm daily*

BIN 707
A formal local favourite for Colorado-sourced farm-to-table fare. No reservations – it's just first come, first served. *www.bin707.com; tel 970-243-4543; 225 N 5th St, Grand Junction; 11.30am-4pm & 5pm-late daily*

IL BISTRO ITALIANO
Italian-born Brunella brings her north-Italian tradition to Grand Junction with such authentically delicious bites as prosciutto platters and butternut-squash ravioli. *www.ilbistroitaliano. com; tel 970-243-8622; 400 Main St, Grand Junction; 5-8.30pm Tue-Sat*

LIVING FARM CAFÉ
Local-farm-fresh food, with some exciting vegetarian and vegan options. The team also runs next-door Remedy – a bike shop with salads, savoury paninis and a juice bar. *thelivingfarmcafe.com; tel 970-527-3779; 120 Grand Ave, Paonia; 7.30am-2.30pm & 5.30-9pm daily*

NEEDLE ROCK BREWERY
Craving a pint after a long day of tasting wines? Seek out this refreshing, locally loved Delta brewpub. *needlerockbrewing. business.site; tel 970-399-3733; 820 CO92, Delta; from 11am*

WHAT TO DO
This region is also a delight for outdoors enthusiasts. There are endless biking and horse-riding trails, hikes within Colorado National Monument, and great tubing down the Colorado River to Fruita. Go rock climbing and kayaking or hike the inner canyon of the Black Canyon of the Gunnison National Park. Or take a break from wineries and visit peach orchards and lavender farms for an inside look at Colorado's other agricultural industries.

CELEBRATIONS
Local festivals range from the July Lavender Festival and Palisade's August Peach Festival to the Colorado Mountain Wine Festival during September harvest. Or kick off the summer with the Palisade Bluegrass and Roots Music Festival in June.

[Idaho]

SNAKE RIVER VALLEY

They won their wine spurs in Napa and Washington, but a new generation of brilliant winemakers are bringing their home-state vines roaring back to life.

Each year, there are more gold medals earned in West Coast competitions by wines from Idaho. A record string of warm vintages in the Snake River Valley have played a key role in these ripe wines. And while the vines are planted in an arid shrub-steppe environment at nearly 3000ft elevation, cool nighttime temperatures help preserve natural acidity in the grapes to create balanced, food-friendly wines.

Few realise Idaho was home to the Pacific Northwest's first commercial wineries, starting in the 1860s, but Prohibition wiped out — until a decade ago — a thriving wine industry in the Panhandle town of Lewiston, 300 miles north of Boise. Ironically, the federal government's establishment of the Snake River Valley AVA in 2007 is viewed as the turning point. A handful of pioneers remain, yet it's the next wave of winemakers who are generating headlines for Idaho, particularly with such varieties as

Malbec, Syrah, Tempranillo, Riesling and Viognier.

'They're very good at winemaking,' says Greg Koenig of Koenig Vineyards. 'They're brilliant at marketing. They've brought the industry a whole new enthusiasm and youthful energy that was lacking.'

Several are women raised in the capital city of Boise who learned their craft in Napa or Washington state. They returned home to raise families and start wineries. Why? It's an all-season recreational paradise.

Moya Dolsby left the Washington State Wine Commission to head up the Idaho Wine Commission. There often are shortages of grapes with just 1300 acres of vines to support the 50 or so wineries, but Dolsby doesn't seem inclined to pull up her roots and leave Boise.

'I first got here in 2008, and it's still all about your friends, your family and your dog – it's not about the shoes you are wearing, your purse or your car,' she says.

GET THERE
Boise is an hour-long flight northwest of Salt Lake City, and less than an hour's drive from more than 30 wineries.

© Shutterstock / Charles Knowles

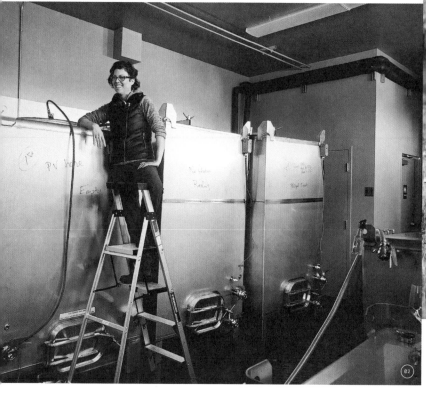

01 Downtown Boise, Idaho

02 Winemaker Leslie Preston at Coiled Wines

03 Winemaker Melanie Krause at Cinder Wines

04 The tasting room at Cinder Wines

① BITNER VINEYARDS

In 1980, Ron Bitner bought a few acres of sagebrush and weeds on the Sunnyslope near Plum Road, on the outskirts of Boise. The state's leading winemaker at the time, Bill Broach, had an idea.

'Ron, you've got a world-class site for Chardonnay there.' Bitner replied: 'That's cool, Bill, but what's Chardonnay?'

Cut to 2018: Greg Koenig, the dean of Idaho winemakers, produces internationally acclaimed Riesling for Bitner, in addition to Syrah (which he labels 'Shiraz'), Merlot, red blends and, yes, Chardonnay. Bitner is fascinated by bees — he has spent much time Australia researching them — which

is why they appear in his branding. The Bitner B&B makes for the complete Snake River Valley wine country experience .
bitnervineyards.com; tel 208-455-1870; 16645 Plum Rd, Caldwell; noon-5pm, Wed-Sun ⑤

② KOENIG VINEYARDS

One of the Northwest's most well-spoken and mild-mannered winemakers, Greg Koenig also ranks among its most talented. A graduate of Notre Dame's famed architecture school, he saved for 20 years to build his Italian-inspired terrace and elegant tasting room.

He's created a following for Williamson Vineyard Syrah and Viognier. Warm vintages allow for

tiny lots of single-vineyard Cabernet Sauvignon and Zinfandel. His Trockenbeerenauslese-style Riesling is a wine he's made twice, in 2010 and 2014, but doesn't expect to again because of climate change.
www.koenigvineyards.com; tel 208-459-4087; 21452 Hoskins Rd, Caldwell; noon-5pm daily

③ STE CHAPELLE/SAWTOOTH

Established in 1975, Ste Chapelle is Idaho's oldest and largest winery, and homegrown winemaker Meredith Smith recently took over its 125,000 cases. She continues to oversee Sawtooth Winery, a storied brand with a new tasting room featuring reclaimed wood and just inside

Ste Chapelle's gate. Smith's stellar reserve-style work with Sawtooth's historic plantings of Syrah, Petite Sirah, Grenache, Tempranillo and Malbec includes Provence-inspired rosé. That expertise shows in Ste Chapelle's portfolio with Chardonnay, Pinot Gris, Riesling and ice wine. *stechapelle.com; tel 208-453-7843; 19348 Lowell Rd, Caldwell, 83607; noon-5pm daily May-Oct, noon-5pm Fri-Sun from Nov-Apr* ✕⑤

04 INDIAN CREEK WINERY

It's a 25-minute drive from Boise to farm-chic, boho-esque Indian Creek Winery in Kuna, where retired Air Force Maj. Bill Stowe,

his daughter, and winemaking son-in-law carry on a 35-year history. They were among the first in the state to bottle Malbec (2004), and the lineup includes Tempranillo, a dry Touriga Naçional, an estate-grown Pinot Noir and Gewürztraminer. Their flagship is the claret-style Star Garnet ($15), which ranks among the Northwest's best bargain reds. *www.indiancreekwinery.com; tel 208-891-7151; 1000 N McDermott Rd, Kuna; noon-5pm Fri-Sun* ✕⑤

05 SPLIT RAIL WINERY

No one in Idaho pushes boundaries as well as Jed Glavin at Split Rail, where a former auto body shop is a tasting room

surrounded by working barrels, amphora and concrete tank to create a winery experience.

'You've got to get wacky sometimes for people to get interested,' he says.

Glavin bottles Gewürztraminer as a *pétillant naturel* ('natural sparkling') called Bruce Lees Brut. His blend of Syrah, Grenache and Mourvèdre, which earned much praise from *Sunset* magazine, is The Horned Beast, depicted by a deer head with grape vines for horns. A three-eyed rabbit touts his Grenache. *www.splitrailwines.com; tel 208-490-0681; 4338 Chinden Blvd, Garden City, 83714; noon-6pm Wed-Sun* ⑤

05 Grapes growing at Bitner Vineyard

06 A bridge over Boise River

06 CINDER WINES

Perhaps the quintessential Idaho wine story belongs to Melanie Krause. She grew up in Boise helping her folks tend their one-acre garden with 40 varieties of grape vines.

Biology and Spanish degrees from Washington State University got Krause a job at Ste Michelle Wine Estates in 2001. Six years at the Northwest's largest wine company led her to launch Cinder with its industrial chic vibe.

'The whole time I was working in Washington I was coming back to Idaho, exploring the vineyards, tasting the wines and thinking, "Hmm, this place has a ton of potential,"' she says.

The celebrated British critic Hugh Johnson has recognised her Syrah, Tempranillo and Viognier. Krause has also earned top awards for Riesling.
cinderwines.com; tel 208-376-4023; 107 East 44th St, Garden City; 11am-5pm daily 💲

07 TELAYA WINE CO

Earl and Carrie Sullivan built a winery for Telaya unlike any in the Northwest. Think of a Montana hunting lodge with only a bike path between it and the Boise River.

'If we can get people walking or riding by to take notice, hopefully they'll say, "OK, I'm going to give Idaho wine a shot,"' Earl says.

West Coast judgings award golds to his Cab, Syrah and Viognier. He plays to Idaho's strengths with Rhône grapes, including Mourvèdre. Earl works with famous Washington vineyards for Bordeaux varieties and Chardonnay. The flagship is Turas, a Syrah-based blend named for a Gaelic reference to 'journey'.
www.telayawine.com; tel 208-557-9463; 240 E 32nd St, Garden City, 83714; noon-6pm daily 💲

08 COILED WINES

Boise native Leslie Preston taught French Literature at the University of California-Davis, where winemaking students would take her class to prep for internships in France. That inspired her to earn a master's in enology, leading to work in famous Napa and Sonoma cellars. By 2012, she'd moved her family back home and produced a bone-dry Riesling lauded by British critic Stuart Pigott.

Preston's bubbly is Rizza, Australian slang for Riesling. Reds include Black Mamba — a Petit Verdot-based blend — and Syrah-influenced Sidewinder. She's the only vintner in Idaho with two tasting rooms: one is a long, narrow wine bar in downtown Boise and the other a winery/cosy tasting gallery in a former Garden City antique warehouse.
www.coiledwines.com; tel 208-820-8466; 3408 W Chinden Blvd, Garden City, 83714; noon-6pm Thursday-Sunday; 813 W Bannock St, Boise; 3-10pm Tue-Sat 🍴💲

WHERE TO STAY

HOTEL 43

Hotel 43 stands out as downtown Boise's boutique destination, unmatched in its urban-chic decor and convenience. It's a short walk from the state Capitol building, art museum, Boise State University, the Boise River Greenbelt and dozens of restaurants. Named for the 43rd parallel and the 43rd state in the Union, the hotel connects with Chandlers Steakhouse. *www.hotel43.com; tel 208-342-4622; 981 W Grove St, Boise*

WHERE TO EAT

FORK

The emergence of the Snake River Valley wine industry synced with Boise's locavore movement led by Fork. The Grown Up Grilled Ham & Cheese sandwich features local cheddar. Local ribs are braised in local ale. Fork's popularity spills out of the historic Boise City National Bank building for sidewalk seating.

boisefork.com; tel 208-287-1700; 199 N Eighth St, Boise

JUNIPER

A block away, gastropub Juniper inspires a toast to Repeal as black letters on the brick wall read VOTE AGAINST PROHIBITION. Craft beverages and local wines rule alongside Hazelnut Crusted Idaho Trout and Lava Lakes Lamb Reuben. *juniperon8th.com; tel 208-342-1142; 211 N Eighth St, Boise*

THE ORCHARD HOUSE

The Sunnyslope Wine District is 30 minutes from Boise, but The Orchard House is a morning-to-night comfort food oasis with the state's best Idaho wine list. *www.theorchardhouse. us; tel 208-459-8200; 14949 Sunnyslope Rd, Caldwell*

PARMA RIDGE

Parma Ridge Winery and bistro is owned by chef Storm Hodge, who fled Seattle to make wine in Idaho. His rosemary truffle fries are sinful. *www.parmaridge.wine/ home.html; tel 208-946-5187; 24509 Rudd Rd, Parma*

WHAT TO DO

The lifeline for Boise outdoor enthusiasts is the Boise River Greenbelt, a network of 25 miles where cyclists

share the paved, tree-lined path with joggers and walkers. Rentals are available downtown, where Idaho Mountain Touring and Boise Bike Tours are among the leaders. *parks.cityofboise.org/ parks-and-facilities/ parks/greenbelt/*

CELEBRATIONS

Savor Idaho (June) is the state's premier wine and food festival, and winemakers from around the state pour alongside chefs at the Idaho Botanical Garden in Boise. It sells out weeks in advance, creating a black market for tickets. *savoridaho.org*

During July's final weekend, Boise's colourful Basque community — at 16,000 strong one of the largest beyond the Iberian Peninsula — gathers downtown at the Basque Block for the annual San Inazio Festival. Malbec is an ideal match with the indigenous cuisine. *www.thebasqueblock. com*

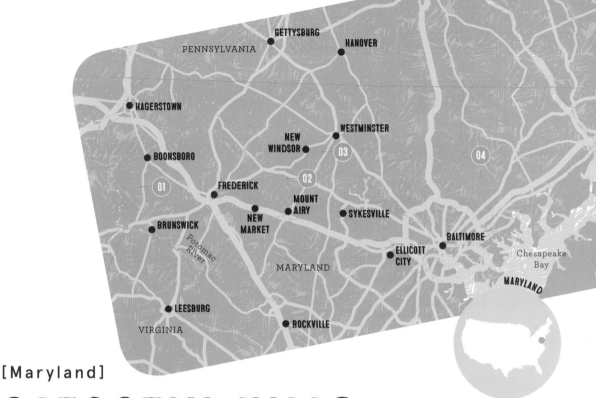

[Maryland]

CATOCTIN HILLS

Part of Maryland's growing wine country, the hillsides of the Catoctin range are dotted with vineyards, producing delicious wines from classic to creative.

Maryland's wine industry has expanded since 2000, spreading across the state from the mountains in the west to the coastal plains of the Eastern Shore. Visiting more than one winery at a time involves a lot of driving, but the reward is a chance to escape the highways for rural back roads and explore the beautiful scenery of the Blue Ridge and Catoctin mountains or the river deltas of Chesapeake Bay.

Maryland's wine history is relatively short, but the state played a major role in promoting viniculture along the east coast following the end of Prohibition in 1933. Philip Wagner, who founded the acclaimed Boordy Vineyards in 1945, was a leading proponent of French-American hybrid grapes such as Seyval Blanc and Chambourcin, which flourish in the challenging humid climate of the eastern

USA. Today, European vinifera varieties thrive here, though some of the old hybrids remain — and produce tasty, inexpensive wines. Meanwhile, wineries continue to experiment with unusual grape varieties to see which will grow well in Maryland's climate and terroir.

The modern renaissance of Maryland wine has been led by Black Ankle Vineyards, which introduced modern viticulture techniques and a culture of sustainability. Others followed suit, including Big Cork Vineyards and Old Westminster Winery. The latter thrills wine fiends with fashionable *pétillant-naturel* sparkling wines from Albariño, Grüner Veltliner and Barbera. Boordy Vineyards, under its current ownership since the early 1980s, updated its winery and now produces subtle, stylish wines with Euro flair. Maryland's modern wine story is in its opening chapters — there's much more to come.

GET THERE
Washington Dulles International Airport and Thurgood Marshall Baltimore–Washington Airport in Baltimore are easy starting points.

Courtesy of Old Westminster

01 BIG CORK VINEYARDS

Perched on a hilltop with 360-degree views of vineyards and mountains, Big Cork Vineyards is a great place to stop and refresh after touring the nearby Antietam and South Mountain Civil War battlefields.

Winemaker Dave Collins spent 14 years at Virginia's Breaux Vineyards (see p236) before joining owner Randy Thompson in 2011 to create Big Cork from scratch. As the winery name suggests, its wines are not shy. Collins has produced award-winning Petit Verdot and Cabernet Franc, but you won't

want to miss his Nebbiolo or his Russian Kiss, a flowery off-dry white made from experimental plantings of Russian grape varieties. The terrace is an ideal picnic spot (bring your own or buy bread, cheese and charcuterie here) and there is often live music in the evenings.
www.bigcorkvineyards.com; tel 301-302-8032; 4236 Main St, Rohrersville; 11am–5pm Thu-Mon ✗⑤

02 BLACK ANKLE VINEYARDS

The husband-and-wife team of Ed Boyce and Sarah O'Herron

The dynamic young siblings behind Old Westminster Winery have succeeded with hard work, social-media savvy and darn good wines

01 Grape picking at
Old Westminster

02 Black Ankle's
sustainable tasting room

03 The science of wine
at Old Westminater

04 Remote Black Ankle
homestead

05 Live music at
Boordy Vineyards

06 Baltimore's Inner
Harbor

ignited the Maryland wine
renaissance in the mid-2000s
when they established Black
Ankle Vineyards on a rocky slope
in central Maryland, east of
Frederick. They took the unusual
step of buying land specifically
with grape-growing in mind,
rather than planting vineyards on
existing family land. They set high
standards, insisting on using only
their own estate fruit and farming
sustainably. Their tasting room
is constructed from materials
they cleared to make way for
the vineyards — straw insulation
in the cutout wall display, a bar

countertop fashioned from pruned vine shoots.

Boyce and O'Herron found they quickly sold out of each new vintage, especially their white wines. So they planted more vines, and, in late 2017, purchased two new plots of land elsewhere in Maryland to expand even further. Highlights among the wines include a Bordeaux-style red blend called Crumbling Rock and a Syrah dubbed Leafstone. Notable whites are Albariño, Grüner Veltliner, Chardonnay and a proprietary blend known as Bedlam.

Speaking of bedlam, GPS systems such as Google Maps are likely to guide you here over twisty, narrow back roads. Best follow the directions on the website and stick to main roads.
www.blackankle.com; tel 301-829-3338; 14463 Black Ankle Rd, Mt Airy; 2–7pm Thu, noon–8.30pm Fri, 10am–5pm Sat & Sun 🟢

03 OLD WESTMINSTER WINERY

Old Westminster Winery burst on to the Maryland scene in 2012 with impressive debut wines and a dynamic trio of young siblings at the helm. Drew Baker, the oldest, is the family vigneron; the middle sister, Lisa Hinton, makes the wines, while the youngest, Ashli Johnson, manages the business and hospitality. They have succeeded with hard work, social-media savvy and darn good wines, and, despite the bucolic family-farm setting, project a lot of youthful energy.

Along with producing the usual Bordeaux-style reds and Chardonnay common in the Mid-Atlantic region, the Bakers love to experiment. Hinton was the first winemaker in the Mid-Atlantic to join the craze for *pétillant-naturel* sparkling wines, or pét-nats, producing them from Albariño, Grüner Veltliner and Barbera. In late 2017, Old Westminster became the first winery in Maryland to release wine in cans, including a skin-fermented Pinot Gris.
www.oldwestminster.com; tel 410-881-4656; 1550 Old Westminster Rd, Westminster; 4–9pm Fri, noon–5pm Sat & Sun 🟢

04 BOORDY VINEYARDS

Boordy is Maryland's oldest winery, dating to 1945 when it was founded in the Baltimore city limits by Philip Wagner, a journalist and wine lover who championed French-American hybrids. Boordy has been owned since 1980 by the Deford family, who moved winery operations to their farm further north in Baltimore County. An ambitious renovation program launched at the turn of the century resulted in new vineyards, new labels and a new winery — and some very elegant wines, especially in the Landmark series. The emphasis is on vinifera varieties, with Merlot and Cabernet Franc shining among reds, and Chardonnay and Albariño leading in whites.

While the Defords and their team have focused on improving quality, Boordy also maintains an active year-round events calendar, including a summer concert series, a weekly farmers' market, seasonal food-and-wine pairings and open-air festivals. The winery isn't far from the city, yet the relaxing pastoral landscape makes the urban hustle seem a world away.
www.boordy.com; tel 410-592-5015; 12820 Long Green Pike, Hydes; 10am–5pm Mon–Sat, 1–5pm Sun ✗ 🟢

From left: courtesy of Boordy; © Shutterstock / f11 photo

WHERE TO STAY

10 CLARKE
This B&B in an old Victorian home sits in charming downtown Frederick, a relaxing area to explore after touring wineries. The contemporary rooms are ornately styled, while a three-course farm-to-table breakfast kicks off the day.
www.10clarke.com; tel 301-660-6707; 10 Clarke Place, Frederick

FREDERICK INN BED & BREAKFAST
Skip the hotels for this 1897 Colonial Revival mansion five miles south of Frederick, which has smartly modernised rooms with Old World charm. Washington DC, Gettysburg battlefield and Leesburg, Virginia, are easy drives from this B&B.
www.frederickinn.com; tel 240-342-2902; 3521 Buckeystown Pike, Buckeystown

WHERE TO EAT

VOLT
Bryan Voltaggio did a star turn on Bravo TV's *Top Chef* before bringing fine dining to his hometown Frederick. Housed in a Gilded Era brownstone mansion, Volt offers bold-flavoured seasonal cuisine with a focus on local ingredients. For a parade of 15 dishes, reserve a month ahead for a seat at the intimate chef's table.
www.voltrestaurant. com; tel 301-696-8658; 228 North Market St, Frederick; 5.30–9.30pm Tue–Fri, 11.30am–2pm & 5.30–9.30pm Sat & Sun

THE WINE KITCHEN ON THE CREEK
This self-styled seasonal chophouse delivers a wine-friendly vibe and hearty meat dishes crafted with local produce. Wines can be enjoyed by the taste, glass or bottle, and several flights are offered. It has two sister restaurants in northern Virginia's wine country — The Wine Kitchen in Leesburg and WK Hearth in Purcellville.
www.thewinekitchen. com; tel 301-663-6968; 50 Carroll Creek Linear Park, Frederick; 11.30am–9pm Tue–Thu, 11.30am–10pm Fri & Sat, 11am–9pm Sun

WOODBERRY KITCHEN
Chef Spike Gjerde set the tone in Baltimore for the farm-to-table movement when he opened Woodberry Kitchen in 2007. His insistence on local ingredients is so strong he foregoes citrus, instead asking Maryland wineries to make verjus from unripened grapes to use in sauces and salad dressings. Meats and produce are locally sourced, and there's a heavy Maryland influence to the drinks list. Gjerde's work earned him a James Beard Foundation Award as Best Chef Mid-Atlantic in 2015.
www.woodberrykitchen. com; tel 410-464-8000; 2010 Clipper Park Rd, Suite 126, Baltimore; 5–10pm Mon–Fri, 10am–2pm & 5–11pm Sat, 10am–2pm & 5–9pm Sun

WHAT TO DO
In downtown Baltimore, explore the Inner Harbor and the National Aquarium, while Fort McHenry tells the story of the Star-Spangled Banner. Downtown Frederick is a charming historical area with lots of shops and a vibrant restaurant scene. And, if fancy a break from all that wine, check out one of Maryland's many craft distilleries (marylandspirits.org).

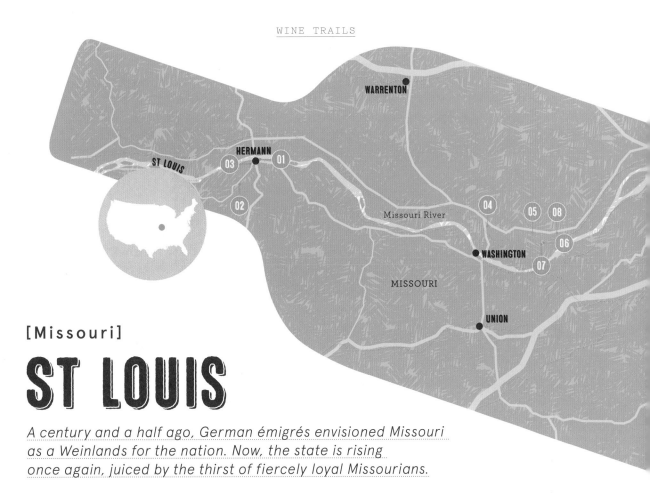

WARRENTON

HERMANN
ST LOUIS
03 01
02
04 05 08
06
Missouri River
WASHINGTON
07
MISSOURI
UNION

[Missouri]

ST LOUIS

A century and a half ago, German émigrés envisioned Missouri as a Weinlands for the nation. Now, the state is rising once again, juiced by the thirst of fiercely loyal Missourians.

Aside from California, Oregon and Washington, no state in the Union buys and drinks as much of its own wine as Missouri. Snooty palates from the coasts might insist that Missourians know no better but, with two major cities (Kansas City and St Louis) and a population of six million served by major universities, people here know a good bottle — they consume 1.5% of all wine drunk in the US.

Wine is in the blood. During most of its history, Missouri has been in and around the top 10 of producing states. Stone Hill is the beacon on the hill, established as a winery in 1847 and then growing to be the second largest in the nation. The nearby town of Hermann was founded in the 1840s on the belief that wine's future in the US lay in the green hills, covering a base of deep limestone, the same sort of soil that can be found under most of Europe's greatest vineyards. The German Settlement Society of Philadelphia, founded in 1836, believed that. They were perhaps misguided but the German émigrés hitched up their lederhosen and transformed the vaunting hillsides into a vinous garden. It grew until the anti-German, anti-immigrant fever of WWI and Prohibition put paid to it all. In the past 50 years or so, it has re-emerged.

With few exceptions, if you see Chardonnay or Cabernet in Missouri wineries, you're looking at out-of-state grapes. What thrives in this harsher climate are lesser-known grapes such as Traminette, Valvin Muscat, Vignoles, Chambourcin or the state's official grape, Norton. Despite the region's reputation for sweet wines, these grapes produce very tart juice, so the habit has long been to leave them a bit sweet. But today wineries are honing their skills at making drier wines with these same varieties.

GET THERE
Fly or drive into St Louis. Take I70 from St Louis to Hermann, then drive to Dutzow and cross the Missouri River for Augusta wineries.

© Shutterstock / Gimas

01 HERMANNHOF WINERY

At least some of the 3 million gallons of wine that were being produced in Hermann by 1904 was produced or stored in these mid-19th century cellars. Though shuttered by Prohibition, the place was purchased in 1974 the Dierberg family (high end, trend-setting St Louis grocers), launching a new era. The vibe is Old World German meets Midwestern, but the facilities are modern.

Hermannhof's award-winning Norton is a great introduction to that sappy, inky, challenging variety. Some Norton producers celebrate the grape's nearly obnoxious intensity, but Hermannhof hews closer to the seductive side of the grape. They are equally skilled with Chardonel, Chambourcin, peachy Vidal Blanc and flowery Valvin Muscat. *www.hermannhof.com, tel 1-800-393-0100; 330 East 1st St, Hermann; 10am-5pm daily except Sun 11am-5pm* $

02 ADAM PUCHTA

Adam Puchta isn't only the oldest family-owned winery in the state, arguably it's the oldest in the country. Tim Puchta is the great-great grandson of German immigrant Adam Puchta.

Puchta describes his campus as 'a mishmash of German-style buildings to early farm homestead to modern machine buildings'. It's a working winery, but also a charming spot with an old press house, everything from pizza to pulled pork on weekends (May to October), picnic grounds next to the creek and an outdoor deck.

Puchta makes two differently styled Norton-based Ports, and their Norton has enough rusticity to show standout complexity. The Dry Vignoles is acknowledged as one of the most exciting dry wines made in the Midwest. *www.adampuchtawine.com, tel 573-486-5596, 1947 Frene Creek Rd, Hermann; 10am-5pm daily except Sun 11am-5pm* ✕ $

03 STONE HILL

Stone Hill sits above it all, high on a hill overlooking the town, and with a restaurant serving country fare with a German connection

atop the sunken, vaulted 19th-century stone cellars. Each wall of its vast tasting room is covered with awards: look for Gold Medals from the Vienna 1873 World's Fair or Philadelphia in 1876. The Held family reopened the winery in 1965 and winery president Jon Held says, 'Our greatest goal is to re-establish Stone Hill to the prominence it had when, prior to Prohibition, it was the second largest winery in America.' It produces dozens of wines in differing styles, including an exciting Germanic style Catawba, but you really can't go wrong with any of them.

www.stonehillwinery.com; tel 573-486-2221; 1110 Stone Hill Hwy, Hermann; 10am to 5.30pm daily except Sat, 10am-6pm ✕⑨

⓸ BLUMENHOF WINERY

Next you'll drive along and across the Missouri River towards Augusta to reach the town of Dutzow, founded in 1834, a few years earlier than Hermann. The Blumenberg family has been here nearly since its inception; farmers by trade, they opened Blumenhof Winery in 1979 and it's an architectural depiction of the region's Germanic heritage, just off Highway 94. Their wines, especially the aromatic Valvin Muscat and the fruity Vignoles, are utterly charming. The Brathaus Grill offers pizzas, sandwiches and sides (May to October).

www.blumenhof.com, tel 636-433-2245, 13699 South Hwy 94, Dutzow; 10.30am–5.30pm daily except Sun noon–5:30pm ✕

01 Route 66 runs through St Louis

02 Germanic Hermannhof winery

03 Historic vineyards at Hermann, Missouri

⓹ NOBOLEIS VINEYARDS

On your drive to Augusta you may have noticed German *namen* morphing into French *nommes*; the French settled this area and birthed their own wineries long ago too. Noboleis Vineyards, however, dates back to just 2004 when Robert and LouAnn Nolan bought the property and turned it into perfect rows of Chambourcin, Norton, Traminette and Vignoles. Their Dry Vignoles may be a trifle sweeter than you expect but it's also far tastier than 99% of the Midwest's current output. The same could be said of their Traminette and in some years their reds set the pace as well. Pizzas and appetisers available, *www.noboleisvineyards.com; tel (636) 482-4500; 100 Hemsath Road Augusta; daily 11am–5pm* ✗ⓢ

06 AUGUSTA WINERY AND 08 MONTELLE WINERY

It wasn't Napa or Sonoma that received recognition as America's first American Viticultural Area (AVA) — it was the vineyards of Augusta. 'We've been growing Norton here for 200 years,' notes Tony Kooyumjian, the same whip-smart winemaker running both Augusta Winery and Montelle Winery. That AVA was 'predicated on the fact that this is the terminal moraine for the last continental glacier and it stopped right here – [so there are a] lot of well-drained, mineral rich soils with a lot of organic matter'.

Kooyumjian's Nortons are as close as the grape gets to elegance. Virtually everything that these two sibling wineries have to offer is on a par with anything made elsewhere in the state and, like Stone Hill, has become legendary for besting California wineries in many national competitions. Montelle Winery encompasses the Klondike Café, with salads, pizzas, sandwiches, wraps and appetisers. *www.augustawinery.com; tel 636-228-4301; 5601 High St, Augusta; 10am–5pm Wed–Sat, 12–5pm Sun. www.montelle.com; tel 636-228-4464; 201 Montelle Drive, Augusta;*

Mon–Fri 11am–5pm, Sat 10am–6pm, Sun 11am–6pm ✗ⓢ

07 MOUNT PLEASANT

The oldest winery in town, Mount Pleasant, was built in 1859 by two German brothers, George and Frederick Muench, and the old cellars here are worth a tour. The place was re-opened in 1966 by the Dressel family who keep moving forward, making a wide variety of wines and styles from 12 different grapes, including some that are unfamiliar to all but the

nerdiest of nerds. Talk to the staff; you'll find them knowledgeable about the history of the region and these grapes. Appellation Cafe is open Thursday through Monday 11am to 4pm. *www.mountpleasant.com; tel 636-482-9463; 5634 High St, Augusta* ✗ⓢ

04 Stone Hill winery sits above Hermann

05 Bike the Katy Trail to Augusta and back

From left: © Don Smetzer / Alamy; © Marek Uliasz / Alamy Stock Photo

www.sillygoosemo.com;
tel 636-482-4667; 5501
Locust St, Augusta;
5am-8pm Wed–Sun, till
9pm Fri and Sat

WHAT TO DO
THE KATY TRAIL
One of the country's
best state-long bike
trails winds its way from
Hermann to Augusta and
back to the St Louis area.
If you're not in a hurry,
this is the most charming
way to traverse these
lush hills. The track is
an old railroad bed so
it's flat and easy, often
meandering alongside the
lazy Missouri River.
mostateparks.com/
park/katy-trail-state-
park

THE HISTORIC DANIEL
BOONE HOME
This site features the
frontiersman's son's
home, where Daniel
spent some of his last
years, along with a
nearby village site.
Tel 636-798-2005;
1868 Hwy F, Defiance;
8.30am–5pm Mon–Sat,
11.30am–5pm Sun,
except Jan & Feb when it
opens half an hour later

WHERE TO STAY
HERMANNHOF WINERY
In a perfect world, you
could drive into Hermann
from St Louis the night
before your wine tour
begins and spend the
night in one of the town's
many B&Bs. They are
too numerous (and too
small) to name here, but
a quick search will turn
up dozens. Hermannhof
Winery has an inn as well
as charming cottages.
www.hermannhof.com;
tel 1-800-393-0100; 237
E 1st St, Hermann

ADAM PUCHTA WINERY
Reserve a room here as
the two-room Guest-
haus books up fast.
www.adampuchtawine.
com; tel (573) 486-5596;
1947 Frene Creek Rd,
Hermann

WHERE TO EAT
VINTAGE 1847
RESTAURANT
Many wineries offer
pleasant lunch fare.
Stone Hill's Vintage 1847
Restaurant is a fun and
homely place for a good
meal. Get there in time
to tour the old vaulted
cellars.
stonehillwinery.com/
vintage-restaurant-
dining; tel 573-486-
3479; 1110 Stone Hill
Hwy, Hermann; 11am-
8pm daily except Wed

BLACK WALNUT BISTRO
Offers solid pasta
with friendly service
and easy demeanour.
www.facebook.com/
blackwalnutbistro; tel
573-486-3298; 222 E 1st
St, Hermann; 4pm–9pm
Wed–Sun

THE PIZZA DOG
Here's a place in which
you can grab great and
creative hot dogs from a
cart, so show up ready
to eat alfresco.
www.wonderwienie.
com; 500 Stewart Circle,
Washington, Missouri,
9am–9pm Wed–Sun

THE BLUE DUCK
Refuel with tasty
sandwiches filled with
fried chicken or, of
course, duck.
blueduckcafebakery.
com; tel 636-390-9131;
516 W Front St Ste 100,
Washington; 10.30am–
2.30pm Tue, 10.30am–
10pm Wed–Sat

THE SILLY GOOSE
To tuck into fun food
with Cajun flair make
your way to the Goose.

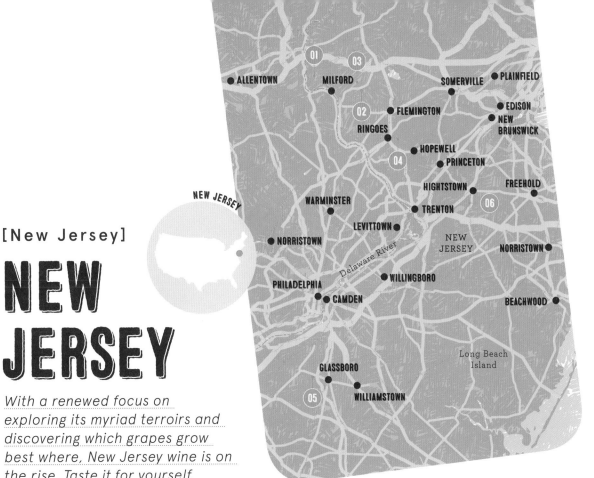

[New Jersey]

NEW JERSEY

With a renewed focus on exploring its myriad terroirs and discovering which grapes grow best where, New Jersey wine is on the rise. Taste it for yourself.

New Jersey's wine industry dates back to the 1700s, when London's Royal Society of the Arts recognised two New Jersey vintners for their success in producing the first bottles of quality wine from the colonies. The state's modern wine industry is much younger, less than 40 years old, and now boasts more than 50 wineries. There is a legacy of sweet, hybrid-based wines that sold — and still sell — well to locals, but today more wineries than ever are focusing on European grapes and pushing the quality envelope.

One of the biggest challenges faced by New Jersey's fine wine producers is that hangover of good-not-great wine. But, though it's the fourth-smallest state in the USA by area, when it comes to wine, New Jersey is hugely diverse. East-coast standards like Chardonnay and Cabernet Franc are grown across the state, but in the southern half, including areas that are essentially Philadelphia suburbs, the terrain is mostly flat with well-drained, loamy sand soils with lots of gravel. There, Bordeaux varieties including Merlot, Cabernet Sauvignon and Sauvignon Blanc dominate along with hybrid varieties like Chambourcin.

The northern half of New Jersey, considered a suburb of New York City, is much more varied in both elevation and soils. This diversity shows in the grapes that shine brightest in these rocky hills — everything from Pinot Noir and Grüner Veltliner to Syrah, Gewürztraminer and Zweigelt.

Wineries cluster in different parts of the state, but, since it's so small, you can easily explore all its terroirs over a weekend, with wineries in the north only a couple of hours' drive from those in the south. Alternatively, stay in Philadelphia and explore the south or visit New York City to study the northern regions.

GET THERE
Fly into Philadelphia or Newark airports and rent a car. Or rely on I80 to get there from points west and I95 to explore from the north or south.

❶ ALBA VINEYARD

Dating back to the 1700s, this 93-acre estate was once a dairy farm. Located in the Musconetcong River Valley (a tributary of the Delaware River), the vineyards are mostly planted on a large hill that features outcroppings of granite and limestone, depending on elevation. The vines themselves rest between 250ft and 750ft above sea level. In a region celebrated for its diversity, the Sharko family focuses on only a handful of varieties, including Chardonnay, Cabernet Franc, Riesling and Pinot Noir. The Chardonnay and Riesling are delicious, but the Pinot Noir is the star — and a bargain to boot. You won't find a better Pinot Noir for the money in the east (and perhaps the entire country).

With a spacious tasting room and a gorgeous outside tasting area with fire pits and a wood-burning pizza oven, Alba Vineyard happily accommodates large crowds. *www.albavineyard.com; tel 908-995-7800; 269 Route 627, Milford; 11am–5pm daily* ⑤

❷ BENEDUCE VINEYARDS

Back in 2001, the Beneduce family originally bought this 51-acre farm to supply their nearby retail gardening business. The greenhouses are still here, but since then the family has planted 16 acres of grapes on a horseshoe-shaped hillside at the top of the property and built a 7000-sq-ft winery and tasting room.

Inspired by wines tasted in Austria, Alsace and northern

01 Tractor tours at Beneduce Vineyards

02 Herbs also grow at Beneduce Vineyards

03 Grapes ripening at Alba Vineyard

04 Vines at Beneduce Vineyard

05 Green views at Unionville

06 The New Jersey Festival of Ballooning

Italy, areas with similar growing conditions to Beneduce's land, vineyard manager and winemaker Mike Beneduce focuses on varieties like Blaufränkisch, Riesling and Gewürztraminer. Flavourful with beautiful balance, the Gewürztraminer is a standout, along with the smoky, spicy Blaufränkisch.

Just 60 miles west of New York City, Beneduce sells most of its wine at the winery itself, where you can enjoy live music every weekend. In warmer months, music acts move outside to the stone patio with bonfire. Families are more than welcome. *beneducevineyards.com; tel 908-996-3823; 1 Jeremiah Lane, Pittstown; noon–6pm Wed, Thu & Sun, to 8pm Fri & Sat* 🟢

03 MOUNT SALEM VINEYARD

Just down the road from Beneduce (it's less than three miles northwest on country roads) lies the historical Abbott Taylor Farmstead, which has been home to Mount Salem Vineyards since 2005, though the farmhouse and its oldest barn date back to 1811. One of the barns is the primary tasting room, while that farmhouse is used for wine dinners, tasting lunches, private tastings and cooking classes.

Austrian varieties dominate the plantings and portfolio here; owner Peter Leitner believes they're an ideal match for the growing conditions in Hunterdon County. A fruity, spicy blend of Blaufränkisch, Zweigelt and St Laurent is delicious with a wide range of food, but don't miss the barrel-fermented Grüner

Veltliner, one of the most striking expressions you'll find of this grape. *www.mountsalemvineyards.com; tel 908-735-9359; 54 Mount Salem Rd, Pittstown; noon–6pm Fri–Sun or by appointment* 🍴🟢

04 UNIONVILLE VINEYARDS

Melding the traditional with the experimental, Unionville Vineyards embodies the true potential of New Jersey wine — and of wine up and down the USA's east coast. Tucked into farmland in Hunterdon County, Unionville is only a 30min drive from the Pennsylvania border and yet only 60 miles southwest of Manhattan.

Managing and sourcing grapes from six vineyards spread over three New Jersey counties, winemaking team Conor Quilty

and Stephen 'Zeke' Johnsen are dedicated to expressing the flavours and textures born from those varied sites and soils. To do so, they employ more old, neutral oak than new, flavourful barrels, and many of the wines are labelled as vineyard designates.

The Pheasant Hill single-vineyard Chardonnay stands up to any made in the USA, while a Syrah from the same vineyard will delight lovers of northern-Rhône wines. For something a little out of the ordinary (by east-coast standards, at least), check out the Mistral Blanc — a blend of Viognier, Marsanne and Rousanne — and the Mistral Rouge, a red blend that changes year to year but often includes the obscure Rhône grape Counoise. Walk-ins are welcome in the tasting room, but for an even more personal experience, book a private tasting. Or come for the spring pig roast; these wines are perfect for roasted meats. *unionvillevineyards.com; tel 908-788-0400; 9 Rocktown Rd, Ringoes; noon–5pm daily* ✕ 💲

05 WILLIAM HERITAGE WINERY

Just over the Delaware River from Philadelphia, and on a popular route to Atlantic City and the Jersey Shore, is William Heritage Winery. The Heritage family has farmed these 150 acres of land since 1853, but in 1999 Penni and Bill Heritage started converting their apple and peach orchards into vineyards. Today, the family grows 40 acres of vines across four distinct terroirs on the property.

True to the region, Bordeaux varieties like Merlot, Cabernet Franc, Sauvignon Blanc and Semillon — as well as other grapes such as Chenin Blanc, Chardonnay and Chambourcin — enjoy the warm growing season and well-drained soils. The high-end red blend BDX will appeal to lovers of brawny reds, but the star of the lineup is a vintage brut sparkling wine made in the tradition of Champagne.

On Saturdays, join the hour-long winery tour to learn about varieties of grapes, the winemaking process and the history of the family's farm.

www.heritagewinenj.com; tel 856-589-4474; 480 Mullica Hill Rd, Mullica Hill; 10am–6pm daily 💲

06 WORKING DOG WINERY

Amid the rolling terrain of Mercer County in central New Jersey, Working Dog started in 2001 with three acres of vines but has since grown to 17 acres and produces 4000 cases of wine each year, including Chardonnay, Cabernet Franc, Syrah, Merlot, Sangiovese, Viognier and Traminette. For anyone with a taste for fruit wines, there's also a fine blueberry wine. The 110-acre property offers walks and wine-tasting sessions on a covered brick patio or even out on the grass.

Don't let the cute dogs on the labels fool you — these are serious wines. The Syrah and Cabernet Franc are concentrated and nuanced, while the Viognier shows great balance and fresh acidity. *www.workingdogwinerynj.com; tel 609-371-6000; 610 Windsor Perrineville Rd, Robbinsville; 2–6pm Fri, 11am–6pm Sat & Sun* 💲

WHERE TO STAY

NASSAU INN

A gorgeous colonial-style inn in the heart of Princeton, New Jersey's first college town, which entices with its world-class dining, Revolutionary War history and neo-Gothic architecture. Elegant yet cosy rooms are dressed in rich woods and warm, earthy tones.
www.nassauinn.com; tel 609-921-7500; 10 Palmer Sq, Princeton

WOOLVERTON INN

Visitors to eastern Pennsylvania and western New Jersey love this deluxe B&B for its three-course breakfasts and 13 cottages and rooms found on 10 park-like acres.
www.woolvertoninn. com; tel 609-397-0802; 6 Woolverton Rd, Stockton

WHERE TO EAT

BRICK FARM TAVERN

Serving farm-to-table tasting menus in an 1880s farmhouse, Brick Farm Tavern is a rare restaurant that also houses a brewery and distillery: Troon Brewing and Sourland Mountain Spirits, respectively.
brickfarmtavern.com; tel 609-333-9200; 130 Hopewell Rocky Hill Rd, Hopewell; 5–9.30pm Wed & Thu, 11.30am–2pm & 5–9.30pm Fri–Sun

MATT'S RED ROOSTER GRILL

Delighting diners with American fare from an open kitchen, this tastefully styled local favourite feels like the home of chef-owner Matt McPherson. It's also BYOB, so you can sample one of the bottles you picked up earlier.
www.mattsredrooster grill.com; tel 908-788-7050;

06

22 Bloomfield Ave, Flemington; 5.30–10pm Tue–Sun

RAT'S RESTAURANT

Within the 42-acre Grounds for Sculpture park, this country-French restaurant is one of the most spectacular places to feast on the east coast. Monsieur Ratty is the main character from *The Wind in the Willows*; dining rooms are themed around scenes from the book.
www.ratsrestaurant. com; tel 609-584-7800; 16 Fairgrounds Rd, Hamilton; 5–9pm Fri, 11am–3pm & 5–9pm Sat, 11am–3pm Sun

CELEBRATIONS

Held each summer at Solberg Airport in Readington, the New Jersey Festival of Ballooning is the largest summertime hot-air-balloon and music festival in North America. With twice-daily mass ascensions of up to 100 hot air balloons, it's a spectacle to behold (balloonfestival.com).

For culinary adventure, check out Shad Fest, which celebrates the annual shad migration every spring in Lambertville. Shad, the largest fish in the herring family, is cooked in a variety of styles and there's also a jam-packed music schedule (shadfest.com).

WHAT TO DO

If Atlantic City and the Jersey Shore don't appeal, maybe delicious cheese will. Across the state, you'll find creameries like Cherry Grove (Lawrence), Valley Shepherd (Long Valley) and Bobolink Dairy (Milford) where you can tour and taste.

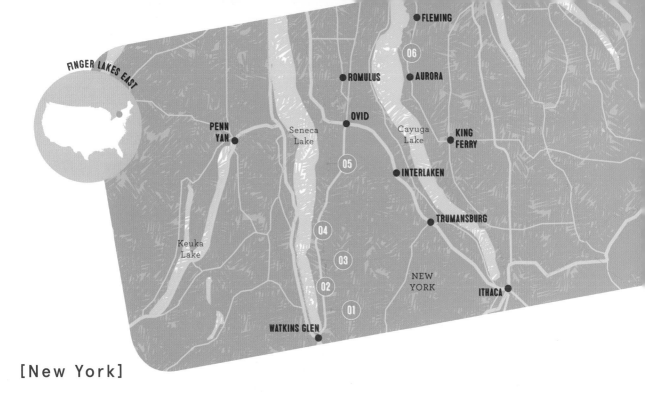

[New York]

FINGER LAKES EAST

In an extraordinary upstate New York landscape of lakes, waterfalls and cliffs, there's a wine boom going on.

Study a map of New York state and beneath Lake Ontario your eye will be drawn to 11 thin, long bodies of water. The distinctive Finger Lakes that rake the land north-south attract all sorts of visitors, from day trippers to second homers. Dotted with gorges and waterfalls, the area is a hiker's paradise. The lakes themselves offer every on-the-water activity imaginable, from fishing to boating.

Then, of course, there's the wine. Depending on your viewpoint, retreating glaciers or the hand of the Great Spirit created these striking features. Either way, the region is blessed with a fortunate series of microclimates. Most of the wineries are clustered on or near the shores of three lakes Keuka, Seneca, and Cayuga, and though white wine, particularly Riesling, made Finger Lakes' reputation, its reds are rising fast. But there is still much good value to be had, says Kelby Russell of Red Newt Wine Cellars: 'In the Finger Lakes you can learn a tremendous amount without spending a tremendous amount. You can almost always do a regular tasting for under $10 and find many bottles for under $20.'

Winters here can be harsh, but these deep lakes moderate temperatures, protecting the grape vines planted there, while also holding the heat of summer well into fall, extending the growing season. Riesling is the quality leader, with excellent wines being made in a variety of styles today. There are standout wines being made from other varieties as well, including Pinot Noir, Gewürztraminer, Cabernet Franc, Chardonnay and Blaufränkisch. Its reputation cemented as one of the finest wine regions in the East, the Finger Lakes and its winemakers continue to experiment, both in the vineyard and in the cellar.

GET THERE
Base yourself at one of the region's city hubs, Watkins Glen, Geneva or Ithaca. Seneca Lake is the boundary between our east and west trails.

01 BARRY FAMILY CELLARS

The winemaking Barry brothers, Ian and Brian, launched their family winery just a few years ago after long stints working at wineries around the Finger Lakes, Oregon and Washington. Though lacking grand lake views, the BFC offers a relaxed, kid-friendly vibe. With vinyl often spinning on the turntable and friendly staff pouring some of the best, small-production wines in the Finger Lakes, this is a must-visit winery for those interested in tasting the next big thing. 'We're at a point in the Finger Lakes where the quality is high and the prices a low in comparison,' says Ian Barry. 'Coming to the Finger Lakes feels like being the first to discover something great.' Don't miss the 'Pastiche' an Alsatian-style blend of aromatic white grapes or Barry's take on funky fresh sparkling wines.

www.barryfamilywines.com; tel 607-569-2352; 3897 Willow Street, Burdett; 11am-6pm Wed-Mon May-Oct, 11am-6pm Fri & Sat Nov-Apr ✕ $

02 FORGE CELLARS

Like a handful of others in the region, Forge Cellars work strictly with Pinot Noir and Riesling, believing that these are the best grapes for Finger Lakes' terroir. This focus allows the winery a meticulous approach to quality. Forge Cellars is an exciting joint venture of three partners: Justin Boyette of Hector Wine Company, New York-based Rick Rainey and Louis Barruol from Gigondas in the Rhône. Working with a number of top growers and terroirs across the Finger Lakes, Forge ensures the grapes are hand-picked and makes its wine with minimal manipulation. The results are gorgeous, and speak for a great ageing potential. A newly opened tasting room is for seated tastings once on Fridays and twice on Saturdays (reservations required). Make those reservations online and use map or satellite navigation to get there as there isn't a sign on the road (or on the building for that matter).

www.forgecellars.com; tel 607-622-8020; 3775 Mathews Rd,

01 Working the land at Heart & Hands

02 The Tasting Room at Forge Cellars

03 Justin Boyette and Rick Rainey of Forge Cellars

04 Guarding grapes at Bloomer Creek

Forge Cellars is an exciting joint venture of three partners working with top growers across the Finger Lakes

Burdett; Tastings by appointment, 5pm Fri, 10.30am & 1.30pm Sat $

03 BLOOMER CREEK

The Bloomer Creek tasting room is a short walk from the Stonecat Cafe (see page 167), and if you visit on a weekend afternoon, you're likely to be served by the tall, affable Kim Engle. Along with his

wife, artist Debra Bermingham, Kim started Bloomer Creek nearly 30 years ago, and continues to make the wine with the help of only one employee. Here, eye-catchingly, the red wines of Loire, France, are the model, and natural methods, including hand-harvest and native yeast ferments, are the goal. Kim makes terrific wines from Gewürztraminer, Pinot Noir, Riesling, and other grapes, but it is his Cabernet Francs that most clearly reflect the Finger Lakes terroir. Be on the lookout for the lip-smacking Bloomer Creek rosé and the elegant, ageworthy 'White Horse' Meritage Red. *www.bloomercreek.com; tel 607-546-5027; 5301 Rte 414, Hector; noon-5pm Sat & Sun* ✕ $

04 RED NEWT WINE CELLARS

Across the street and up the hill from Bloomer Creek sits Red Newt Cellars. Harvard-educated winemaker Kelby Russell makes something for everyone, and he firmly believes that it's an exciting time to make and drink wine in the region: 'Visiting the Finger Lakes now feels like visiting Napa Valley in the 1970s or Oregon in the 1980s; you are catching the burst and growth of a wine region that is finding itself.' Taste in the tasting room and then move to a wide deck for a glass or into the attached bistro for lunch — both offer expansive views of Seneca Lake. His skills shine brightest with a series of single-vineyard reserves. Look for vineyard

05 The tasting room at
Barry Family Cellars

06 Basket pressing at
Barry Family Cellars

07 Watkins Glen south
of Barry Family Cellars

designations such as Sawmill
Creek and Glacier Ridge and
Curry Creek, regardless of variety.
The Rieslings in particular are
intricate and detailed.
*www.rednewt.com; tel 607-546-
4100; 3675 Tichenor Rd, Hector;
11am-5pm daily* ✕Ⓢ

05 BOUNDARY BREAKS

Kelby Russell also makes the wine
for this ambitious newcomer,
which started in 2008 when
owner Syracuse businessman
Bruce Murray planted six acres of
Riesling on his 120-acre farm. The
vines are situated on a sloping site
between two ravines,

so-called boundary breaks.
Single-vineyard Riesling, from
bone dry to succulent and sweet
— all good — started as the sole
focus, but they've added small
production Gewürztraminer
and Cabernet Franc. Just north
of Lodi State Park, well off the
main road and about as close
to Seneca Lake as you can get
without getting wet, Boundary
Breaks offers a quiet, no-crowds
tasting experience with, naturally,
beautiful views of the lake.
*www.boundarybreaks.com; tel
607-474-5030; 1568 Porter Covert
Rd, Lodi; 11am-5pm daily* ✕Ⓢ

06 HEART & HANDS WINERY

Though a bit out of the way, this
small winery that started the
Riesling-and-Pinot revolution
is well worth the trip. A winding
road takes you along the lake,
past a wildlife refuge, beside
open fields and through cute
historical towns, until you reach
the Union Springs, and the winery
of Tom and Susan Higgins, Heart
& Hands. Consummate hosts,
the Higgins' are passionate
about three things: limestone
soil, Pinot Noir and Riesling. Just
over a decade old, the winery
is quietly making a convincing
case for vineyard-specific Pinot
and Riesling as the Finger Lakes'
signature varieties; they also
craft an extraordinary vintage
sparkling Brut.
*www.heartandhandswine.com;
tel 315-889-8500; 4162 Rte 90,
Union Springs; noon-5pm Fri-
Sun, or by appointment* Ⓢ

WHERE TO EAT

DANO'S HERIGER ON SENECA

Arrive here early in the evening: this traditional Austrian *heuriger* (wine tavern) offers stunning views of the sun setting over Seneca Lake. The food is classic – staples such as schnitzel, currywurst, spätzle and sacher torte – and the exciting wine list offers a selection of Austrian and German wines alongside a range of the best from the Finger Lakes. *www.danosonseneca. com; tel 607-582-7555; 9564 Rte 414, Lodi*

STONECAT CAFE

All the locals swing by the Stonecat at some point; it's like a *Cheers* bar for winemakers, relaxed and casual, with an excellent selection of Finger Lakes wines and beers. The back dining room opens on to a sloping garden where most of the food on the menu is sourced. It doesn't get more 'farm-to-table' than that... *stonecatcafe.com; tel 607-546-5000; 5315 Rte 414, Hector*

WHERE TO STAY

HUMBLE HILL LODGE AND FARM STAY

A short drive south of Ithaca, down Hwy 96B, this homey lodge is located on a small, chemical-free family farm, and offers affordable stays, both short- and long-term, for individuals or groups. The breakfasts are particularly delicious. *www.humblehill.com; tel 607-738-6626; 467 Tallow Hill Rd, Spencer*

THE WILLOWS ON KEUKA LAKE

Located directly on Keuka Lake, with a beautiful waterfront deck and available pontoon boat. Host Kathy Yonge goes out of her way to give her guests the most comfortable stay possible. *tel 315-536-5653; 6893 East Bluff Dr, Penn Yan*

WHAT TO DO

WATKINS GLEN STATE PARK

Enjoy a morning hike through otherworldly cliffs, where 19 waterfalls crash along a 2-mile course, and learn about the Finger Lakes' unique geology. (Don't forget to take a quiet moment to admire the Central Cavern Cascade.)

WALK THROUGH THE TOWN OF SKANEATELES

Hugging the north end of Skaneateles Lake, this charming small town, home to some of the region's best shopping and lakeside strolls, is a living testament to the virtues of old America.

CELEBRATIONS

In the middle of July, Watkins Glen hosts the terrific Finger Lakes Wine Festival, where over 80 wineries pour their new releases in a cheerful Woodstock-like scene of campers, wine lovers, and live music. Ravines Cellars hosts a crowded Fall Harvest Festival at their Seneca Lake tasting room in late September, and every weekend in December, Skaneateles is transformed into a Dickensian Christmas celebration, with costumed characters roaming the snowy streets.

07

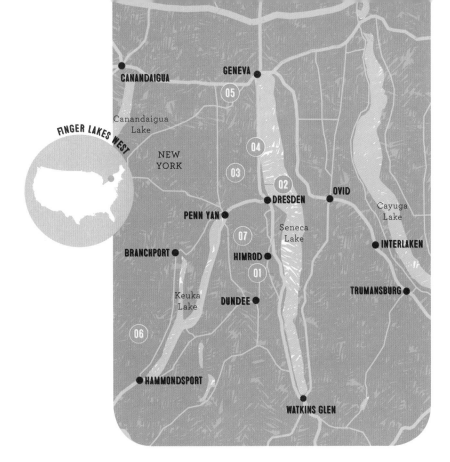

Canandaigua Lake

CANANDAIGUA

GENEVA

05

NEW YORK

04

03

02

DRESDEN

OVID

Cayuga Lake

PENN YAN

Seneca Lake

07

INTERLAKEN

BRANCHPORT

HIMROD

01

Keuka Lake

DUNDEE

TRUMANSBURG

06

HAMMONDSPORT

WATKINS GLEN

FINGER LAKES WEST

[New York]

FINGER LAKES WEST

An infectious sense of freedom – and gorgeous lakeside views – await here,
where European vines grow at the northern limit of American winemaking.

With such a bounty in this corner of New York state, there are sufficient wineries and wines to explore that even on repeat visits you need not stop at the same place twice. Our second Finger Lakes trail focuses on the west shore of Seneca Lake where the early days of Finger Lakes' serious wine scene dawned. It was in the 1960s, after the twin plagues of phylloxera and Prohibition, that vinifera grapes began to be taken seriously in this region. Dr Konstantin Frank planted some of the earliest vines here (his winery was founded in 1962). These days there's no doubt that grapes can thrive. Some wineries prefer to remain experimental

and cultivate a number of varieties – such as Cabernet Franc and Blaufränkisch – while adapting how the wines are made by considering questions of which yeast (native or laboratory), how to harvest (by hand or machine) and whether to mature in oak or steel. Others focus on honing just a couple of grapes, typically Pinot Noir and Riesling. Whatever the approach taken, it's an exciting and interesting time to taste Finger Lakes' wines.

The glacier-carved lakes are narrow (and deep) so on this trail base yourself either at the southern tip of Seneca around Watkins Glen or midway up the west side at Penn Yan in the heart of the wineries.

GET THERE
JFK or Toronto are the nearest major airports. Flights go from JFK to Ithaca, 85km from Hammondsport. Car hire is available.

01 HERMANN J WIEMER

In 1979 German-born Hermann Wiemer, one of the first to push for vinifera varieties in the region, founded his eponymous estate. Since then, his winery has earned a reputation among the best in the United States. Hermann retired in 2007 and his former assistant, Fred Merwarth, has taken over the winemaking, focusing on terroir, matching variety and style to the estate's varying vineyard sites. Oskar Bynke is Fred's partner in this project and serves as the public face for the estate — his wine presentations are keenly insightful. All the wines here are made with an eye for detail, but don't miss the Magdalena Vineyard Riesling, the Magdalena Vineyard Cabernet Franc and the sparkling wines. Bynke is also keenly aware that this fast-rising region benefits his and other wineries in many ways. 'With quite a few options including outdoor and water activities, museums, and authentic farm-to-table dining experiences that don't feel contrived, there is something for everyone,' he says. 'It just takes a drive around the lakes to see the abundant resources available.' *www.wiemer.com; 3962 Rte 14, Dundee; tel 607-243-7971; 10am-5pm Mon-Sat, 11am-5pm Sun* ✕⑤

02 ANTHONY ROAD WINE CO

Anthony Road's story is something of a mirror to the Finger Lakes' as a whole. Ann and John Martini planted their first vines — all hybrids — in 1973, and have since replanted nearly all the vines to vinifera variety such as Chardonnay, Riesling, Pinot Gris, Cabernet Franc, and Merlot. Today, the great majority of their delicious bottlings are strictly vinifera, but they also offer a semi-sweet hybrid wine (of Vignoles), giving a window to the recent past.

Anthony Road is a super visit to make for wine education (especially after Hermann Wiemer), and much

more. Very close to Seneca Lake, the bring-your-own-picnic-friendly open-lawn patio (local cheese also available) offers spectacular views. Inside, a frequently changing gallery features the work of local artists. Don't miss the Artist Series Riesling and winemaker Peter Becraft's 'Grey Series' experimental wines. *www.anthonyroadwine.com; 1020 Anthony Rd, Penn Yan; tel 315-536-2182; 10am-5pm Mon-Sat, noon-5pm Sun* ✕⑤

⑬ RED TAIL RIDGE WINERY

Weave through the vines on the west side of Seneca Lakes and you will come upon Red Tail Ridge

Winery, whose winery in 2011 earned the LEED Green Building Certification. Owners Nancy Irelan and Mike Schnelle — she makes the wines, he grows the grapes — produce outstanding Riesling and Pinot Noir, but RTR fascinates because of what it's doing with its Obscure Varietal Series. For any given vintage, you might find Teroldego, Dornelder and Blaufrankisch. An unoaked Chardonnay is one of the great value buys of the region. *www.redtailridgewinery.com; tel 315-536-4580; 846 NY-14, Penn Yan; 10am-5pm Mon-Sat, 11am-5pm Sun* ✕⑤

01 The tasting room at Dr Konstantin Frank

02 Ranks of vines at Red Tail Ridge Winery

03 Wine pioneer Dr Konstantin Frank

⑭ FOX RUN VINEYARDS

Fox Run is situated in a converted century-old dairy barn overlooking Seneca Lake. It includes a market and a cafe where artisanal Finger Lakes cheeses are paired with Fox Run wines. Here, it's possible to taste one of the widest stylistic arrays from a single estate in the Finger Lakes, from red and white to sparkling, from rosé to port styles. Winemaker Peter Bell has seen a transformation in Finger Lakes as a wine destination: 'Good

food and lodging were pretty scarce 10 years ago. Now it's easy to find both,' he says. Bell's most exciting tier of wines is the Geology series. Its object: to learn about the expression of single-vineyard sites through separate Riesling and Chardonnay bottlings. Kick your feet up with a glass of Riesling or Lemberger and enjoy the views of Seneca Lake on the back patio.
www.foxrunvineyards.com; tel 315-536-4616; 670 Rte 14, Penn Yan; 10am-6pm Mon-Sat, 11am-6pm Sun ✗⑤

⑤ RAVINES WINE CELLARS

Ravines Cellars' Morten Hallgren's entré into winemaking was at his family's Provence estate, Domaine de Castel Roubine. In 2000 Hallgren

and his wife Lisa secured a set of vineyards in the Finger Lakes, between two large ravines on the eastern shores of Keuka Lake.

Since then, they've prospered, and today, thanks to wide distribution and a popular wine club ('Ravinous') run one of the most representative Finger Lakes wineries. Ravines' wines have a direct, uncomplicated appeal, and while proud of his Riesling and Pinot Noir, Hallgren also bottles Cabernet Franc and Gewürztraminer. The Argetsinger Vineyard Dry Riesling and Maximillien red blend are two of their finest bottlings to date.

Located in a converted old barn, the tasting room oozes memories of generations past, and the kind,

knowledgeable staff are eager to please. After your visit, take a short drive to the historic city of Geneva. *www.ravineswine.com; tel 315-781-7007; 400 Barracks Rd, Geneva; 10am-5pm* ✗⑤

⑥ DR KONSTANTIN FRANK

Founded in 1962 by Ukrainian immigrant Dr Konstantin Frank, this pioneering estate is home to some of the first vinifera plantings in the region. Currently transitioning into a fourth generation of family ownership, Dr Frank is now home to three tiers of wine: the old-vine, estate-driven Dr Konstantin Frank, value-oriented Salmon Run, and sparkling-exclusive Chateau Frank. The wines to watch for here are Rkatsiteli, Grüner Veltliner, Riesling

Founded in 1962 by a Ukrainian immigrant, Dr Konstantin Frank is now into a fourth generation of family ownership

Semi-Dry and Chateau Frank Vintage Brut — all best enjoyed on an expansive deck that offers panoramic views of Keuka Lake. *www.drfrankwines.com; tel 800-320-0735; 9749 Middle Rd, Hammondsport; 9am-5pm Mon-Sat, noon-5pm Sun* ✕⑤

07 KEUKA SPRING VINEYARDS

In the early 1980s, Len and Judy Wiltberger bought 30 acres of land perched above the east shore of Keuka Lake and planted a variety of grapes. Today, their small winery is one of the state's most celebrated. Winemaker August Deimel is an iconoclast. He favours aromatics and freshness and has eliminated oak barrels from his red wines but uses them for his Gewürztraminer and dry rosé, which should not be missed, along with his juicy, snappy Cabernet Franc and Merlot bottlings. *www.keukaspringwinery.com; tel 315-536-3147; 243 Route 54 East Lake Rd, Penn Yan; Dec, Feb & Mar 10am-5pm Fri-Sun; Apr-Nov 10am-5pm Mon-Sun* ✕⑤

WHERE TO EAT
FLX WIENERY
From the road, it looks like a run-of-the-mill hotdog stand and it is that, but it's also so much more. Enjoy a variety of elevated dogs, sausages and burgers with toppings such as kimchi, smoked ketchup, and truffle mayo. The proprietors also own Element Winery, so you can taste their wines. *flxwienery.com; tel 607-243-7100; 5090 NY-14 Dundee*

WHERE TO STAY
NEW VINES BED & BREAKFAST
Due to the presence of seven wineries within two miles, and a line of its own estate-grown wines, New Vines offers an immersive Finger Lakes wine experience on Seneca Lake. Many of the rooms offer lake views. *newvinesbnb.com; tel 315-536-4087; 1138 Travis Rd, Penn Yan*

WATKINS GLEN HARBOR HOTEL
Named one of USA Today's 10 Best Waterfront Hotels in 2016, it's in the heart of downtown Watkins Glen on Seneca Lake. A large, full-service hotel, it offers an on-site restaurant. A great option if you plan to explore Keuka and Cayuga Lakes. *watkinsglenharborhotel.com; tel 607-585-6116; 16 N Franklin St, Watkins Glen*

04 Views over the Finger Lakes at Dr Konstantin Frank

05 Red Tail Ridge

[New York]
LONG ISLAND

Much more than beaches, celebrity-filled mansions and sleepy fishing villages, Long Island's ocean-washed East End is one of the world's finest places to make wine.

Long Island wine country is just an 80-mile drive east from Manhattan's skyscrapers, but it might as well be another country. The Atlantic waters fringing its grape-growing areas are the key to Long Island's outstanding wines: they moderate spring and autumn temperatures, extend the growing season, protect vineyards against frost, and minimise winter-cold damage. A lengthy growing season, with plentiful summer sun and cool overnight breezes, makes Long Island's maritime climate unlike any other in the world.

Surrounded by water to the north, east and south, the East End's North Fork is home to most of the region's 50-plus producers. In fact, the industry was born here in the early 1970s when Alex and Louisa Hargrave planted the first commercial vineyard. Today, you'll find bucolic villages bordered not only by vineyards but by farms of every kind — a reminder of Long Island's agricultural heritage. The South Fork (better known as The Hamptons) is home to a few wineries, but most famous as the summer home of athletes, film stars, music moguls — and beautiful east-coast beaches.

There was a time when Long Island compared itself to both Bordeaux and California, and its grapes reflect that. Merlot is the most-planted red, and there are significant plantings of Cabernet Sauvignon and Cabernet Franc. Chardonnay dominates local whites, but Sauvignon Blanc is becoming more common and compelling with every vintage. Winemakers continue to explore what makes Long Island drops delicious, leading to plantings of Albariño, Teroldego, Syrah, Tocai, Malbec, Grüner Veltliner and Chenin Blanc. With more than 25 grape varieties grown across 2500 acres, diversity rules Long Island wine.

North Fork wineries lie on one of two roads: Rte 48/Sound Ave (north) and Rte 25/Main Rd (south). Wineries on the South Fork are off its lone primary road, Rte 27a/Montauk Highway.

GET THERE
If your budget doesn't stretch to a helicopter or limo, you can take a bus or the Long Island Rail Road from Manhattan – or drive yourself.

01 PAUMANOK VINEYARDS

Winemaker Kareem Massoud was just 10 years old when his parents, Ursula and Charles Massoud, planted Paumanok's first vines on this former potato farm in 1983. Though he started a career in finance, he eventually found his way back to the family business. In the early 2000s, he took over the winemaking duties from his father and has worked to further cement Paumanok's place among Long Island's elite wineries. A converted barn serves as the tasting room but even better is a large deck overlooking the vines where you can enjoy a tasting, a glass or a bottle of wine with friends. In season, the Massouds invite oyster farmers to shuck their shellfish to order — a fine pairing with the winery's terrific Chenin Blanc or Sauvignon Blanc.
www.paumanok.com; tel 631-722-8800; 1074 Main Rd, Aquebogue; 11am–5pm daily Nov–Mar, 11am–6pm daily Apr–Oct ✕ ⑤

02 MACARI VINEYARDS

After many years of making wine in his basement in Queens, Joseph Macari Sr bought a 500-acre former potato farm in Matticuck. Thirty years later, his son and daughter-in-law, Joseph Macari Jr and Alexandra Macari, planted the first vines; vineyards now stretch all the way to Long Island Sound.

Macari Jr has long treated his vineyards and the surrounding land in a holistic manner with an eye toward biodynamics. He's

developed a complex composting programme that includes a herd of Long Horn cattle and a field devoted to compost, emphasising that the health of the plants and the character of the grapes depend on well-nourished, living soil, and that each step in the process contributes to the final product. Two large, energy-filled tasting rooms, in Mattituck and Cutchogue, offer the opportunity to taste a diverse portfolio of wines made with both traditional and more experimental techniques. The Katherine's Field Sauvignon Blanc is a local benchmark, while the Life Force wines, another Sauvignon Blanc and a Cabernet Franc, are fermented in concrete eggs. The Cabernet Franc is particularly delicious with a little something from the on-site pizza truck behind the Mattituck tasting room.

macariwines.com; Macari Vineyards Mattituck: tel 631-298-0100; 150 Bergen Ave, Mattituck; 9am–5pm Mon–Fri, 11am–5pm Sat & Sun. Macari Vineyards Cutchogue: tel 631-734-7070; 24385 Main Rd, Cutchogue; 11am–5pm daily May–Nov ✕ $

03 BEDELL CELLARS

Owned by film executive and art collector Michael Lynne, Bedell is one of the east coast's most celebrated wineries. At Barack Obama's 2013 inauguration, its Merlot became the first New York wine in history to be served at the inauguration of the President of the USA. Winemaker Rich Olsen-Harbich has been producing wine on Long Island since the 1980s and was one of the first winemakers here to move entirely to ambient yeasts for fermentation. The tasting room — and wine labels — are adorned with work by famous artists, and there is a sincere focus on hospitality, which gives the entire Bedell experience a luxurious feel. Cabernet Franc, Merlot and Sauvignon Blanc are standouts, but Museé, a red blend, is the splurge-worthy jewel of the portfolio.

For a more casual sampling and wines served exclusively on tap, visit The Tap Room at Corey Creek, where you can taste some of Olsen-Harbich's more experimental trials, listen to live music and enjoy a rotating schedule of food trucks. www.bedellcellars.com; tel 631-734-7537; 36225 Main Rd, Cutchogue; 11am–5pm daily The Tap Room at Corey Creek: tel 631-765-4168; 45470 Main Rd, Southold; noon–5pm Sun–Thu, to 7pm Fri & Sat Jun–Oct ✕ $

At Paumanok, oyster farmers shuck their shellfish to order — a fine pairing with the winery's terrific Chenin Blanc or Sauvignon Blanc

01 Windows with views
at Kontokosta Winery

02 Rosé research at
Wölffer Estate

03 Outdoor wine
tasting at Lieb Cellars

04 The tasting room at
Paumanok Vineyards

05 The tasting room
interior at Lieb Cellars

06 Fireside fun at Lieb
Cellars

04 LIEB CELLARS

Lieb Cellars is operated by an innovative team with a single goal: produce wine it's proud to serve. With its two tasting rooms — one for its Lieb Cellars estate wines, another for its Bridge Lane second label — Lieb has something for everyone, served in comfortable, unstuffy tasting rooms. With the main Lieb Cellars line, Australian winemaker Russell Hearn shows off what Long Island can do best, focusing on Merlot, Cabernet Franc, a red blend, Chardonnay and one outlier: a fresh, expressive Pinot Blanc that should not be missed. The Bridge Lane is the crazy little sister — these are charming, easy-drinking wines that are available in bottle, but also in 3L bag-in-box, disposable kegs and four-packs of cans — perfect for that day on one of Long Island's beaches or out on a boat.
Lieb Cellars: liebcellars.com; tel 631-734-1100; 13050 Oregon Rd, Cutchogue; noon-7pm daily. Bridge Lane Wine: bridgelanewine.com; tel 631-298-1942; 35 Cox Neck Rd, Mattituck; noon-7pm Wed-Mon May-Nov, noon-7pm Fri-Mon Oct-Apr $

05 KONTOKOSTA WINERY

Just outside the fishing-turned-tourist village of Greenport and its shops, bars and restaurants, Kontokosta is remarkable for any wine region — a waterfront tasting room and winery. Situated on 62 acres with more than a quarter-mile of Long Island Sound seafront, this is the only place in Long Island wine country where you can sit and enjoy a tasting or glass of wine up on the bluffs, with views that stretch to Connecticut on a clear day. The beautiful tasting room and winery are powered entirely by the near-constant winds that cross the property. Visit for the views, but not just for them: try out the Cabernet Franc and rosé, which stands out among other local pink wines thanks to its heavy dose of Syrah.
kontokostawinery.com; tel 631-477-6977; 825 North Rd (Rte 48), Greenport; 11am-5pm Sun-Thu, to 6pm Fri & Sat May-Dec; 11am-5pm Sun, Mon & Thu, to 6pm Sat Jan-Apr $

06 WÖLFFER ESTATE

In the heart of the Hamptons, Wölffer Estate was founded in 1988 by German-born Christian Wölffer. These former potato fields are home to a 55-acre vineyard, as well as Wölffer Estate Stables, which provides training, schooling, year-round boarding and instruction, in a facility with the east coast's largest indoor riding ring. The equestrian theme carries over into the winery, where horses adorn each wine label. Today, Mr Wölffer's children, Joey and Marc Wölffer, along with winemaker-partner Roman Roth, oversee the estate, which produces more than 50,000 cases of wine and hard cider each year. With a distinctly European aesthetic, the tasting room and adjacent terrace offer breezy yet cosy spaces and views of the vineyard, while table service delivers a refined tasting experience that matches the winery's Hamptons location.

Wölffer rosés, both the regular bottle and the Summer in a Bottle label, are Hamptons summer classics, but don't miss one of Long Island's top wines, Christian's Cuvée, a Merlot named after the winery's late founder.
www.wolffer.com; tel 631-537-5106; 139 Sagg Rd, Sagaponack; 11am-6pm Sun-Thu, to 8pm Fri & Sat $

Courtesy of Lieb Cellars; Wolffer Estate / Mark Louis Weinberg

WHERE TO STAY

CEDAR HOUSE ON SOUND

Just east of Macari Vineyards' Mattituck tasting room, this potato-sorting barn turned modern B&B has rooms washed in warm tones and bathed in natural light. The hearty two-course breakfast is an ideal way to start a day of wine touring. *www.cedarhouseon sound.com; tel 631-298-7676; 4850 Sound Ave, Mattituck*

HOTEL INDIGO EAST END

If a more traditional hotel with extras like a gym and swimming pool appeals, this is a pet- and family-friendly pick conveniently located at the gateway to wine country. Clean lines and splashes of colour dominate the comfortable rooms, and the on-site restaurant serves local wines. *www.ihg.com; tel 631-369-2200; 1830 West Main St, Rte 25, Riverhead*

WHERE TO EAT

NORTH FORK TABLE & INN

Founded by four veterans of Manhattan's high-end fine dining scene, this is arguably the best restaurant on all of Long Island. Farm-to-table tasting menus offer elevated Long Island classics as well as innovative contemporary cuisine. The four-room inn upstairs includes delicious breakfasts. *northforktableand inn. com; tel 631-765-0177; 57225 Main Rd, Southold; 5.30–10pm Mon–Fri, 11.30am–2.30pm & 5.30–10pm Sat & Sun*

LOVE LANE KITCHEN

Whether you're looking for morning coffee, breakfast, lunch or dinner, this family-friendly restaurant on a charming country street will satisfy. In the warmer months, sit outside with a glass of local wine or beer. *lovelanekitchen.com tel 631-298-8989; 240 Love Lane, Mattituck; 7am–9.30pm Mon–Fri, 8am–9.30pm Sat & Sun*

NORTH FORK ROASTING COMPANY

Head here the morning after a day of wine tasting for coffee roasted on-site or for a sustaining breakfast before returning to the wine trail. Don't miss the duck-egg burrito made with eggs from just down the street. *www.noforoastingco. com; tel 631-876-5450; 55795 Main Rd, Southold; 7am–5pm Mon–Sat, to 3pm Sun*

WHAT TO DO

MONTAUK SKATE PARK

Known as 'The End', Montauk hosts the fourth-oldest active lighthouse in the USA — you can climb to the top for 360-degree views — as well as hiking and fishing. Visit from mid-November to May and you might see some seals on the rocks.

CELEBRATIONS

Every June, when local strawberries are at their sweetest, the Mattituck Lions Club hosts the four-day Mattituck Strawberry Festival (*mattituckstrawberry festival.org*). Later in the summer, the Long Island wine industry gets together for Harvest East End to celebrate its past, present and future with a walkaround tasting of top wines and local foods.

[North Carolina]

YADKIN VALLEY

The hills of western North Carolina provide a scenic setting for delving into wineries that have found the elevation and sloping terrain ideal for growing grapes.

Winemaking in North Carolina carries a similar trajectory to many other east-coast states, drawing on historical roots dating back centuries, yet also with a contemporary industry that takes in only a few decades. Where it differs is in the national perception: this a state more famous for its tobacco and moonshine and the bootlegging runs that led to the development of auto racing than for a wine industry that is far more prominent to the north.

Yet the numbers suggest a business growing just as quickly as other neighbouring states, with nearly 200 wineries and vineyards across 2300 acres by 2017, producing 1.1 million cases annually; ranking North Carolina 11th most-productive on a national scale.

Many of these wineries are located in the Yadkin Valley, North Carolina's first federally recognised American Viticultural Area (AVA). Situated in the foothills of the Blue Ridge Mountains, it's a short drive from several of North Carolina's major cities (such as Winston-Salem, Greensboro and

Charlotte), but one that offers a dramatic change in topography and, in summer, comfort.

While North Carolina still squeezes juice out of some of its native American varieties like Muscadine, most areas of the Piedmont grow vinifera grapes. This includes the usual suspects of Chardonnay, Riesling, Sauvignon Blanc, Cabernet Sauvignon, Cabernet Franc and Merlot, with some southeast-coast favourites such as Viognier, Syrah and Petit Verdot also thrown in. The mix also features hybrids such as Chambourcin, Seyval Blanc, Chardonel and Traminette.

A few wineries have cultivated their own niche. Foremost and most successful among these is Raffaldini, sinking its Italian roots into the North Carolina mountains to plant Vermentino, Nero d'Avola, Sagrantino and Sangiovese as part of 27 acres of vines. Its Bella Misto is a field blend of eight grapes that incorporates many of these varieties, including Montepulciano.

GET THERE
The nearest airports are at Charlotte and Winston-Salem/Greensboro, both less than an hour's drive from at least one of these wineries.

01 RAFFALDINI

Transporting Tuscany to the Yadkin Valley could be this star winery's tagline. That's until you approach the villa with its stone facing, Italian roof tiles, and broad patio overlooking the distant mountains, and you taste the Vermentino and Montepulciano.

Named after its owners, with a heritage tied to the Roman city of Mantua, Raffaldini's 40 acres of vineyards are home to a mix of Italian varieties. The winery is one of a few regional advocates of the *appassimento* drying process, promoting higher concentration of colour and taste. Owner Jay Raffaldini says it took a while to eschew the north-Italian grapes his forefathers grew. 'In northern Italy, you're protected by the Alps; it's a much cooler climate. So, say if I was in Pennsylvania, I might be growing northern-Italian, but down in North Carolina it's more like the climate of Tuscany and Rome south,' he explains.

When you aren't sampling the Pinot Grigio or Sagrantino, take a guided vineyard tour (1pm or 4pm Wednesday to Sunday), or stroll through grounds designated a wildlife sanctuary. The winery's deli stocks gourmet produce. *www.raffaldini.com; tel 336-835-9463; 450 Groce Rd, Ronda; 11am–5pm Wed–Mon* ✕🅢

02 JONES VON DREHLE

Chuck Jones, one of the family members who founded Jones von Drehle in 2007, explains how years

of research brought them to this far upper-western corner of the Yadkin Valley. 'Our wine style showcases the benefits of this special terroir while embracing the centuries-old traditions of winemaking,' he says. 'Careful use of French oak creates just the right hint of influence while keeping the fruit to the forefront. As a pure estate winery, we purchase no fruit, juice or concentrates from anywhere.'

This producer has found a home 1500ft up, and sources a 30-acre vineyard made up largely of French grapes. Tables line the patio fronting the tasting room; inside, choose from regular or reserve tastings and accompanying snacks. Among Jones von Drehle's award-winning wines are white varietals Petit Manseng and Viognier and reds Petit Verdot and Cabernet Franc. *www.jonesvondrehle.com; tel 336-874-2800; 964 Old Railroad Grade Rd, Thurmond; 11am–5pm Wed–Sun* ✕🅢

03 MCRITCHIE

It's a five-minute, two-mile trip south from Jones von Drehle to McRitchie. Sean McRitchie has worked in wineries and vineyards

Finding JOLO, the 2016 North Carolina winegrower of the year, is easy – just look for the peak of Mt Pilot, which rises over 2400ft

vineyards, was voted the fourth-best winery restaurant in the country by *USA Today* in 2017) and accommodations on the grounds.

Shelton's 100-acre vineyard sits on a landscaped 200 acres of rolling land tucked into the foothills of the Appalachians, on a spot where tobacco once flourished, just minutes from the Blue Ridge Parkway. The 12th-oldest winery in North Carolina, it grows many recognisable varieties, including Chardonnay, Viognier and Cabernet Franc, plus a few less-common picks such as Malbec and Tannat. Numerous regional awards have been bestowed on its Riesling, Chardonnay, Cabernet Sauvignon, Tannat and port. Tastings include guided tours. *www.sheltonvineyards.com; tel 336-366-4724; 286 Cabernet Lane, Dobson; 11am–5pm daily* ✕ $

in the Willamette Valley of Oregon and in other premier wine regions around the world. He and Patricia (formerly an attorney and judge) moved from Oregon to North Carolina in 1998 just as the local wine industry was forming. Within 10 years, they had opened a winery, emphasising wine over everything else.

'We are not an event centre and encourage a more relaxing, zen experience,' Patricia says. 'We want our guests to slow down and enjoy the peacefulness and beauty of the location. We encourage picnics and relaxing on our porches; intimate

experiences, not group-focused.'

Highlights among McRitchie's small-batch beverages are its Chardonnay, Traminette and Sapere Aude red blend, as well as its hard ciders. Cheese and meat platters accompany the wines. *www.mcritchiewine.com; tel 336-874-3003; 315 Thurmond PO Rd, Thurmond; 10am–5pm Wed–Sat, 1–5pm Sun* ✕ $

04 SHELTON

If you're splitting your Yadkin Valley wine tour, Shelton is the stopping point, with outstanding dining (the Harvest Grill, huddled amid

05 JOLO

Finding this winery should be easy: just look up at the peak of Mt Pilot, which rises more than 2400ft amid 3700 acres of state-park grounds. Visitors will get an eyeful

of both this scene and Cox Lake, an attractive reservoir in an area with trails and campgrounds.

From a production standpoint, JOLO stands in no one's shadow, its wines recognised by a number of national and international competitions and poured in some of the state's top restaurants and hotels. It was North Carolina's wine grower of the year in 2016.

Founded by entrepreneurs Kristen and JW Ray, JOLO gets its name from their two sons, Joey and Logan. The tasting room hosts a restaurant specialising in tapas, with wines that run the gamut from frizzante to Chambourcin to compelling blends. Book ahead for a tour or barrel tasting.
www.jolovineyards.com; tel 336-614-0030; 219 JOLO Winery Lane, Pilot Mountain; 10.30am-6pm Thu-Sun ✗ 🟊

06 RAYLEN

For years a dairy farm, this 115-acre property (18 miles southwest of Winston-Salem) was bought in 1998 by Joyce and Joe Neely. The first vines were planted a year later, and the vineyard that visitors pass today on the way to the tasting room is an assortment of European vinifera, from Pinot Grigio and Chardonnay to Syrah and Petit Verdot.

You'll arrive into one of North Carolina's loveliest tasting rooms, with its patio and second-storey porch overlooking the vines, and plenty of lawn to lay out a blanket. A cupola atop the building adds charm to the countryside setting, and you can stock up on meats and cheeses while popping in for a tasting.

Raylen's signature wine is a Bordeaux blend called Category 5, with the drawing of a hurricane's

outer bands making for one of the region's most distinctive labels.
www.raylenvineyards.com; tel 336-998-3100; 3577 US158, Mocksville; 11am-6pm Mon-Sat, noon-5pm Sun ✗ 🟊

07 CHILDRESS

Richard Childress was a NASCAR driver whose career exploded after he retired in 1981 and became a car owner, teaming up with legendary driver Dale Earnhardt to win six titles, propelling him into the sport's Hall of Fame in 2017. By then, his North Carolina winery was well on its way towards similar success.

Headquartered in a gorgeous building in Lexington, 22 miles south of Winston-Salem, Childress operates a state-of-the art winemaking facility to handle grapes from its 72 acres of vineyards.

Beyond the premium dry wines offered for tastings, the portfolio also salutes the area's history. 'Richard's long standing as a Southern sports hero positions us to reach many non-traditional wine drinkers. We maintain our roots by producing a line of Muscadine varietal wines and preserve the grape species that is native to the American southland,' says winemaker Mark Friszolowski.
www.childressvineyards.com; tel 336-236-9463; 1000 Childress Vineyard Rd, Lexington; 10am-5pm Mon-Sat, noon-5pm Sun ✗ 🟊

WHERE TO STAY

VINTAGE INN B&B

Surrounded by large willow oaks and maples, this 85-year-old structure in Yadkinville offers four elegant rooms, a large living room and a veranda. Stay two nights and gain transportation to three or four selected wineries. *www.vintageinnbedand breakfast.com; tel 866-219-0696; 705 E Main St, Yadkinville*

CABINS AT ELKINS CREEK

These four intimate, creekside cabins provide a rustic getaway with modern conveniences, amid the woods and sounds of flowing water. A short walk takes you to an old mill, a waterfall, a vineyard and a winery. *www.elkincreekvineyard. com; tel 336-526-5119; 318 Elkin Creek Mill Rd, Elkin*

WHERE TO EAT

SWEET POTATOES

This award-winning restaurant in Winston-Salem's downtown Arts District has been delighting customers

and critics alike since 2003. From fried green tomatoes and okra basket to collard green dip, experience soul food at its finest thanks to owners Vivian Joyner and Stephanie Tyson, who also added a fried-chicken eatery next door in 2017. *www.sweetpotatoes. ws; tel 336-727-4844; 607 N Trade St, Winston-Salem; 11am-10pm Tue-Sat, 10am-3pm Sun*

THE TAVERN IN OLD SALEM

Winston-Salem's historic district of Old Salem showcases the culture of the Moravian settlement in North Carolina during the 18th and 19th centuries, and this family-operated

restaurant specialises in dishes inspired by those long-ago residents. Look for locally farmed food, wine, craft and draft beers and mixed drinks in an upscale-casual environment. *thetaverninold salem.ws; tel 336-722-1227; 736 S Main St, Winston-Salem; 11am-3.30pm & 5-9pm Tue-Sat, 11am-3pm Sun*

WHAT TO DO

If you're in an urban mood, swing by the NASCAR Hall of Fame (*www.nascarhall.com*) in Charlotte, the Old Salem Museum (*www.oldsalem. org*) and Foothills Brewing (*www.foothillsbrewing. com*) in Winston-Salem, and the Greensboro Science Center (*www. greensboroscience.*

org). Less than an hour away is Hamptonville, where the Shiloh General Store (*www. shilohgeneralstorenc. com*) sells fresh-baked food; it's one of a number of Amish-run merchants here and in nearby Windsor's Crossroads. If you're looking to add some outdoor adventure to that wine tasting, Stone Mountain State Park (*www.ncparks.gov*) offers some of the best hiking in North Carolina. About 150 miles west lies hip Asheville (*www. exploreashvile.com*).

CELEBRATIONS

Festivals abound during spring and summer, beginning with MerleFest every April in Yadkinville (*www.merlefest.org*), then the Yadkin Valley Wine Festival in Elkin in May (*www.yvwf.com*), a Salute North Carolina Wine Festival in Winston-Salem in June (*www. visitwinstonsalem.com/ special-events/view/ salute*), and Raffaldini's seasonal wine-and-dinner pairings and Italian wine festival every September (*www.raffaldini.com*).

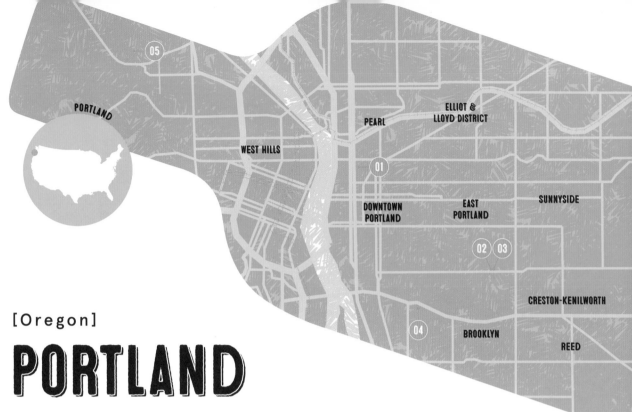

05 PORTLAND

PEARL

ELLIOT &
LLOYD DISTRICT

WEST HILLS

01

DOWNTOWN
PORTLAND

EAST
PORTLAND

SUNNYSIDE

02 **03**

CRESTON-KENILWORTH

04

BROOKLYN

REED

[Oregon]

PORTLAND

World-class food, wines for every palate and a tantalising
side order of urban cool? We have just the city for you...

Known the world over for its vibrant food
scene, the city of Portland celebrates its
funky food trucks as much as its traditional
restaurants. As the food scene has exploded, so has
the region's wine. Portland is a perfect city for making
an urban adventure out of your love for both. Thanks
to their proximity to one of the world's renowned
Pinot Noir regions, as well as the smaller, warmer
Columbia Gorge, Portland's urban wineries offer both
the cool-climate wines of Willamette Valley, and the
more robust flavours of the Gorge. In exploring the
city's winery scene you'll find tasting rooms for every
preference: cooperative warehouse-style tasting
rooms where you can taste multiple labels under one
roof; wine bar-style rooms where a winery offers its
own wines by the glass alongside wines of the
world; traditional tasting rooms adjoining
their respective wineries.

Portland is surrounded by the beauty
of the Pacific Northwest. On a clear day,
you'll see multiple mountain peaks in

the distance, including Mt Hood and Mt St Helens.
The northern edge of the city is bound by the
Columbia River, which divides the state of Oregon
from Washington. That's also where the Willamette
River flows into the Columbia after its meandering
progress from the south. In doing so, it bisects
the city: higher-end homes and boutique style
shopping characterise west Portland, while the
east has transformed into a newly reinvigorated, if
still slightly edgy, neighbourhood, thanks to former
warehouses that are now creative mixed-use spaces.
The tasting rooms tend to be found in the east, but
the food trucks and plenty of wine bars are in the
west, so you'll be criss-crossing the bridges over
the Willamette. Temperatures in the area can vary
significantly. In the summer you can expect
relatively warm, though rarely hot, days.
Winter brings the notorious Portland rains,
so pack your rain boots and rain jacket
if you're in the area any time between
November and March.

GET THERE
Fly directly into the
Portland International
Airport to visit the city. If
you're in Seattle, its just a
four-hour drive south
along Interstate 5.

01 FAUSSE PISTE

Located in the formerly industrial south-east of Portland, winemaker Jesse Skiles was one of the first to establish a winery in the city. Jesse draws on the warmer growing regions to the east of the city, on varieties such as Viognier, Grenache, and Syrah; he also makes small quantities of a Chardonnay and Pinot Noir. All his wines are informed by Jesse's background as a chef. 'Although I am a cook by heart and trade, a series of events in 2008 led me to switch to crafting wines,' he says. 'From the beginning, my wines have been driven by locale, climate, and cuisine.' To visit the tasting room you'll need to make an appointment; just call ahead. The winery adjoins a restaurant, Holdfast, whose menu of local seafood, meats and produce changes every two weeks. The wine list includes some of the most hard-to-find wines of the west coast, including Fausse Piste (advance reservation advised). *www.faussepiste.com; tel 971-258-5829; 537 SE Ash St, Portland; 5pm–10pm Tue-Sat* ✕ 💲

02 DIVISION WINE CO

Winemakers and partners Thomas Monroe and Kate Norris have one goal: to find the best vineyards that have excellent farming so they can intervene as little as possible in the cellar. As Thomas explains: 'There is no mystery in the winemaker. The mystery is the connection to the land. It is all

01 Explore Oregon wine at Division Wine

02 The 'I love Gamay' event at Division Wine

03 Disgorging sparkling wine at Division Wine

04 Southeast Wine Collective's interior

05 Crushing grapes for rosé at Division Wine

Clockwise from bottom left: courtesy of Division / Cremant: Division / Cheryl Juetten: SEWine Collective / Dina Avila: Division

about finding the vineyard that we want to work with.'

The result is a bevy of playful and delicious wines from varieties from all over Oregon and Washington. Mouthwatering, mineral-driven Chenin Blanc from the Columbia Valley AVA in Washington. Single-vineyard Pinot Noirs are from Willamette Valley. Floral and herbal Cabernet Franc from the Applegate Valley AVA to the south. The wines are all small production and hand crafted. Stop in any time to the Southeast Wine Collective retail shop (see below) to taste and purchase wines from Division. For an in-depth experience with the winemakers, call ahead to schedule a tasting appointment for one to 10 people. *www.divisionwineco.com; tel 503-887-8755; 2425 SE 35th Pl, Portland; 4pm–9pm daily* 🍴

03 SOUTHEAST WINE COLLECTIVE

The Southeast Wine Collective is a shared-space winery where some of Portland's best wineries make their wine. For an exciting glimpse at the region's growing community of young winemakers, drop into the tasting room, which doubles as a retail space and wine bar for the collective's members. There, with guidance from the servers, you can put together a flight of wines from multiple wineries, or wine-by-the-glass (the wine bar is also a small-scale restaurant).

The Collective was founded by the Thomas Monroe and Kate Norris, of Division Wine Co (see above). As Kate Norris explains: 'The purpose of having an urban winery is not only to live in town, but also to welcome the entire community into the winemaking process from start to finish.' Keep

an eye on the event schedule hosted by the Collective as well. *sewinecollective.com; tel 503-208-2061; 2425 SE 35th Pl, Portland; 4pm–9pm daily* 🍴💲

04 TEUTONIC WINE COMPANY

Classic rock and classic cars — it's clear what fires up Barnaby and Olga Tuttle when you step into Teutonic's comfortable tasting room. They bring the same conviction to their wines, which are inspired by the brightness and texture of German and Alsatian wines. The duo seek out vineyards,

'An urban winery welcomes the entire community into the winemaking process from start to finish'

*– Kate Norris,
Southeast Wine Collective*

primarily in the Willamette Valley, that offer tons of flavour at lower alcohols. To further showcase Oregon's riches, the Tuttles focus largely on single-vineyard wines. This approach also reveals how wines from various vineyards age. A visit to the tasting room brings a good chance of meeting the Tuttles themselves, who bootstrapped their winery from scratch. Stop into the tasting

room for a flight across the portfolio (cheese and charcuterie available) and a peek into the adjacent winery.
teutonicwines.com; tel 503-235-5053; 3303 SE 20th Ave, Portland; 12–9pm daily ✕ ⑤

⑤ BOEDECKER CELLARS

Pop across one of the bridges to the northwest side of Portland for a visit to the Boedecker Cellars tasting room. The winery keeps its focus on Pinot Noir from the Willamette Valley offering a range of single-vineyard examples. Husband-and-wife team, Stewart and Athena Boedecker started in 2003 at a collective-style winery in the Willamette Valley before launching their own cellar in Portland. The tasting room is in a converted warehouse space, and the Boedeckers are frequently on hand as they're often working in the winery next door. You're welcome to visit on weekends, or throughout the week at busier times of the year (such as the holiday season). Call ahead for accompanying plates of local charcuterie and cheeses.
boedeckercellars.com; tel 503-224-5778; 2621 NW 30th Ave, Portland; 4pm–7pm Fri, 1pm–6pm Sat–Sun ✕ ⑤

Ø6 Kate Norris (left) of Division Wine

Ø7 Tasting at Teutonic Wine Company

Ø8 Food trucks are a feature of Portland

WHERE TO STAY

HEATHMAN HOTEL

The Heathman Hotel is a Portland institution. Its classic styling has been updated with modern comforts, and the bar and restaurant are worth a visit. Its downtown location puts the Heathman within easy walking distance of the popular shopping district, The Pearl, or just across the bridge from the southeast industrial district where many tasting rooms are located.
portland.heathmanhotel. com; tel 503-241-4100; 1001 SW Broadway, Portland

THE BLUEBIRD GUEST HOUSE

To stay in the heart of the quirky, up-and-coming southeast industrial district of Portland check out this boutique-style hotel. There are only seven guest rooms in the Arts & Crafts era building so be sure you reserve well ahead of time. Once there you'll be in easy walking distance of incredible food, wine, and shopping.
www.bluebirdguesthouse. com; tel 866-717-4333; 3517 SE Division St, Portland

WHERE TO EAT

POK POK AND WHISKEY SODA LOUNGE

One of Portland's great success stories, Pok Pok started as a food cart serving Thai street food before becoming a full restaurant in Portland's southeast industrial quarter. It's a short distance from most of the tasting rooms. Put your name on the waiting list and enjoy a cocktail at the adjoining Whiskey Soda Lounge (take-away available).
pokpokrestaurants.com; tel 503-232-1387; 3226 SE Division St, Portland; 11.30am–10pm daily

SALT & STRAW

Another Portland food success story, Salt & Straw got started making mind-bending flavours of ice cream like Chocolate Caramel Potato Chip Cupcake, or Meyer Lemon Meringue Pie, sold from a push cart. So popular were these crazy but delicious combos that Salt & Straw now has its own proper scoop shop in Portland and several others in cities across the United States.
saltandstraw.com; tel 503-208-2054; 838 NW 23rd Ave, Portland; 10am–11pm daily

WHAT TO DO

POWELL'S CITY OF BOOKS

A visit to Portland is not complete without a detour to Powell's. The flagship store, stocking more than a million books, is in The Pearl district, and on the edge of the food-truck quarter. It stocks more than a million books.
www.powells.com/ locations/powells-city-of-books; tel 800-878-7323; 1005 W Burnside St, Portland; 9am–11pm daily

CELEBRATIONS

OREGON WINE MONTH

May is considered Oregon Wine Month throughout the state, and the city of Portland leads the festivities, hosting a range of activities, including special tastings at wineries, and by-the-glass pours at restaurants.

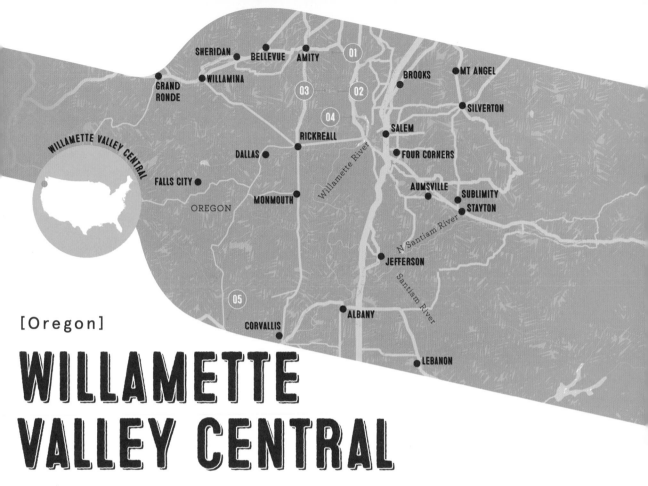

The map shows the following locations: SHERIDAN, BELLEVUE, AMITY, 01, BROOKS, MT ANGEL, WILLAMINA, GRAND RONDE, 03, 02, SILVERTON, 04, SALEM, RICKREALL, DALLAS, FOUR CORNERS, WILLAMETTE VALLEY CENTRAL, FALLS CITY, OREGON, Willamette River, AUMSVILLE, SUBLIMITY, STAYTON, MONMOUTH, N Santiam River, JEFFERSON, Santiam River, 05, ALBANY, CORVALLIS, LEBANON

[Oregon]

WILLAMETTE VALLEY CENTRAL

From the winding roads, charming towns and remote-feeling vineyards around Salem hail some of the wines that America's loves best

The Willamette Valley is some of the richest farmland in the Pacific Northwest. It's an enviable combination of row crops, orchard fruits, and nut trees on the valley floor, and vineyards on the steeper slopes. In between you'll find dairy farms, pastures, and sheep. Half way down the valley, along the banks of the Willamette River sits the city of Salem, the capital of Oregon, north of which lies the Eola-Amity Hills AVA - and some of the most exciting new growth in the region. Despite its proximity to Salem, the area feels remote, and is more farmland than residential. Vineyards have long been a feature around Salem, yet only recently have a few tasting rooms appeared. Be sure to check out the town of Corvallis too for a charming look at small town life.

Plan to base yourself Salem, and then drive from there to the tasting rooms. Destinations in wine country here appear more remote than they are. Even so, ensure that you have your GPS or road map with you. The hills and tight canyons here can make the area confusing to drive without directions.

There are only a few full-fledged restaurants in the hills north of Salem so if you're planning on being in that area during lunch, bring along a picnic or head for a food destination such as Brooks Winery or The Blue Goat (both listed in this chapter). Once you're into Salem or Corvalis there will be plenty of food choices. Even with a little extra planning required, this wine trail will reward the curious traveller interested in a glimpse of farm life. Wines through the area are celebrated, and the old-growth oak and pine forests through the hills are stunning.

GET THERE
Fly into Portland International Airport then drive 60 miles south on I5 to the city of Salem, at the south of Central Willamette Valley.

01 BROOKS

Brooks has swiftly become the prime destination winery of the Central Willamette Valley. The winery and adjoining tasting room are on a hill on the eastern side of the Eola-Amity Hills AVA, giving incredible views of Mount Hood, Mount Jefferson, the Three Sisters, and, on a clear day, Mt St Helens. Its impressive portfolio is built around single-vineyard wines from Pinot Noir and Riesling. Janie Brooks Hueck took on the winery when her brother and founder Jimi Brooks died, and hired Jimi's close friend Chris Williams to lead winemaking.

The duo continue Jimi's passion for small-lot fermentations, single-vineyard wines, Riesling, and biodynamic viticulture. Set into the side of the hill with a roomy patio, the comfortable tasting room is designed with reclaimed elements, including wood from a local barn. Select from a range of tasting flights from current releases, or library wines. Estate tours are available. Or buy a glass of wine with lunch made by the in-house chef. *www.brookswine.com; tel 503-435-1278; 21101 SE Cherry Blossom Ln, Amity; 11am–5pm daily* ✕ ⑤

02 CRISTOM

Cristom has been recognised as one of the most popular wines served in restaurants across the USA. It has also become one of the most celebrated Pinot Noir producers of the Willamette Valley. The winery is now managed by Tom Gerrie, who is the son of the founders Paul and Eileen Gerrie. The vineyards' winemaker, Steve Doerner, moved from California to Cristom in the early 1990s. 'Pinot can combine power and finesse,' says Steve. 'I try to emphasise the elegance but I don't mind having the power.'

> 'Teekayian traditional wine is family wine where it is made with special care and the expecta drinks it will be filled with joy.'
>
> –Archil Natsvishvili, Kakheti

A visit to the tasting room includes the Seasonal flight, tasting across the portfolio of current-release wines. Or you can schedule in advance for an in-depth tasting of the single-vineyard Pinot Noirs while learning all about the history of the winery. The grounds here include an outdoor patio and beautiful gardens. Consider reserving a picnic experience to accompany your tasting. *www.cristomvineyards.com; tel 503-375-3068; 6905 Spring Valley Rd NW, Salem; 11am–5pm daily*

03 BETHEL HEIGHTS

At Bethel Heights the Casteel family planted vineyards that are now some of the oldest vines in Central Willamette Valley. According to winemaker Ben Casteel: 'We want the wines to be driven by the place, not defined by different styles. We want the estate itself to show through.' A tasting of these distinct cuvées reveals the influence of vine age on wine quality. Located in the southern hills of Eola, the tasting room and its outdoor patio offer breathtaking views of the region. Walk in to enjoy a tasting from a mix of current release wines, or

call ahead to arrange a private tasting. Options include a look at older vintages and the history of the family's winemaking. Or, get to know how location can change the character of a wine by doing an estate tasting of wines from the specific blocks of their vineyards. *www.bethelheights.com; tel 503-581-2262; 6060 Bethel Heights Rd NW, Salem; 11am–5pm daily*

04 EVESHAM WOOD & HADEN FIG

Founded in the mid-1980s by Russ and Mary Raney, Evesham Wood handcrafts small-lot wines

(05)

from the region's flagship variety, Pinot Noir, from different sites. It's a wonderful opportunity to consider how a vineyard and its subregion inform the flavours and structure of the final wine. The Raneys began working with winemaker Erin Nuccio and his wife Jordan, who purchased the project when the Raneys retired and continued the spirit of Evesham Wood. Tastings include Nuccio's other label, Haden Fig, which delivers small production, playful wines from organic and biodynamically farmed vineyards of the region. Evesham Wood also offers bottlings of Grüner Veltliner, a variety rarely seen in the region. The tasting room is in a converted wood cabin on the property. It's rustic, simple and

friendly, and one of the owners will often be hosting. Drop in during opening hours, or plan ahead for a private tour of the vineyard and winery. *eveshamwood.com; tel 503-371-8478; 3795 Wallace Rd NW, Salem; 12–4pm Fri–Sun* 💲

05 LUMOS WINE CO

Set deep in the forested hills of Willamette Valley, Lumos Wine Co is an unexpected treat outside the town of Corvallis. It was one of the first family-owned tasting rooms in these coastal hills, from a second-generation winery on their third-generation farm. Set into a hill, the tasting room is in a converted barn that was part of the historic H bar H Dude Ranch in the 1940s. From its outdoor patio there's

01 Misty vines at Lumos Wine Co

02 The tasting deck at Brooks

03 New life at rural Lumos Wine Co

04 Antipasti platters at Brooks

05 Sampling the juice at Cristom

06 Willamette Valley Cheese Company

a beautiful view of the Oregon coastal mountains and nearby Mary's Peak. The peacefulness is worth the drive and the family even more so — one or other of the founders Dai and PK Crisp are often pouring the wines. Tastings include their current-release wines and a look at the Crisps' Wren vineyard directly beside the tasting room, which tends to close in January, usually opening again mid-February. *lumoswine.com; tel 541-929-3519; 24000 Cardwell Hill Dr, Philomath; 1–6pm Sat–Sun* 💲

WHERE TO STAY

GRAND HOTEL SALEM
Located in downtown Salem, Oregon's capital, the comfortable Grand Hotel brings classic styling renovated with modern conveniences, while downstairs is Bentley's Grill. It's a simple drive from this location to any of the tasting rooms of the the Eola-Amity Hills AVA. *grandhotelsalem.com; tel 503-540-7800; 201 Liberty St SE, Salem*

WHERE TO EAT

THE BLUE GOAT
In the tiny town of Amity the destination restaurant The Blue Goat is casual dining with country charm. The menu centres around the wood-fired oven and features a rotating selection by seasons. All meats, produce, and cheeses are locally sourced, as is everything on the wine list. *www.amitybluegoat. com; tel 503-835-5170; 506 S Trade St, Amity*

WILD PEAR
Combining fresh

Northwestern ingredients with Vietnamese flavours, the Wild Pear has become a locals' favourite. The restaurant is only open into the early evening so don't plan on a late dinner. Check out the events schedule for occasional seasonal dinners served family style. *www.wildpearcatering. com; tel 503-378-7515; 372 State St, Salem*

WHAT TO DO

WILLAMETTE VALLEY CHEESE COMPANY
Family-owned Willamette Valley Cheese Company works with a local dairy to source the highest-quality milk to produce their artisanal cheeses. Their Gouda, Havarti, and Fontina cheeses are award winning. The tasting room is located at the family farm. Take a gander at the collection of handmade cheese or learn a bit more about how each is made. *www.wvcheeseco.com; tel 503-399-9806; 8105 Wallace Rd NW, Salem*

CORVALIS HISTORIC TREES
The Willamette Valley has some of the biggest trees in the state of Oregon. In the city of Corvalis locals even offer a self-guided tour to some of the heritage trees that they help to conserve. Get started on the Oregon State University campus to view several of the oldest trees in the area, including a historic white oak outside Magruder Hall, the giant Douglas Fir locals call the Moon Tree, and a less-common Metasequoia near Benton Hall, Oregon State University *visitcorvallis.com/ explore-nature/ corvallis-heritage-trees*

Ø6

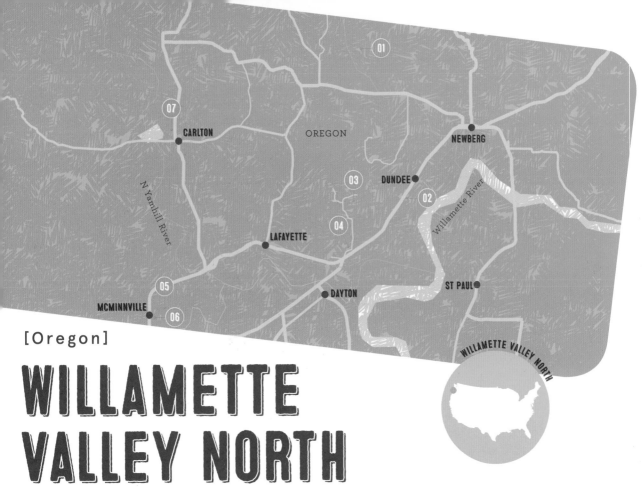

[Oregon]

WILLAMETTE VALLEY NORTH

World-class Pinot Noir lies in rolling hills just an hour from Portland – but don't forget the excellent Chardonnay, Riesling and fizz.

Sandwiched between the Coastal Mountains in west Oregon and the Cascade Range to the east stands the Willamette Valley, in several ways the heart of Oregon. At the bottom of the valley sits Portland, where the Willamette River flows into the Columbia River, and upstream are the state's two next largest cities, Salem and Eugene, where a quarter of the state population dwell. The valley is also the farming capital of Oregon. Busy place! Despite all this, conditions are perfect for grape vines and much of the Willamette Valley retains the feel of an idyllic farming community. Even the winter rains bring an undeniable beauty to the rolling hills and mixed forests of the valley.

Stick to the northern portions of the Willamette Valley to visit the founding wineries of the region, the highest concentration of tasting rooms are to be found here in the lower part of the valley and all are within striking distance of Portland. The Willamette Valley houses two-thirds of Oregon state's wineries, with over 500. The defining variety of the region is Pinot Noir but Pinot Gris, Chardonnay, Riesling, and a handful of other varieties in small plantings are also grown. If you really want to see the variety of the valley, make your way to Remy Wines, which is entirely devoted to Italian varieties.

In the tasting rooms, expect Burgundy and other cool-climate varieties showing off the vibrant acidity of the region. Besides the wealth of still table wines you might expect, there has recently been an explosion of sparkling wine production and plenty of experimentation.

GET THERE
Fly into Portland International Airport and then head southwest along I5 for less than an hour.

01 ADELSHEIM

Fewer than 10 wineries could be found in the region when David Adelsheim began establishing his vineyards. His influence on the growth of the region is immeasurable. He found some of the earliest investors from Burgundy, brought in key varieties from France and expanded the region's reputation to international proportions.

The tasting room includes options from the region's flagship variety, Pinot Noir, as well as Pinot Gris, Chardonnay, Pinot Blanc and even a bit of Syrah. The food options include charcuterie, a snack 'Nosh Box' or a cheese plate, Schedule in advance to include a tour of the winery and vineyards as well.
www.adelsheim.com; tel 503-538-3652; 16800 NE Calkins Ln, Newberg; 11am–4pm daily ✕⑤

02 DAY WINES & DAY CAMP

Day Camp was founded as a winemaking cooperative by winemaker Brianne Day, owner of Day Wines. The winery collective serves as an incubator for smaller-production labels which, by sharing equipment, space and winemaking help, are able to afford to launch their boutique-sized wines and grow their businesses. Head into the tasting room for the opportunity to taste either a mixed flight from multiple labels made at Day Camp, or target a particular winery. The minimalist aesthetic is clean and welcoming. Sidle up to the bar, relax in the lounge seating, or head into the courtyard where there are also various garden games. Keep an eye out for seasonal events in the space. Day Camp is also working on partnering with food trucks.
www.daywines.com; tel 971-832-8590; 21080 OR-99W, Dundee; 11am–4pm Fri–Sun ⑤

03 DOMAINE DROUHIN

One of the region's true destination wineries, Domaine Drouhin stands at the top of the Dundee Hills with exceptional views of the entire valley. On a clear day, Mt Hood, Mt Jefferson and the Three Sisters are all visible from the deck. Domaine Drouhin is the Oregon outpost for Burgundy's famed Joseph Drouhin winery, and it is here that Veronique Drouhin brings the finesse of French winemaking to

01 Sundowners at Day Wines

02 Checking the vines at Adelsheim

03 Winemaker Jason Lett at Eyrie Vineyards

(03)

the fruit of Oregon. The high-ceilinged tasting room is one of the more palatial experiences in Willamette Valley. Soak it all up as you enjoy a flight of wines from its Pinot Noir and Chardonnay or, on a nice day, taste them on the deck beside the vineyard. In exchange for the full tasting fee you will experience a tour of the winery and the grounds, in addition to an educational comparative tasting. *www.domainedrouhin.com; tel 503-864-2700; 6750 NE Breyman Orchards Rd, Dayton; 11am–4pm daily* $

04 REMY WINES

When you're ready to taste more than the valley's signature Pinot, make your way to a historic house at the foot of the Dundee Hills that is Remy Drabkin's tasting room and the fulfilment of a long-held ambition. 'This has been a dream for the last 10 years. I am excited to bring this new vision to life,' says winemaker Remy. She has one of the more eye-catching wine portfolios in the region, focused entirely on single-vineyard, single-varietal wines made from Italian varieties. Most are farmed in the Willamette Valley itself. In a region

celebrated for its French heritage, it's a refreshing surprise to find a tasting room entirely devoted to the Italian counterparts. The surrounding gardens and forest add a rustic dimension to this new vision. Drop in, or schedule ahead for a personalised experience. *www.remywines.com; tel 503-560-2003; 17495 NE McDougall Rd, Dayton; 12–5pm daily* $

05 EYRIE VINEYARDS

Eyrie was the first to plant vines in the Willamette Valley in the 1960s. Founder David Lett recognised the potential of the region's cool climate for making Pinot Noir and its sibling varieties Chardonnay and Pinot Gris — which are what Eyrie is renowned for to this day. Today, son Jason Lett leads Eyrie, making wine in the historic winery space started by his father. The tasting room maintains its historic feel but with its location in the heart of McMinnville is also an easy walk to local food favourites, coffee shops, and other tasting rooms. Best of all, a stop into the tasting room includes not only four or seven wine flights from across the Eyrie portfolio, but also the option to add from a revolving collection of older vintages. With a library of

wines from over 50 vintages, there is no better place to taste wines built to age.
eyrievineyards.com; tel 503-472-6315; 935 NE 10th Ave, McMinnville; 12–5pm daily 🌑

06 R STUART & CO

In the middle of downtown McMinnville, R Stuart & Co's tasting room is designed to feel more like a relaxing wine bar than winery stop. Tastings include the collection of single-vineyard Pinot Noirs made by winemaker Rob Stuart, as well as their signature sparkling wine and their founding, flagship wine, Big Fire. 'Our aim is to offer an inviting, bistro-style experience. You can have a glass of wine, an espresso, or microbrew in a relaxed atmosphere,' explains co-owner Maria Stuart. Local fare is at the centre of the experience with a small collection of local microbrews, and locally roasted espresso. Maria offers charcuterie and cheese pairings, as well as ever-changing local snacks and recipes to enjoy at home and pair with R. Stuart & Co wines.
rstuartandco.com; tel 866-472-8614; 528 NE 3rd St, McMinnville; 12–5pm daily 🍴🌑

07 CARLTON WINEMAKERS STUDIO

Founded in 2002, this is the region's original cooperative winery, and one of the very first on the west coast. The result is some of the most experienced and varied winemakers in the state all working in the collective space. The tasting room is next to the collective winery and through large windows you'll see activity in the barrel room, where wines are aged (if it's not too busy you can take a winery tour). Together the producers of the Studio make wines both classically and experimentally (fermenting in clay or concrete vessels, for instance). Winemakers in the studio don't just stick to Pinot Noir either, though there is plenty of that to taste as well. In the tasting room you can find everything from Rhone or Bordeaux varieties to obscure cool-climate selections, in a dynamic range of more than 40 wines.
www.winemakersstudio.com; tel 503-852-6100; 801 N Scott St, Carlton; 11am–4pm daily 🌑

04 The tasting room at Remy Wines

05 Red Hills food market in Dundee

WHERE TO STAY

THE ALLISON

For a bit of luxury in wine country, check into The Allison in Newberg. The guest rooms are spacious and comfortable complete with Jacuzzi tub, fireplace, and balcony. The restaurant includes an impressive wine list focused primarily on regional wines, as well as a selection of classic cocktails. Food focuses on garden-to-table seasonal cuisine. *www.theallison.com; tel 503-554-2525; 2525 Allison Ln, Newberg*

MCMENAMINS OREGON HOTEL

Stay right in the heart of it in downtown McMinnville. The historic hotel McMenamins includes a range of fun in-house activities from the rooftop bar, basement wine cellar, and street-level restaurant. Within easy walking distance of a mix of restaurant, local shops, and tasting rooms. *www.mcmenamins.com; tel 503-472-8427; 310 NE Evans St, McMinnville*

05

WHERE TO EAT

THE VALLEY COMMISSARY

Enjoy a casual lunch that's full of flavour from seasonal ingredients. The menu is a mix of fresh local fare with a side of comfort food. The fried chicken sandwich is a local favourite. You can also grab food to-go. *www.valleycommissary. com; tel 503-883-9177; 920 NE Eighth St, McMinnville*

RED HILLS MARKET

As you drive through Dundee, grab breakfast, take-away or quick espresso here. If you have time for lunch, be sure to check out the wood fired pizza. The deli case offers a fresh mix of options to take home or on a picnic. You can also step into the retail section to grab bottles of wine to take with you. *www.redhillsmarket. com; tel 971-832-8414; 155 SW 7th St, Dundee*

WHAT TO DO

TOUR DEVINE BY HELI

Tour and taste one of Willamette Valley's smaller AVAs by helicopter. Each tour will bring you to taste at three different wineries, include a picnic lunch, and a greeting with sparkling wine. An unforgettable way to get to know the valley. *tourdevinebyheli.com; tel 503-537-0108; 17770 NE Aviation Way, Newberg*

VISTA BALLOON

Start at dawn for a three-hour experience seeing the Willamette Valley by air. You'll watch the sun come up and experience 360-degree views including 10 mountain peaks, the Willamette River, and a glimpse over the Coastal Mountains towards the Pacific Ocean. After landing guests are brought back to the launch site to enjoy a celebratory brunch. Weather permitting. *vistaballoon.com; tel 503-625-7385*

[Pennsylvania]

PA'S ATLANTIC UPLAND

Take a trip through some of America's oldest farmland to experience one of America's best wineries and arrive on the doorstep of one of America's great cities.

One of the 13 original colonies, Pennsylvania is a state where you're enveloped in the past, from the Liberty Bell and Independence Hall in Philadelphia to the weathered log cabins at Valley Forge to the silence of the open fields at Gettysburg.

Amid the refurbished buildings and historic markers that reflect the deep ties to America's history are a group of pioneers with comparatively shallow roots. While grape growing and winemaking date back to the 1600s, the Limited Winery Act was passed as recently as 1968. Today, around 250 wineries operate statewide.

Many benefit from the rolling terrain spilling off the Allegheny and Pocono Mountains that provides elevation and a drying breeze. Pennsylvania's diverse topography also produces a variety of climates, but don't worry — though cold winters and humid summers are typical, extremes in those seasons rarely endure.

Most of the state's wineries are clustered across the eastern and south central sections and along Lake Erie, in the northwest corner. A vast majority of operations are family-owned, many with vineyards. While you'll find vinifera such as Chardonnay, Cabernet Sauvignon and Cabernet Franc, you'll also come across samples of hybrids such as Chambourcin and Traminette, both made in a variety of styles and improving in quality by the year. Native American grapes such as Niagara and Concord satisfy a local sweet tooth.

That said, the greatest gains are being made in the production of premium dry wines, from red and white blends to experimentation with newcomers such as Grüner Veltliner, Albarino, Zweigelt and Blaufrankisch.

Weekends from March through October offer a variety of events, from summer concerts to harvest festivals.

GET THERE
Allentown has an airport or use Philadelphia. It's a good base or try Jim Thorpe as an historic option or West Chester in the reverse direction.

01 GALEN GLEN

It may be one of the state's most rural wineries, but it sports an international reputation for its Riesling and Grüner Veltliner. Tucked into a valley between the Blue and Mahoning mountains, Galen Glen offers an airy tasting room and a 20-mile view from the back patio.

Galen Troxell tends the vines on a farm that has been in his family for generations. His wife, Sarah, makes the wine. Both come from scientific backgrounds. 'We farm wine. Period. Not grapes. Responsibly and sustainably,' says Sarah. 'We are obsessed with aromatic white wine: Riesling, Grüner Veltliner and Gewürztraminer.'

Try Galen Glen's reds, too, such as Zweigelt and Chambourcin. *www.galenglen.com; tel 570-386-3682; 255 Winter Mountain Drive, Andreas; noon-5pm Wed-Sun, with some seasonal variance* ✕ $

02 CLOVER HILL

It was several years after the passage of the Limited Winery Act that Pat, a teacher, and John Skrip, a civil engineer, decided to plant grapes as a hobby at their home outside Allentown. Today, they are among the state's biggest producers, operating out of a spacious, modern tasting room that looks out over the hilly terrain of eastern Pennsylvania. Visitors will find a diverse list of products, with several styles of Chambourcin, a low-tannin

'We farm wine. Period. Not grapes. Responsibly and sustainably. We are obsessed with aromatic white wine'

– Sarah Troxell, Galen Glen

red hybrid that grows plentifully throughout the region, and offerings such as frizzante, ice wine and port. Meats and cheeses are available for purchase. *www.cloverhillwinery.com; tel 610-395-2468; 9850 Newtown Road, Breinigsville; 10am-5.30pm Mon-Sat, noon-5pm Sun* ✕ $

01 Historic Jim Thorpe town in Pennsylvania

02 The tasting room at Galer Estate

03 Winemaker Sarah Troxell at Galen Glen

04 Antipasti platters at Folino Estate

03 FOLINO ESTATE

A head-turner. There's no other way to describe the Tuscan-style villa that comprises Folino Estate's winery, tasting room, market, restaurant and events hall, built on a 54-acre property, half of which will be vineyard when the planting is completed.

Around the winery are a sprawling patio and bocce court. 'Seeing our dream come to life has been an experience like no other,' says Andrea, Marco's wife.

You can count on one hand the number of regional wineries that have full-service restaurants, so Folino Estate focuses on Old World-style wines to pair with the pizzas and pastas produced on site. Wines range from Pinot

Grigio and Moscato to Pinot Noir and a Bordeaux red blend called Lorenzo Forte.

www.folinoestate.com; tel 484-452-3633; 340 Old Route 22, Kutztown; 11am–8pm Wed–Sun, winery and restaurant ✗ ⑤

04 SETTER RIDGE

Many regional wineries shy away from Pinot Noir; Setter Ridge, operated by the Blair family, embraces this finnicky grape, not only growing it on parts of 30-plus acres but using it in several wines, including a varietal.

'We're blessed with a climate that allows us cooler days, with less humidity than surrounding areas,' says Rich Blair, who opened the winery in 2010.

At the end of a twisting driveway, past the vines, is an A-frame with a covered porch. Pick your spot to sample a list of quality dry wines (the winery name recognises the family's fondness for English setters).

www.setterridgevineyards.com; tel 610-683-8463; 99 Dietrich Valley Road, Kutztown; 11am–5pm daily ✗ ⑤

05 VA LA

Va La is not merely recommended, it is unmissable. The winery is unparalleled in its consistency for excellence — indeed, a national website annually lists it among America's top wineries.

Owner Anthony Vietri is the fifth-generation of his family to

05 Tasting choices at
Clover Hill

06 Longwood's
ornamental gardens

899-8013; 700 Folly Hill Road,
Kennett Square; noon-8 pm,
Fri-Sun ✕Ⓢ

⓪⑦ PENNS WOODS

A former wine-importer, Gino
Razzi earned 95 points from *Wine
Spectator* magazine for his first
commercially produced wine. Still,
he says that there were plenty
of self-doubts when he created
Penns Woods in 2001.

Razzi's winery, which now involves
daughter Carley in many aspects of
the operation, first and foremost
sells the consistent quality of its full
line of wines, mostly vinifera and
primarily estate-grown. 'I think for
my father the most satisfying part
of opening his winery was allowing
his hobby and dream to become
a true reality,' Carley says.

The tasting room and wine shop
overlook rolling vineyards. While
some are drawn by a busy events
schedule that includes music and
yoga in the vineyard, many just
spread a blanket or park at one of
the lawn picnic tables.
*www.pennswoodevents.com; tel
610-459-0808; 124 Beaver Valley
Road, Chaddsford; noon–5.30pm
Tue-Sun* ✕Ⓢ

farm the seven acres of northern
Italian and French varieties of
grapes on a farm that dates back
to the original 1000 acres of the
John Miller estate, deeded to
him by William Penn, founder of
Pennsylvania, in 1713.

Also the winemaker, Anthony
makes just six or seven field blends
a year. 'We strive to offer dry table
wines that are unique to this site
and specifically designed to shine
with food,' he says.

Wines are offered by the glass
or bottle in the two-level tasting
room inside the century-old barn.
A $20 flight features four wines
accompanied by bites of local
specialities and seasonal tidbits
from the farm. Out the back,
a porch and lawn puts visitors
alongside the vineyard.
*www.valavineyards.com;
tel 610-268-2702; 8822 Gap
Newport Pike (Rt 41), Avondale;
12-6pm Fri-Sun* ✕Ⓢ

⓪⑥ GALER ESTATE

The tagline for this suburban
Philly winery is 'Blending Nature,
Science and Art', appropriate
for a producer that neighbours
the nationally known Longwood
Gardens in Chester County.

Wine-tech connoisseurs will
appreciate the gravity-flow winery
with a specialised fermentation
room that feeds into a subterranean
barrel room. Lele and Brad Galer
run the place, which brings us to
the art: artist Lele shows her own
work and that of regional artists and
craftsmen in a rustic tasting room.
(Accompanying charcuterie and
local cheeses available.)

Dry premium vinifera make up
the wine list, with Chardonnays
from several vineyards and rosé
along with Bordeaux blends
accounting for the more than 100
awards garnered during a handful
of years in business.
www.galerestate.com; tel 484-

From left: courtesy of Clover Hill; Mira / Alamy Stock Photo

WHERE TO STAY

THE PARSONAGE

A must-stay B&B in the must-see Victorian town of Jim Thorpe. Though the structure was built in 1844, owners Michael and Jeffri have turned it into their own trip through time with bits and pieces of their 40 years of collecting and travel. Galen Glen co-owner Sarah Troxell rates the place as a 'stunning place to stay that looks like a movie set, and breakfast is ridiculously amazing'. *www.the parsonagebandb.com*

WHERE TO EAT

The marriage of a couple's love for food, Bolete (*www.boleterestaurant. com*) is meant to be an escape from the hurried world we live in. Says owner Lee, the chef, and Erin of their Bethlehem farm-to-table venue: 'We do not rush what we do and we don't want you to rush through your dining experience with us.' The result has drawn praise regionally and nationally. Also along the way options include the equally high-profile Savona Bistro (*www. savonabistro.com*) in Kennett Square; the Marion Hose Bar (*www. marionhosebar.com*), a renovated vintage fire-company-turned-pub in Jim Thorpe; and the Kutztown Pub Taphouse & BBQ (*www.ktownpub. com*).

WHAT TO DO

There's something for everyone's tastes. On the northern end are the Valley Preferred Cycling Center (*www. thevelodrome.com*), a world-class biking facility in Trexlertown, and Hawk Mountain Sanctuary in Kempton (*www.hawkmountain. org*), a nonprofit, 2600-acre wild bird sanctuary since 1934 featuring a visitor centre, trails and overlooks. Farther south is Kennett Square (*www. historickennettsquare. com*) and the world-famous mushroom country that surrounds it, gorgeous Longwood Gardens (*www.long woodgardens.org*), and the Brandywine River Museum of Art (*www.brandywine. com/museum*), which specialises in Wyeth family artworks and art of Chester County. If you head into the city, stop at the National Constitution Center (*www.constitutioncenter. org*) and Reading Terminal Market (*www. readingterminalmarket. org*). To the west is Amish Country (*www. discoverlancaster.com*) and the splendour of Hershey and its huge theme park (*www. hersheypa.com*).

CELEBRATIONS

The Lehigh Valley Wine Trail (*www. lehighvalleywinetrail. com*) is one of the region's most active. Harvest Weekend is usually held in early September, and features tastings, vineyard and winery tours, food and wine pairings and live entertainment. Other wine-related festivals can be found on the state's wine association website (*www.pennsylvaniawine. com*). Among the metro events worth checking out are Philly Wine Week (*www.phillywineweek. org*) in March and Philly Beer Week (*www. joesixpack.net*) in June.

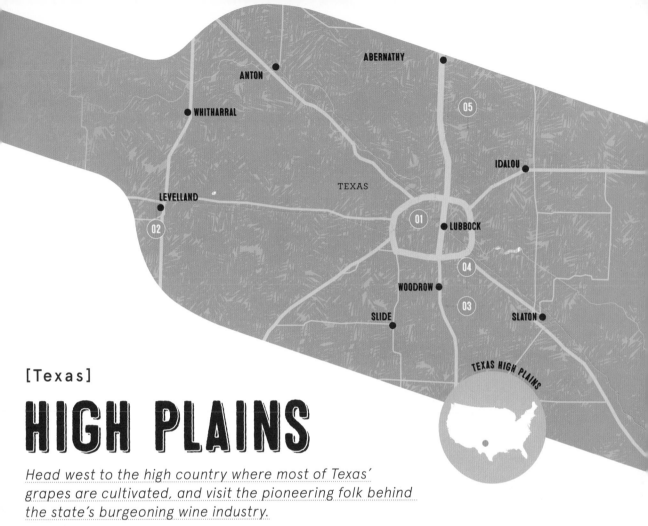

ABERNATHY

ANTON

05

WHITHARRAL

IDALOU

TEXAS

LEVELLAND

01

LUBBOCK

02

04

WOODROW

03

SLIDE

SLATON

TEXAS HIGH PLAINS

[Texas]

HIGH PLAINS

*Head west to the high country where most of Texas'
grapes are cultivated, and visit the pioneering folk behind
the state's burgeoning wine industry.*

Vast tracts of cotton and peanut fields stretch
into a distant horizon under an overarching
brilliant-blue sky. The joke in Lubbock, the
centre of the Texas High Plains growing region, is that
you can watch your dog run away...for a week. This
vastness is what defines the High Plains. And yet, in
a place where cotton- and peanut-farming are the
mainstays, viticulture has become a growth area
for farmers over the last 10 years. The majority of
Texas' wine grapes are grown in the High Plains and
this region is recognised for producing the highest-
quality grapes in the state from its deep
sandy loam soils, disproving the notion that
slopes are required to produce fine wine.

Talk to any of the grape-growers and
winemakers here and you'll quickly learn
that the attraction of the Texas High Plains

GET THERE
The closest
international airport
is Dallas–Fort Worth, a
350-mile drive east. Or use
multiple regional flights
from Dallas.

is not just the scenery, but also the people. Sit with
the McPherson family at La Diosa for an evening,
tasting tapas, sipping excellent Rhône-style blends
and listening to music; or make the trip to Levelland
to chat with three visionary farmers turned grape-
growers, who started their own wine brand, opened
a tasting room and, in the process, helped revive
the town square; or sidle into the tasting room at
CapRock Winery to be greeted by one of the top
hospitality teams in the Texas wine business.

The best part of the Texas High Plains is that all
of these people are accessible to visitors.
There's no marketing scene, just real people
warmly welcoming you to their far western
part of the state in hopes that you will
become as enthralled as they are with the
quality of its wines.

Llano Estacado excels at education and has tours on offer several times a day, encompassing the stages of wine production and how the process relates to what's in your glass

01 MCPHERSON CELLARS

University of California at Davis-trained Kim McPherson is Texas wine royalty, and arguably the state's finest winemaker. Kim's father 'Doc' McPherson was one of the founders of the legendary Llano Estacado winery, and the first winemaker in Texas to plant Sangiovese, considered amongst the state's best varieties. Kim was winemaker at both Llano Estacado and renowned Texas High Plains winery CapRock before starting his own business in 2008. For all his credentials, Kim retains his penchant for telling stories and his wines are a direct reflection of his character: accessible and fun with a core of integrity and substance.

Grape varieties used here tend towards Italian, Spanish and southern French varieties. The Les Copains line of white, rosé and red wines are Cotes-du-Rhône-inspired blends and the McPherson Cellars' most recognised wines. Single-variety reds from Cinsault and Sangiovese are standouts, but the real stars are the single-variety whites: Albariño, Viognier and especially Roussanne. Enjoy your sampling in the winery's tasting room or courtyard located in an old Coca-Cola bottling plant in the hot Depot District of downtown Lubbock. *www.mcphersoncellars.com; tel 806-687-9463; 1615 Texas Ave, Lubbock; 11am–5.30pm Mon–Sat* $

02 TRILOGY CELLARS

Make a trek to Levelland, 30 miles west of Lubbock, for a taste of the future of Texas wines. Three farmers, Steve Newsom, Chace Hill and Rowdy Bolen, diversified from cotton and peanuts into grapes. The largest cotton-producing area in the world centres on Lubbock, so most grape-growers originally converted from other crops. What makes these three special is the collaborative nature of Trilogy Cellars. A conversation that began with the idea to contribute Malbec grapes and have the wine jointly bottled turned into opening a winery and tasting room.

Trilogy Cellars, named in honour of its three founders' families, is located in a cosy, refurbished 1926 building on Levelland town square. The project was not only collaborative among the three prospective winery owners, but also between them and the town: 'When we decided to renovate an old building on the town square for our winery and tasting room, the town rallied around the idea,' explains Steve. With many Texas settlements losing their town-square identity, Trilogy Cellars is seen as having revived the character of the downtown area.

And the wines are a real draw to the tasting room. The Malbec is bright, fine and well balanced, offering complexity beyond many Malbec wines. The Gewürztraminer, modelled on an Alsace style, hits the marks, both refreshing and layered. Roussanne continues to be a star, with a nutty, textured offering. *trilogycellars.com; tel 806-568-9463; 618 Ave H, Levelland;*

Courtesy of Llano Estacado

01 Cotton is a key crop in Texas

02 The tasting room at Llano Estacado

03 The interior of
Llano Estacado

04 The American
Windmill Museum

production and how the process relates to what's in your glass. Post-tour, try a six-wines tasting.

Italian varieties such as Trebbiano and Sangiovese are consistently good, but the Tempranillo and especially the flagship Viviano blend are the best of the broad range here. Viviano is considered one of Texas' icon wines, and for good reason. *llanowine.com; tel 800-634-3854; 3426 E FM, Lubbock; 10am–5pm Mon–Sat, noon–5pm Sun* 🟑

noon–7pm Tue & Wed, to 8pm Thu, to 10pm Fri & Sat, 1–5pm Sun

03 CAPROCK WINERY

One of the pioneering wineries of Texas' wine industry, CapRock has enjoyed a few incarnations over its more-than-30-year history. What has not changed are the contemporary southwestern winery architecture and grounds, which rank amongst the most beautiful in Texas. The real attraction here are estate sommelier and tasting-room manager Tim Abascal and his team. Book in advance for the Private Food and Wine Experience: Tim offers an in-depth lesson in food-and-wine pairing ($35) through six seasonal selections of wine and bite-sized culinary creations with advanced booking. Red wines revolve around Zinfandel, Cabernet Sauvignon and Merlot, while Riesling, Viognier and Chardonnay

feature among the whites. *www.caprockwinery.com; tel 806-863-2704; 408 E Woodrow Rd, Lubbock; noon–5.30pm Tue–Thu, to 6.30pm Fri & Sat* 🍴🟑

04 LLANO ESTACADO WINERY

Founded in 1976, Llano was the first of the modern-era Texas wineries. It has kept up with the times, expanding and renovating with a stylish, contemporary tasting room and the latest technology in wine production. Executive winemaker Greg Bruni has stewarded the winemaking since 1993. 'We want to offer an experience that ranks among the best in the world,' explains President and CEO Mark Hyman, offering an insight into the celebrated winery's drive.

Llano Estacado excels at education with tours on offer several times per day, encompassing the stages of wine

05 PHEASANT RIDGE WINERY

Bobby Cox is the heart and soul of Pheasant Ridge, having planted the vineyards and founded the winery in 1978. Since then, it has changed ownership a couple of times, but Bobby returned as owner and winemaker in 2015. Bobby's gregarious nature makes him one of the best ambassadors of Texas wines, with his outgoing personality reflecting the welcoming hospitality for which Texas is known. A tasting at Pheasant Ridge (six to eight wines) is a rustic, genuine experience. Be sure to sample the Chenin Blanc, the benchmark wine for the variety in the state and a personal favourite of Bobby Cox. *www.pheasantridgewinery.com; tel 806-746-6033; 3507 E County Rd 5700, Lubbock; 3–8pm Fri, noon–7pm Sat & Sun* 🟑

WHERE TO STAY

OVERTON HOTEL
Modern and centrally located for roaming the frontier of the Texas Hill Country, the Overton Hotel is the place to stay in Lubbock, with crisp, business-like, stripy-floored rooms. Its restaurant serves both local cuisine and Texas wines.
www.overtonhotel.com; tel +806-776-7000; 2322 Mac Davis Lane, Lubbock

WHERE TO EAT

COCINA DE LA SIRENA
This casual Lubbock spot is run by mother-daughter duo Cat Traxler and Jessica Fultz in the historical Cactus Alley courtyard. The menu showcases Fultz's inventive, modern takes on Latin American fare and also offers updates to Tex-Mex staples such as tostadas and enchiladas. The stacked enchilada, a family recipe, is a must-try.
www.lasirenacocina.us; tel 806-368-7960; 2610 Salem Ave, Lubbock; 4–10pm Mon–Thu, to midnight Fri & Sat

LA DIOSA CELLARS
The creation of interior designer Sylvia McPherson, wife of winemaker Kim McPherson, La Diosa offers a complementary food experience to the local wine scene. The laid-back vibe, eclectic design and authentic Spanish tapas make the bistro a staple of the fashionable Depot District. Live music sets from Thursday to Sunday feature some of Lubbock's best musicians.
www.ladiosacellars.com; tel 806-744-3600; 901 17th St, Lubbock; 4–11pm Tue–Thu, noon–midnight Fri & Sat

WHAT TO DO

Travel to the American western frontier of the 1780s–1910s by visiting the National Ranching Heritage Center and the American Windmill Museum, which complement each other to tell the story of the move west and the adaptions and innovations made by frontierfolk. Experience the life of the early settlers of the High Plains with a chronological tour of the homes, barns and other structures that shaped life here. Learn about one of the most critical aspects of life on the plains, where surface water is scarce: the windmill. The American Windmill Museum traces the history of this design masterpiece, which was at the time the most efficient method for retrieving water from the Ogallala Aquifer beneath the High Plains.

NATIONAL RANCHING HERITAGE CENTER
www.depts.ttu.edu/ nrhc; tel 806-742-0498; 3121 4th St, Lubbock; 10am–5pm Mon–Sat, 1–5pm Sun

AMERICAN WINDMILL MUSEUM
windmill.com; tel 806-747-8734; 1701 Canyon Lake Dr, Lubbock; 10am–5pm Tue–Sat

CELEBRATIONS

LUBBOCK UNCORKED
This event takes place each April at the American Windmill Museum, with an evening of toasting the grape-growing and winemaking of the Texas High Plains. Around 25 wineries take part and the event also showcases local food and music.
lubbockchamber.com/ lubbock-uncorked

[Texas]
HILL COUNTRY

Travel the beautiful Texas Hill Country on the USA's second most-visited wine road,
Hwy 290, for a taste of wines as varied as the wildflowers that dot the roadside.

West of Austin, the Texan capital, and north of San Antonio lies the second-largest grape-growing region in the USA. As the saying goes, 'everything is bigger in Texas,' and the Texas Hill Country spans nine million acres, which means plenty of room to accommodate numerous soils and climates. This has led to several smaller wine regions existing within the larger Texas Hill Country, and also to a wonderful variety of grapes thriving here. These range from Bordeaux varieties Cabernet Sauvignon and Merlot to Italian Sangiovese and Vermentino, and even cool-climate Chenin Blanc.

Fredericksburg is the heart of the region, and an easy, scenic drive from Austin along Hwy 290, which winds its way through the region's namesake hills. Limestone slopes dotted with cedar and scrub oak are interspersed with ravines lined with cypress and brushy thickets. Oaks and elms provide shade at wineries along the way, wildflowers bloom in the fields, the bright Texas sky shines soft-blue above, and at Becker Vineyards the gentle breezes rustle expanses of lavender. This is the Texas seldom seen in cinema, and one of the most scenic parts of the state.

The wine industry is well established here and the area is oriented towards wine. Many of the state's most recognisable wine-industry names have wineries or tasting rooms in or around Fredericksburg. Opportunities for tasting are plentiful and varied. The wines, scenery and — as epicentre of the outlaw country movement in the 1970s — the music make the Texas Hill Country one of the most visited attractions in Texas, and indeed the whole USA.

GET THERE
Austin has the closest airport, around 70 miles (a 1.5hr drive) east of Fredericksburg via Hwy 290, along which lie the wineries.

Courtesy of Pedernales

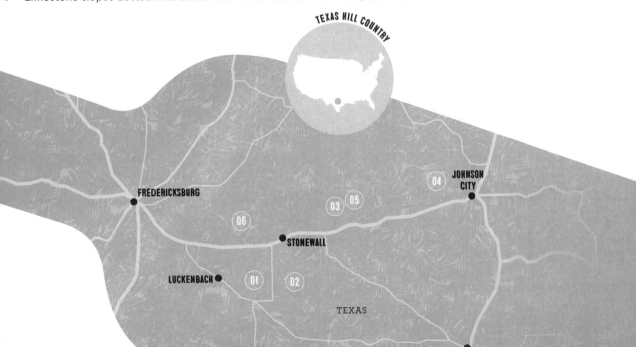

TEXAS HILL COUNTRY

FREDERICKSBURG

JOHNSON CITY

04

03 05

06

STONEWALL

LUCKENBACH   01   02

TEXAS

BLANCO

01 BECKER VINEYARDS

Dr Richard and Bunny Becker established Becker Vineyards in 1992, making them visionaries of the modern era in the Texas Hill Country. What started as a search for an authentic cabin getaway turned into a vineyard and winery. The original 1890s log cabin still sits on the property, now joined by a German stone barn-styled winery and Lavender Haus reception hall, a replica of a limestone barn in the LBJ National Historical Park.

The attractions here, aside from the wines, are the native wildflowers, peach orchards and fields of lavender. But the wines are the stars, of course, and the multiple tasting options include a six-wines walk-in tasting and a booked-ahead Reserve Library tasting with a behind-the-scenes tour and a wine-and-cheese pairing session. The Malbec and Petite Sirah are an essential Becker Vineyards experience, while lavender sachets, linen sprays and soaps allow you to take home a piece of the Hill Country.
www.beckervineyards.com; tel 830-644-2681; 464 Becker Farms Rd, Stonewall; 10am–5pm Mon–Thu, to 6pm Fri & Sat, noon–6pm Sun 💲

02 PEDERNALES CELLARS

Pedernales Cellars has groomed the founders at two other wineries along this trail, and its legacy extends beyond the excellent wines produced here. The Tempranillo and Viognier Reserve established the winery's stellar reputation, so savour these on the oak-shaded deck of the tasting room.

Alternatively, opt for either the six-wines tasting or the weekends-only Reserve Tasting (also six wines), which includes a friendly, knowledgeable wine expert to guide you through some of Pedernales' rare and limited-production wines.
www.pedernalescellars.com; tel 830-644-2037; 2916 Upper Albert Rd, Stonewall; 10am–5pm Mon–Thu, to 6pm Fri & Sat, noon–6pm Sun 💲

03 KUHLMAN CELLARS

Kuhlman Cellars prides itself on European-inspired styles crafted by winemaker Benedicte Rhyne, formerly of Ravenswood Winery in Sonoma. Recognising the complementary nature of food and wine, the Signature Tasting here pairs five wines with five seasonal small bites from chef Chris Cook.

From left: courtesy of Pedernales Cellars (2); William Chris Vineyards / Miguel Lecuona / Hill Country Light

01 The Pedernales
River in Texas

02 Sorting grapes at
Pedernales Cellars

03 Food and wine at
Pedernales Cellars

04 Steel tanks at
Becker Vineyards

05 Evening at William
Chris Vineyards

06 Enchanted Rocks
State Natural Area

Kuhlman's signature wines are based on Rhône Valley natives, with Cinsaut rosé and Roussanne leading the way. A personal sommelier guides you through your tasting, providing a thorough wine education.

Kuhlman Cellars' educational leanings can also be experienced in other ways, such as the Vina Vita University program. On select dates, you can learn about, say, vine-pruning and maintenance or deductive tasting while sipping Kuhlman Cellars libations. *www.kuhlmancellars.com; tel 512-920-2675; 18421 East US290, Stonewall; 11am–6pm Thu–Sat, noon–5pm Sun & Mon* ✕ ⑤

04 LEWIS WINES

The centrepiece of Lewis Wines is a pavilion tasting room overlooking the vineyards — a modernist-style barn of steel, concrete and glass with weathered repurposed boards. On a pristine Hill Country day, the whirring fans of the pavilion porch and the rustling of the surrounding oaks provide plenty of incentive to sit and sip Lewis drops. Or book in for an in-depth Winemaker Reserve tasting of reserve, single-vineyard and library offerings (minimum eight people). All tastings provide an exciting overview of Doug Lewis' and Duncan McNabb's success in crafting top-quality wines from the finest Texas grapes.

Doug and Duncan both worked at Pedernales Cellars, before founding Lewis Wines in 2010. They planted unconventional varieties that grow well in Texas soils, such as Touriga Nacional, Tinta Cao, Tannat and Arinto. Since then, they have worked with growers around the state to add other offerings such as Tempranillo, Mourvèdre and Petite Sirah. *www.lewiswines.com; tel 512-987-0660, 3209 US290, West Johnson City; 10.30am–5pm daily* ⑤

05 WILLIAM CHRIS VINEYARDS

William Chris Vineyards is as renowned for its exceptional hospitality as for its quality wines. Sitting on the patio or in the pavilion allows for both wonderful vistas of rolling hills dotted with oak and elm, and, if you're visiting on a weekend, some fantastic tunes, as the winery hosts live music. Snack plates are more substantial here than at many other local wineries, which means you'll want to linger.

Chris Brundrett, a Texas wunderkind of winemaking, and wine-grower William 'Bill' Blackmon established the vineyard in 2008. Showing that they're at the forefront of trends, in 2015 Brundrett produced a *pétillant-naturel* rosé. Book ahead for a five-wine tasting. *www.williamchriswines.com; tel 830-998-7654; 10352 US290, Hye; 10am-5pm Mon-Wed, to 6pm Thu-Sat, noon-5pm Sun; reservations required Fri-Sun* ✗⑤

⑥ 4.0 CELLARS

A hit collaboration among three of Texas' most highly regarded winemakers: Pat Brennan of Brennan Vineyards, Gene Estes of Lost Oak Winery and Kim McPherson of McPherson Cellars. As their Texas Hill Country outpost, 4.0 Cellars is the fourth winery in this group; each of the others lies in a different part of the state.

The tasting room carries not only 4.0 Cellars' wines but also drops from the other three wineries — the perfect opportunity to sample a spread of wines from across Texas. Try Brennan Vineyards' Viognier, McPherson Cellars' Reserve Roussanne or Lost Oak's Cabernet Franc. In homage to traditional Hill Country architecture, the tasting room is a stylish, light-flooded modern building of corrugated metal and sandstone, and the inviting park-like setting has wrought-iron tables and benches under crepe myrtles.

Reserve ahead for the Texas Cheese and Wine Experience, which pairs five artisan Texan cheeses from Veldhuizen Cheese Company with five wines, or the Texas Chocolate and Wine Experience starring six chocolate truffles from local chocolatier Cathy Locke; or just drop in for a tasting of six wines. *www.fourpointwine.com; tel 830-997-7470; 10354 East US290, Fredericksburg; 11am-5pm Sun-Thu, 10am-6pm Fri & Sat* ✗⑤

WHERE TO STAY

BARONS CREEKSIDE

The rustic luxury of a Swiss mountain village, just minutes from downtown Fredericksburg. Each of the 18 cabins is different, though all have jetted tubs, modern amenities and authentic charm. Most offer a private porch with views of a stream and lawn, where you might spot deer grazing in the morning. *www.baronscreekside. com; tel 830-990-4048; 316 Goehmann Ln, Fredericksburg*

HOFFMAN HOUSE

Take your pick of a room, a suite or a house at this cosy B&B one block away from downtown Fredericksburg. The soft, natural Hill Country colours and comfortable furnishings in each individually styled room offer a respite after long days of touring and tasting. A day spa is available by appointment. *www.hoffmanhaus. com; tel 830-997-6739; 608 East Creek St, Fredericksburg*

WHERE TO EAT

HYE MARKET

Whether on your way to Fredericksburg or during your wine-tasting sojourn, don't miss a stop at historical Hye Market in the small community of Hye. The market offers a counter-service menu of Texas-sourced ingredients and local wines to match. An array of sandwiches, pizzas, and salads is available. *www.hyemarket.com; tel 830-868-2300; 10261 West US290, Hye; 11am–7pm Wed–Sat, to 4pm Tue, to 5pm Sun*

VAUDEVILLE BISTRO/V SUPPER CLUB

Vaudeville plays many roles, from interiors showroom to bistro to supper club. Beneath the Main St showroom, the bistro serves modern-US comfort food, such as gumbo and pork-belly tacos. A more luxurious culinary experience, the in-demand V Supper Club cooks up a tasting menu on Friday and Saturday, brunch on Sunday, and prix-fixe delights on Monday evening; local ingredients are the focus of dishes like crab cannelloni, and reservations are a must. *www.vaudeville-living. com; tel 830-92-3234; 230 E Main St, Fredericksburg. Bistro opens 10am–4pm Sun–Thu, to 9 pm Fri & Sat; V Supper Club opens 6.30–9.30pm Fri, Sat & Mon, 11am–3pm Sun*

WHAT TO DO

ENCHANTED ROCKS STATE NATURAL AREA

Hikers and climbers will want to tackle the granite domes of Enchanted Rock State Natural Area, 18 miles north of Fredericksburg. Miles of hiking trails, including the four-mile Loop Trail, and climbs such as the 5.10 Texas Crude, offer a day's worth of activities.

CELEBRATIONS

FREDERICKSBURG FOOD & WINE FEST

Held each October, this festival features over 20 Texas wineries, a cooking school, and Texan specialities. Local chefs and winemakers host events, adding to the down-home feel. Immerse yourself in the best of Texas' culinary scene, starting with Thursday and Friday dinners and culminating in Saturday festivities. *fbgfoodandwinefest.com*

[Vermont]

VERMONT

*In the unspoilt hills where the
farm-to-table food revolution stirred,
the same mouthwatering integrity
is being applied to the art of the grape.*

Vermont's natural beauty and welcoming communities attract travellers from the nation and around the globe. They come to this small state to immerse themselves in the terrain and to discover a myriad of tiny treasures; culinary, cultural and historic. Two great valleys on its eastern and western boundaries rise through rolling foothills and river valleys, populated by picturesque small villages, which gather along winding roads through old hill farms into a high alpine spine that runs north to south and marks the region's namesake. Long recognised for its agricultural identity and opportunities for outdoor recreation, the Green Mountain State also offers visitors distinctive and fulfilling eateries, artisan cheese and food producers, remarkable visual and performing arts, as well as a innumerable historic sites.

While Vermont is a late-comer to the United States' commercial wine making

boom, it draws on centuries of farm-house fermentation and spirit-making. Where home-made wild grape, apple and fruit wines were once the norm for its citizens, modern winemaking technology and a revolution in winter-hardy grape varieties have enabled Vermont to elevate itself as a groundbreaking and premier producer of cold-climate wines. These food-friendly and industry-leading wines are a natural extension of a farm-to-table movement that took root in Vermont, decades before that term was coined.

Given Vermont's varied, mountain and valley geography, it's recommended to aim for just a couple of tasting targets each day, and to leave space in the itinerary for exploring the many other attractions each neighbourhood has to offer. Nominal tasting fees apply at most, some tasting rooms are open daily and year-round, while others vary with the seasons, so plan your schedules and visits accordingly.

GET THERE
Burlington is the accessible fly-in city, and Vermont is a spectacular drive from New York City, Boston and Montreal via Interstate Highways.

① SHELBURNE VINEYARD

What began as just a dream in Ken Albert's hobby vineyard has grown to become the state's largest wine producer. An easy-access and well-appointed tasting space awaits on RT 7 just south of Burlington, in close proximity to the historic grounds of Shelburne Farms and the extensive collections of the Shelburne Museum. A standard bearer for Vermont's growing wine industry, Shelburne Vineyard bottles a wide array of award-winning dry, off-dry, and ice wines to serve a diversity of tastes. Winemaker Ethan Joseph believes he's 'fortunate to follow a passion dedicated to highlighting the rich geologic and agricultural history of the state through the lens of wine' and his recent expansion into wild fermentations is exciting those eager for wines with even greater transparency to origin. *www.shelburnevineyard.com; tel 802-985-8222; 6308 Shelburne Rd, Shelburne; 11am-5pm daily Nov-Apr, 11am-6pm May-Oct* 🔘

② LINCOLN PEAK VINEYARD

The Granstrom family farmed strawberries for 20 years before transitioning to a cold-hardy grape vine nursery and then a vineyard and winery. Their dry red wines made from the Marquette grape are a bold statement about what is possible in the north country, while their white varietals and proprietary white blends are aromatically intense and palate refreshing. Owner and winemaker Chris Granstrom says, 'I enjoy pouring a sample for someone who has never tasted a Vermont wine and seeing this reaction: "Oh... oh! This is actually very good!" A winemaker could take offence at that but I look at it the opposite way – I've made a new convert!'

Lincoln Peak is a must-stop spot on Middlebury's Tasting Trail, which includes three spirit producers, two breweries and a major cider maker. The vineyard also hosts a talented, family-friendly music series that invigorates the neighbourhood throughout summer and autumn. *www.lincolnpeakvineyard.com; tel 802-388-7368; 142 River Rd, New Haven; 11am-5pm Fri-Sun* 🔘

③ LA GARAGISTA

'We try to let the field and the cellar speak for themselves, while providing stewardship,' says La Garagista's Deirdre Heekin. In doing so she successfully blends modern sensibilities with ancient methodologies through an alchemy that intends to tap the raw terroir of Vermont. Lauded by critics and colleagues, this little winery has been embraced by the natural segment of the global wine scene. Farming with organic and biodynamic principles, and minimal-intervention winemaking, enables La Garagista to produce precise 'tastes of place' based on a 'wine is food' ethos. Tastings are by appointment; sign up to the mailing list. RSVP for one of the scheduled bottle tastings, or the

01 The historic farm at
Boyden Valley Winery

02 Maple dessert wine
at Boyden Valley Winery

03 New vines at
Boyden Valley Winery

04 Snapshots of life at
La Garagista

05 Lake Champlain

tapas and dinner events that chef Caleb Barber serves up at the farm and taverna. He is proud to provide local charcuteries, Vermont's famous cheeses, as well as breads and pizzas baked in the vintage oven that now resides in the winery. *www.lagaragista.com; tel 802-291-1295; 1834 Mt Hunger Rd, Barnard; open by appointment* ✕⑤

⑭ PUTNEY MOUNTAIN WINERY

The Connecticut River Valley is home to this innovator and baton bearer for Vermont's long history of foraged fruit and farmhouse fermentation. Putney harnesses the seasonal abundance of local orchards and regional farms, from which they bottle an impressive portfolio. Sparkling apple, dry Asian pear, blueberry, and lauded rhubarb wines, as well as fortified pommeau and cassis, can be sampled at the landmark Basketville Store that houses the winery and main tasting room. There are satellite tasting locations: the southernmost is in Wilmington, another is in the Cabot Cheese Store adjacent to impressive Quechee Gorge, and a third in Windsor, at Artisans Park (also home to Harpoon Brewery, Silo Distillery and the Vermont Farmstead Cheese Company). *www.putneywine.com; tel 802-387-5925; 8 Bellows Falls Rd, Putney; 11am-5pm daily* ⑤

⑮ FRESH TRACKS FARM

Sustainability and eco-friendliness guide Fresh Tracks Farm's diversified agricultural operation. Owner and head winemaker Christina Castegren and her team strive to deliver high-quality beverages to community members and visitors alike. The fruit from 14 acres of cold-climate vines and the sap from 1000 maple taps are collected and prepared in a state-of-the-art facility supported by geothermal climate-control systems and solar-power production. The comfortable and welcoming tasting room is located just a few miles from the golden dome of the Vermont statehouse building, as well as the shops and eateries of downtown Montpelier, the nation's smallest capital city. *www.freshtracksfarm.com; tel 802-223-115; 4373 VT-12, Berlin; 1-8pm Wed-Sat, 1-6pm Sun*

⑯ BOYDEN VALLEY WINERY

Boyden is a century-old, four-generation farm. Once a dairy and sugarbush (a stand of sugar-maple trees), many of its 10,000 maple taps have turned from syrup making to fermentation at one of

Vermont's foundational wineries. Set in a magnificent location, Boyden produces a wide range of libations from cold-climate grape wines and fruit wines, including a seasonal favourite cranberry, to ciders and spirits. The harvest from Boyden's trees and vines is supplemented by the orchards of local farmers, to acquire the best raw materials and support an agricultural economy. Sustainability and accessibility direct a style that shows in both their products and their public spaces. Visit the renovated 1875 carriage barn in Cambridge or the annex tasting space in Waterbury's landmark Cold Hollow Cider Mill.

www.boydenvalley.com; tel 802-644-8151; 64 VT-104, Cambridge; 10am-5pm daily 💲

07 SNOW FARM WINERY

Snow Farm is Vermont's oldest continually operating winery dedicated solely to traditional cool-climate varieties and modern cold-climate grapes. It was planted on land purchased from the Lane family's Dairy farm on South Hero Island and had blazed the trail for two decades when the Lanes acquired the operation; they continue to produce wine with guidance from the project's original winemaker. Happily, it's sited along one of the most captivating bicycle routes in the northeastern United States. 'Many people are attracted to the seven-day-a-week bicycle ferry, love the quest of travelling around the islands on their bikes, and visit for a wine tasting and a bite to eat,' says proprietor Julie Lane. 'We have guests from all over the world who come to the summer concert series.' Snow Farm also offers B&B lodging at their neighbouring 1820s farmhouse with a view of Mt Mansfield, the state's highest peak.

www.snowfarm.com; tel 802-318-3208; 190 W Shore Rd, South Hero; 11am-5pm daily May-Dec, rest of year Sat & Sun only

WHERE TO STAY

HOTEL VERMONT
Cosmopolitan style meets woodsy allure at this independently operated boutique lodging on the beautiful Lake Champlain waterfront. Amazing views and an easy walk to the downtown marketplace. www.hotelvt.com; tel 855-650-0080; 41 Cherry Street, Burlington

WOODSTOCK INN & RESORT
Central location in a classically quaint village known for shopping, architecture and the Marsh-Billings-Rockefeller National Historic Park. Dining, golf, ski hill and trails, fitness centre and spa. www.woodstockinn.com; tel 888-338-2745; The Green, Woodstock

WHERE TO EAT

HEN OF THE WOOD
This multiple James Beard Award-winning restaurant inhabits an old mill building in Waterbury and captivated diners with a mission based on farm-sourced ingredients and elegant but unpretentious dining. A second, more urban location in Burlington serves the same sensible, seasonal cuisine and maintains an equally impressive wine list and cocktail bar. www.henofthewood. com; Waterbury: tel 802-244-7300; 92 Stowe St. Burlington: tel 802-540-0534; 55 Cherry St

AMERICAN FLATBREAD
These wood-fired pizzas have been Vermont favourites for over three decades. With the belief that good health and good lives come from good food, the makers employ organic flours and a network of local farms and dairies to source the cheeses, vegetables and meats. Ovens are located in downtown Burlington, Middlebury and the original home at Lareau Farm in Waitsfield, where lodging is available in a historic 18th-century farmhouse. www.americanflatbread .com; tel 802-496-8856

WHAT TO DO

Rising above the Lake Champlain Valley, just off VT RT7, Mt Philo was designated as Vermont's first state park in 1924. A notable geographic feature, it has twice been an island in the past 12,000 years. A short trail hike or ride up the seasonal access road provides views of the valley, the lake, the Adirondack Mountains and the spine of the Green Mountains. View raptors there and witness the annual bird migrations. www.vtstateparks.com/ philo; tel 802-425-2390

CELEBRATIONS

THE VERMONT CHEESE-MAKERS FESTIVAL
Sample and purchase from the state's world-class cheese producers at this summer event in the Coach Barn of historic Shelburne Farms. Many of Vermont's wineries attend, as do a number of craft-beer, cider and spirit makers. www.vtcheesefest.com; tel 866-261-8595

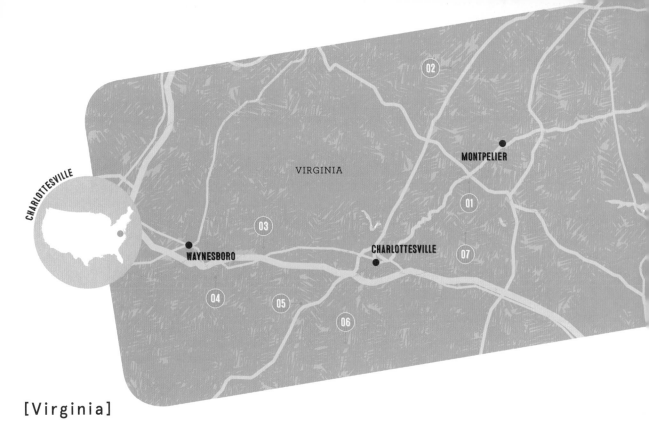

VIRGINIA

MONTPELIER

CHARLOTTESVILLE

WAYNESBORO

01

02

03

04

05

06

07

[Virginia]

CHARLOTTESVILLE

Once a sleepy college town, Charlottesville is now the epicentre of a thriving viticultural and culinary renaissance with an enjoyably varied selection of drops.

The spirit of Founding Father Thomas Jefferson infuses central Virginia's wine country – so much so that the Monticello American Viticultural Area (AVA) is named for his estate just south of Charlottesville. Jefferson planted European grape varieties three different times on his property, but never succeeded in making wine — the grapes were ravaged by birds, Hessian war prisoners and the phylloxera root louse. Today, however, the region's vintners are producing first-class wines. Bordeaux-style blends based on Merlot shine, but central Virginia refuses to be pigeonholed. Look for delicious Vermentino, flowery and fruity Petit Manseng, and brawny Tannat.

In Charlottesville, you can rub shoulders with students from the University of Virginia while wandering shops and testing out restaurants along the downtown pedestrian mall, or explore the local-food bounty at the Saturday morning farmers' market. A short drive from town puts you in the countryside, where you might catch a polo match at a local winery or sip a Cabernet Franc while enjoying the views of the Blue Ridge Mountains to the west.

This area is also riddled with history. Local cideries are reviving the heirloom apple varieties Jefferson and his contemporaries used to make cider, their daily tipple. And the homes of Jefferson, James Madison and James Monroe, three early American presidents, are open to visitors. Even modern politics intrudes — Trump Winery is here, after all.

GET THERE
Charlottesville has a small airport. It is a 90-minute drive from Richmond Airport and two hours from Washington Dulles Airport.

Courtesy of Early Mountain Vineyards / Andrea Hubbell

01 BARBOURSVILLE VINEYARDS

Barboursville, owned by the Zonin family of Italian wine fame, ignited Virginia's wine industry when it was founded in 1976. It has succeeded in embodying the ethos of Mr Jefferson. The estate was once owned by James Barbour, a governor of Virginia and friend of Jefferson's. The ruins of Barbour's mansion, designed by Jefferson, grace the grounds and the winery's labels. Barboursville's icon wine is called Octagon, after the shape of the rotundas Jefferson designed at Monticello and Barboursville.

With more than 180 acres under vine, Barboursville is one of Virginia's largest wineries and the most important commercially. Virginia's preference for Bordeaux grape varieties is apparent here, particularly in the Cabernet Franc and Merlot-based Octagon. More recently the emphasis has been on Italian grapes such as Vermentino, Fiano, Ribolla Giallo and Nebbiolo.

The Barboursville tasting room can get crowded. Slip away to the Library 1821, open on weekends, for a reserve tasting of older vintages in a more relaxed atmosphere. And don't miss the dessert wine Paxxito, made from air-dried Muscat Ottonel and Vidal grapes. The winery also has a small, elegant inn and a north-Italian restaurant. *www.bbvwine.com; tel 540-832-3824; 17655 Winery Rd, Barboursville; 10am–5pm Mon–Sat, 11am–5pm Sun* ✖💲

02 EARLY MOUNTAIN VINEYARDS

Around 30 miles northeast of Charlottesville, Early Mountain is a great stop for wine-lovers heading to wine country from Washington along US29. The winery was bought in 2011 by Steve and Jean Case, two founders of America Online, and has been renovated and rejuvenated since. The tasting room serves a Best of Virginia selection, allowing visitors to sample wines from other producers around the state, along with gourmet snacks and, often, live music. The winery has a small cottage if you fancy staying overnight, too.

The Cases have also invested in new vineyard sources for the wines. Star drops include savoury Cabernet Franc, racy Chardonnay and a delightful white blend based on Petit Manseng. *www.earlymountain.com; tel 540-948-9005; 6109 Wolftown-Hood Rd, Madison; 11am–5pm Wed–Mon* ✖💲

03 KING FAMILY VINEYARDS

Care for some polo during your winery tours? On Sundays from late May to mid-October, King Family Vineyards morphs into Roseland Polo, with matches providing a genteel and wine-soaked diversion. Polo enthusiasts David and Ellen King were looking for a flat space for a polo field when they bought the property in 1995; fortunately, there was also excellent vineyard territory on more sloping land just out of sight of the tasting room.

Today, King Family Vineyards produces some of Virginia's finest Viogniers and Bordeaux-style red wines. The Meritage, a red blend, is re-released six years after vintage to show how the wine ages. Winemaker Matthieu Finot tinkers with what he calls a 'small-batch series' of experimental wines that are a good incentive to join the winery club. *www.kingfamilyvineyards.com; tel 434-823-7800; 6550 Roseland Farm, Crozet; 10am–5.30pm Thu–Tue, to 8.30pm Wed* 💲

04 VERITAS VINEYARD & WINERY

Veritas was part of the Virginia wine boom that ignited at the turn of the 21st century. It started with five acres under vine but now has more than 50 acres planted. Winemaker Emily Pelton consistently produces outstanding Viognier and Sauvignon Blanc among white wines; her Petit Verdot and Cabernet Franc shine among the reds. Linger over a bottle on the veranda while soaking up the view of the Blue Ridge Mountains to the west.

Veritas is a popular event and wedding venue, and the tasting room gets busy on weekends. Starry Nights see live concerts and revelry on the second Saturday of the month from June to September, and, on New Year's Eve, the winery hosts a masked ball.

The Farmhouse at Veritas, a small inn with eight rooms, provides a comforting oasis.

Courtesy of Early Mountain Vineyards / Tom McGovern

01 The interior at Early Mountain Vineyards

02 Outdoor scene at Early Mountain Vineyards

03 Accommodation at Barboursville

www.veritaswines.com; tel 540-456-8000; 151 Veritas Lane, Afton; 9.30am–5.30pm Mon–Fri, 11am–5pm Sat & Sun 💲

05 ALBEMARLE CIDERWORKS

When Thomas Jefferson wasn't drinking wine, he drank cider, as many did in colonial times. Today, Virginia is at the heart of the cider renaissance that has gripped the USA since the late 2000s. Albemarle Ciderworks uses some of the same apple varieties Jefferson employed to make cider, such as Hewes Crab and Royal Pippin. Apple orchards rather than vineyards grace the views here, but sampling its various tipples might well convince you that cider and wine have a lot in common.

The Shelton family has worked to preserve heirloom cider apple varieties and make them available to other cider growers. These are not the common eating apples we know today, but more tannic varieties that need fermentation to release their goodness.

www.albemarleciderworks.com; tel 434-297-2326; 2545 Rural Ridge Lane, North Garden; 11am–5pm daily, closed Mon & Tue Jan–Jun 💲

06 MICHAEL SHAPS WINEWORKS

Michael Shaps came to Virginia in 1995 after learning enology in Burgundy and played a major role in starting several wineries in the Charlottesville area. Since 2007 he has been at Wineworks, in an old winery building carved into a hill south of town. As a custom crush facility, it serves as an incubator for new labels that don't yet have their own wineries.

Shaps can innovate in a crunch: during one particularly rainy vintage, he installed two old tobacco-drying sheds to get water off the grapes before pressing. He still uses them today to help concentrate some wines. He is best known for his Cabernet Franc and a dry version of Petit Manseng, but also produces a lush Viognier and one of Virginia's best Chardonnays. The latter should

come as no surprise, as he also makes wine in Burgundy under the Maison Shaps label. Visitors to this winery can sample both. There's also a Charlottesville tasting room, Wineworks Extended, for anyone who can't make it to the winery. *www.virginiawineworks.com Michael Shaps Wineworks: tel 434-529-6848; 1781 Harris Creek Way, Charlottesville; 11am–5pm daily Wineworks Extended: 1585 Avon Street Extended, Charlottesville; 1–7pm daily* 💲

07 KESWICK VINEYARDS

In the rolling countryside northeast of Charlottesville, Keswick Vineyards produces some of Virginia's most medal-awarded wines, including outstanding Viognier (both oaked and unoaked), and deep reds from Cabernet Sauvignon and Cabernet Franc. Keswick also makes a fine Touriga, from the Portuguese grape.

Aspiring winemakers can join Keswick's wine club and participate in an annual blending competition: the winning wine is sold as Consensus Red. The tasting room has an outdoor space for picnicking. *www.keswickvineyards.com; tel 434-244-3341, 1575 Keswick Winery Dr, Keswick; 10am–5pm daily* 💲

WHERE TO STAY

THE 1804 INN AND COTTAGES

Barboursville Vineyards' Georgian inn was built in 1804, before the winery's Jefferson-designed mansion, whose ruins lie next door. Today, the inn and its historical cottages provide a luxurious country hideaway with Italian flair.
www.bbvwine.com; tel 540-832-5384; 17655 Winery Rd, Barboursville

THE FARMHOUSE AT VERITAS

This plushly styled B&B adjacent to Veritas Winery has mountain and vineyard views along with bountiful breakfasts and dinners. Choose from six elegant rooms with 19th-century inspiration, or a two-room, kitchen-equipped cottage.
www.veritasfarmhouse. com; tel 540-456-8100; 72 Saddleback Farm, Afton

BOAR'S HEAD

An elegant resort with classically styled rooms on 573 green-clad acres just west of Charlottesville, convenient to wineries and downtown, while also giving you a sense of the country. Try golf, tennis or squash, then unwind with a spa treatment.
www.boarsheadresort. com; tel 844-611-8066; 200 Ednam Drive, Charlottesville

WHERE TO EAT

PALLADIO

Palladio offers refined north-Italian cuisine at Barboursville Vineyards, plus the chance to taste some older reserve vintages of Barboursville wine. The chefs get immersion training, with the restaurant closing each January and the entire crew taking a culinary tour of Italy.
www.bbvwine.com; tel 540-832-7848; 17655 Winery Rd, Barboursville; noon–2.30pm Wed, Thu & Sun, noon–2.30pm & 6.30–9.30pm Fri & Sat

BBQ EXCHANGE

Worth seeking out for its fine Virginia 'cue, the BBQ Exchange is just a short detour from the eastern edge of the Monticello Wine Trail.
www.bbqex.com; tel 540-832-0227; 102 Martinsburg Ave, Gordonsville; 11am–8 pm daily

FLEURIE

Intimate modern-French restaurant steps from Charlottesville's pedestrian-only downtown mall, with a terrific wine list, including many Virginia labels.
www.fleurierestaurant. com; tel 434-971-7800; 108 3rd St NE, Charlottesville; 5.30–9pm Mon–Thu, to 10pm Fri & Sat

THE ALLEY LIGHT

Hard to find and harder to get into, this quirky venue offers small plates with French flair, along with a great wine selection. It's the place to see and be seen in C'ville.
www.alleylight.com; tel 434-296-5003; 108 2nd St SW, Charlottesville; 5-11pm Tue & Sun, to midnight Wed & Thu, to 2am Fri & Sat

TASTINGS OF CHARLOTTESVILLE

The retail section of this restaurant-shop hybrid is in effect a self-serve wine list, with plenty of selections to match the robust cuisine of chef-owner Bill Curtis.
www.tastingsofcville. com; tel 434-293-3663, 502 E Market St, Charlottesville; 11.30am–2.30pm Tue, Wed & Thu, 11.30am–2.30pm & 6-9pm Fri & Sat

WHAT TO DO

History buffs will want to visit Montpelier, the home of James Madison, the country's fourth president. The area's main historical attraction, of course, is Jefferson's home at Monticello, just south of Charlottesville. A little further down the road from Monticello is Jefferson Vineyards, on land where Jefferson actually planted vines. Music fans may want to continue on to Blenheim Vineyards, owned by rock musician Dave Matthews.

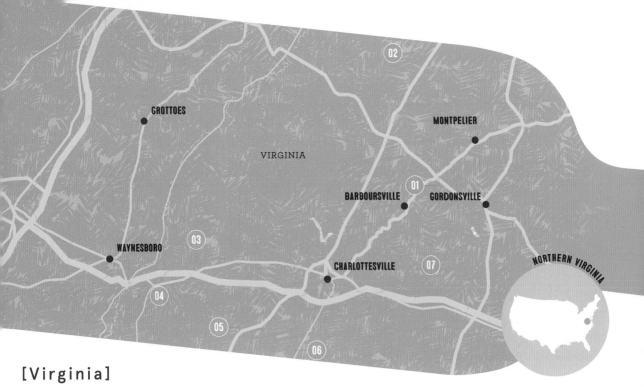

[Virginia]

NORTHERN VIRGINIA

West of Washington DC's political drama, northern Virginia's tranquil wine country turns out top-quality Bordeaux blends and Viogniers amid sprawling vineyard views.

Venture west from Washington DC and, traffic willing, within an hour you'll escape the suburban sprawl into farmlands, with the Blue Ridge Mountains looming on the horizon. Veer off the main roads and you'll find yourself in hunt country or in small Federal-era towns. This is Civil War territory, from the Manassas battlefields to Harper's Ferry, where Mosby's Rangers bedeviled Union troops defending the capital.

But this is also wine country. Virginia's wine industry exploded in the early 2000s, growing from 120 to 280 wineries and becoming the fifth-largest wine-producing state in the USA. The growth centred on the eastern slopes of the Blue Ridge. Virginia's bid for quality focuses on Bordeaux-style red blends, but there's still a frontier spirit of experimentation. Petit Verdot and Tannat do well here among red grapes, while Viognier,

Petit Manseng and Albariño thrill among white wines.

Quality-minded vintners continue scouting out steep slopes with rocky soils of granite or sandstone to provide drainage as a guard against Virginia's sometimes rainy summers. These sites often produce fantastic Cabernet Sauvignon and Petit Verdot. As you explore the region, ask your hosts what excites them. They may tell you about a new vineyard being planted, something to look forward to next time.

In northern Virginia, you'll find wineries that provide a diversion from city life — a place to picnic or enjoy live music. You'll also uncover an iconoclastic vintner championing Virginia's native wine grape, the Norton, and mountain rebels planting vines on sheer slopes to push Virginia wine's quality ever higher. While you're here, check out Virginia's equestrian events, arts and crafts, and its exciting craft beer, cider and spirits.

GET THERE
Washington Dulles International Airport is minutes from northern Virginia's wine country. Or take a day trip from Washington DC.

01 CHRYSALIS VINEYARDS

Jennifer McCloud is so enthusiastic about Norton, the grape developed in the 1820s by Dr Richard Norton in Richmond, Virginia, that she trademarked the phrase: 'Norton – the REAL American grape!' At Chrysalis, she also boasts the world's largest planting of Norton at more than 40 acres. Chrysalis produces it in a variety of styles, from a light, gulpable rosé called Sarah's Patio Red to a serious Bordeaux-like Locksley Reserve. Chrysalis also demonstrated that Albariño can flourish in northern Virginia, and other white wines here include a top-notch Viognier and a Petit Manseng.

At her ambitious new tasting facility (with an adults-only tasting space), dubbed The Ag District, McCloud is embracing the idea of farm as ecosystem. An artisan cheesemaking facility is in the works, and culinary surprises use eggs from free-range chickens and beef from heritage cattle reared on the estate.
www.chrysaliswine.com; tel 540-687-8222; 39025 John Mosby Hwy, Middleburg; daily, hours vary by season 💲

02 BOXWOOD ESTATE WINERY

The genteel hunt country town of Middleburg has lost some luster since its heyday when John and Jackie Kennedy had an estate nearby, but it's still a destination for wine-lovers. Thanks largely to the efforts of Rachel Martin, executive vice president of Boxwood Estate, Middleburg became Virginia's seventh American Viticultural Area (AVA) in 2012.

Boxwood is owned by John Kent Cooke, a communications magnate and former owner of the Washington Redskins football team. With famed Bordeaux enologist Stephane Derenoncourt consulting, Boxwood emphasises stylish Bordeaux blends based on Cabernet Sauvignon, Cabernet Franc and Merlot. Recent expansions include Sauvignon Blanc and Sauvignon Gris. You can easily pop in for a tasting, though reservations are required for groups of 10 or more.
www.boxwoodwinery.com; tel 540-687-8778; 2042 Burrland Ln, Middleburg; 11am–6pm Fri-Sun 💲

03 RDV VINEYARDS

When Rutger de Vink abandoned corporate life to become a vigneron, he looked briefly at land in California but settled on

(03)

a rugged hill of decomposing granite in northern Virginia that the previous owner had only deemed suitable for grazing sheep. RdV is now Virginia's most renowned winery, and, from its initial launch of the 2008 vintage, its wines have stood among the best in the world.

Huddled into the hillside, the winery resembles a barn — a tribute to the region's agriculture. The minimalist interior, however, displays an intense modernist focus on quality at any expense but without unnecessary frills. Visits are by appointment only, with parties limited to four guests, and include a tour of the winery and its 16 acres of meticulously planted vineyards, amid 360-degree views of the Blue Ridge foothills. And, of course, there's a tasting of RdV's two Bordeaux-style red blends: Lost Mountain, based on Cabernet Sauvignon, and Rendezvous, based on Merlot. This is an in-depth experience for those serious about their wines, rather than the casual visitor.

www.rdvvineyards.com; tel 540-364-0221; 2550 Delaplane Grade Rd, Delaplane; Thu–Sun by appointment $

04 LINDEN VINEYARDS

Jim Law is a modern-Virginia wine pioneer, having established Linden Vineyards on a hillside east of Front Royal in 1982, following a stint in the Peace Corps and a few years learning about wine-growing in Ohio. He named his vineyard Hardscrabble, a reflection both of the soil and his work ethic. From this vineyard and with fruit grown by two nearby vintners, Law produces single-vineyard wines intended to express the terroir.

Law's outstanding Chardonnays are often mistaken in blind tastings for fine Burgundies, and his Sauvignon Blancs combine the mineral smack Loire Valley fans crave with American ripeness. Meanwhile, his Cabernet Sauvignon-based blends just keep getting better.

You pass Law's own home as you approach the winery, which resembles a mountain cabin in its elegant rusticity; the spare but comfortable tasting room sits above the crowded cellar and production space. A note for visitors: large groups are discouraged and the porch with its vineyard views is reserved for winery club members (buy a case and you're a member). Reserve

tastings in the cellar are offered on Saturday so seize the opportunity! www.lindenvineyards.com; tel 540-364-1997; 3708 Harrels Corner Rd, Linden; 11am–5pm Fri–Sun Apr–Nov, 11am–5pm Sat & Sun Dec–Mar ⑤

⑤ GLEN MANOR VINEYARDS

Settle into a chair with a glass of Jeff White's award-winning Hodder Hill red blend and you might spot a parasailor floating over the vineyards on the slopes above you. Glen Manor, seven miles southwest of Front Royal, lies just below the Skyline Trail, a scenic byway along the Blue Ridge Mountains in Shenandoah National Park. Don't get so distracted that you forget to try the excellent Petit Verdot and Petit Manseng...

It's an intimate tasting experience here with a maximum of six people per group.
www.glenmanorvineyards.com; tel 540-635-6324; 2244 Browntown

Rd, Front Royal; 11am–5pm Mon & Fri–Sat, noon–5pm Sun ⑤

⑥ BREAUX VINEYARDS

With more than 100 acres under vine, Breaux is northern Virginia's biggest winery, producing delicious Cabernet Franc, sophisticated red blends and one of Virginia's finest Viogniers, all of which you can sample on tours and tastings. There's even a tasty tongue-in-cheek sparkling wine called Breauxmance.

Despite its size, Breaux remains a family operation under the watch of Jennifer Breaux. In keeping with the family's Cajun roots, many of the live music and festival events that pepper the winery's calendar have a New Orleans vibe, though the view is of colourful mountains and sweeping vineyards rather than the wrought-iron balconies of the French Quarter. Breaux also offers wine-appreciation classes through its Virginia School of Wine and, given

its location near the West Virginia–Maryland border, makes an ideal stop for combining a wine-tasting jaunt with historical sightseeing in the town of Harpers Ferry. www.breauxvineyards.com; tel 540-668-6299; 36888 Breaux Vineyards Lane, Purcellville; daily, hours vary ⑤

⑦ TARARA VINEYARDS

Just west over the Potomac River from Maryland, Tarara Vineyards is one of Loudoun County's oldest wineries and entertainment venues. The focus for the last decade has been heavily on the wines, and it has certainly paid off in improved quality and wider variety. Winemaker Jordan Harris emphasises single-vineyard blends to express terroir under the Tarara label. He also makes varietal wines, sometimes with out-of-state fruit, called Killer Cluster, and collaborates on another project called Boneyard, whose wines are you can taste at Tarara.

Fun fact: the name Tarara is Ararat spelled backwards, a reference to Mt Ararat, where legend says Noah's Ark came to rest and Noah planted a vineyard. And on Saturdays and Sundays from 11am to noon, tastings are only a penny.
www.tarara.com; tel 703-771-7100, 13648 Tarara Lane, Leesburg; 11am–5pm Mon–Thu, to 6pm Fri & Sun, closed Tue & Wed Nov–Mar ⑤

ESSENTIAL
INFORMATION

WHERE TO STAY

THE ASHBY INN
In the tiny hamlet of Paris, the Ashby Inn offers smart rooms with old-charm hints, plus a restaurant and a little history. Confederate General Thomas Jackson rested on the original porch on his way to the battle of First Manassas, where he earned his famous nickname, 'Stonewall'. *www.ashbyinn.com; tel 540-592-3900; 692 Federal St, Paris*

SALAMANDER RESORT & SPA
Modern luxury in Middleburg, at the heart of Virginia's hunt and wine country, along with spa treatments, cooking classes and elegant, soothing-toned rooms with fireplaces. Local wines feature in the Gold Cup Bar. *www.salamanderresort. com; tel 844-303-2723; 500 North Pendleton St, Middleburg*

WHERE TO EAT

FIELD & MAIN
Just a stone's throw from the I66 highway, the sleepy Federal-era hamlet of Marshall has morphed into a gastronomic hub. Leading this revival is Field & Main, which personifies the farm-to-table zeitgeist with locally raised meats and produce cooked on an open hearth. Proprietor Neal Wavra is a champion of Virginia's wine industry, and offers several of the Commonwealth's top vinos, including some on tap. If you pass through too early for dinner, stop in at the nationally acclaimed Red Truck Bakery across the street. *www.fieldandmain restaurant.com; tel 540-364-8166; 8369 W Main St, Marshall; 5.30–9pm*

Thu, Fri & Mon, 11am–2pm & 5.30–9pm Sat & Sun

MONK'S BBQ
Monk's is the go-to place for sustenance when you haven't got time to linger over a long lunch between wineries. Smoked brisket, pulled pork and the meat-lover's delight, bacon-on-a-stick, are for the asking, along with a tantalising assortment of barbecue sauces. No fancy place settings here, just tin trays and butcher paper. But Monk's takes no shortcuts with its food and offers plenty of local brews and spirits. *www.monksq.com; tel 540-751-9425; 251 N 21st St, Purcellville; 5–10pm Mon & Tue, 11.30am–*

11pm Wed & Thu, 11.30am–midnight Fri & Sat, 11.30am–9pm Sun

THE RESTAURANT AT PATOWMACK FARM
For a relaxing dinner of refined modern-American cuisine after a long day of winery hopping, look no farther than The Restaurant at Patowmack Farm, which, in true farm-to-table spirit, grows most of its own produce. *www.patowmackfarm. com; tel 540-822-9017; 42461 Lovettsville Rd, Lovettsville; 5.30–8.30pm Thu & Fri, 11am–1.30pm & 5.30–8.30pm Sat, 11am–1.30pm Sun*

WHAT TO DO
Nature lovers will want to journey along the Skyline Drive or hike part of the Appalachian Trail, especially in October when autumn leaves tinge the mountains in a riot of colour. Fans of aviation should not miss the spectacular exhibits at the National Air and Space Museum's Steven F Udvar-Hazy Center near Dulles airport.

05

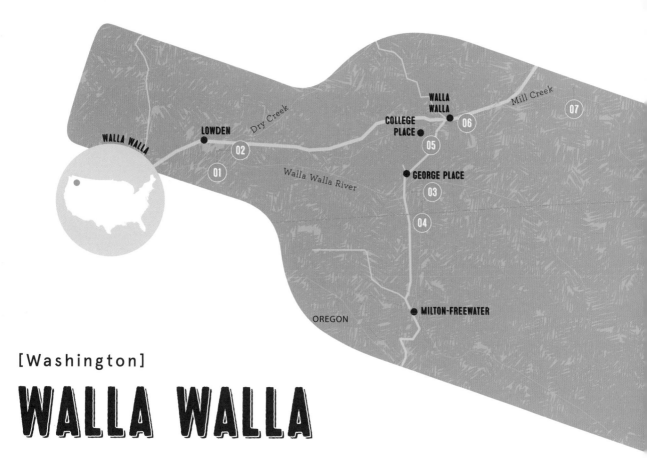

[Washington]

WALLA WALLA

A breadth of world-class wines, first-rate dining and spectacular scenery — this is Washington at its best. As one winemaker says: 'We sold everything we had in New York and moved to Walla Walla.'

Beneath the Blue Mountains on the eastern side of Washington, the Walla Walla Valley has become a remarkable story of rural transformation. The area has always been known for its agriculture, but three decades ago the valley and the town were struggling. Then the grape vines arrived. Today, Walla Walla is one of Washington's most celebrated wine regions. It is also the best equipped for wine-country travel, with an enticing mix of tasting rooms, charming local eateries, comfortable bed & breakfasts and new luxury hotels. Washington's desert country is quite a landscape, too: sweeping, arid, with wide open, sunny skies. The road from Seattle takes you over the Cascade Range, which in winter has some of the best downhill skiing in the Pacific Northwest (if driving at that time of year,

check the roads are open and you have snow tyres).

In the town of Walla Walla itself, tasting rooms can be found throughout the downtown area as well as at some wineries on the outskirts. Almost half of the Walla Walla AVA sits below the Oregon border just a few minutes south of town, but most of the wineries are located in the Washington half. If you're in the market for world-class Syrah, the Rocks District of Milton-Freewater AVA has become one of the new hot spots of the region.

While tasting through the region, be sure to allow some time to enjoy a walk around the town of Walla Walla itself. The town has developed a justified reputation for good wine and food. Some of the best chefs in the state have relocated to open newer restaurants in the eastside town.

GET THERE
Fly directly into Walla Walla regional airport, or drive east four hours over the Cascade Mountains from Seattle.

01 WOODWARD CANYON

Founded by Rick and Darcey Fugman-Small in 1981, Woodward Canyon was only the second winery in Walla Walla. Today their daughter Jordan works in the vineyards and winery alongside her father. The vineyards on the family farm are located in the Woodward Canyon for which the winery is named. The Smalls have kept their focus on small-production, artisanal wine meant to celebrate the distinctive character of Washington. The tasting room stands in the family's restored 1870s farmhouse, and inside you'll find charming and well-informed staff. Keep an eye out for their Cabernet and Merlot, but you can also expect a few unusual varieties such as Charbonneau made in small lots.
www.woodwardcanyon.com; tel 509-525-4129; 11920 US-12, Lowden; 10am–5pm daily ✕ 💲

02 L'ECOLE NO 41

West of Walla Walla, the small community of Frenchtown was founded in the 19th century by French Canadians. Today the village is called Lowden and the original L'Ecole No 41, which became the Lowden Schoolhouse, serves as the tasting room for this third-generation family-owned winery. The Clubb family established L'Ecole No 41 in the early 1980s and led the charge for sustainable farming. When it comes to winemaking, L'Ecole believes 'in well-balanced wines, good acidity and firm but not overpowering tannins'. You'll find that class in their Ferguson Estate red, a blend of Bordeaux varieties grown in the region's highest vineyard. It's one of Washington's most distinctive wines and ages well.
www.lecole.com; tel 509-525-0940; 41 Lowden School Rd, Lowden; 10am–5pm daily ✕ 💲

03 AMAVI CELLARS

The name Amavi is a combination of 'amor' and 'vita'. And no one has done more than the winery's founder, Norm McKibben, to support the life of Walla Walla wine. He got started in grapes by getting started with apples. 'All I meant to do was help out a couple of friends who had [an apple] packing house and were struggling,' he says. Norm then got talked into planting wine grapes. Now, Amavi concentrates on wines made entirely from the Amavi Vineyards in Walla Walla, all certified sustainable. One of the state's most celebrated winemakers, Jean-François Pellet, maintains the soils; in the cellar

01 The exterior of Seven Hills Winery

02 Woodward Canyon Cabernet Sauvignon

03 Learn about wine at L'Ecole No 41

04 The crush at L'Ecole No 41

05 An aerial view of L'Ecole No 41

06 The Marcus Whitman Hotel

the goal is transparency. A visit to the tasting room also offers beautiful vistas of that Walla Walla sky. Pop in for a flight of wines, or call ahead for a tour of the winery and vineyards followed by a private tasting in the barrel room. *www.amavicellars.com; tel 509-525-3541; 3796 Peppers Bridge Rd, Walla Walla; by appointment* ✕ 💲

04 PEPPERBRIDGE

Pepperbridge is a collaboration between three families: the McKibbens, Goffs and Pellets. 'Terroir is a vague word but it means a lot to me,' says winemaker Jean-François Pellet. 'We all want that sense of place.' The wine programme is dedicated to Bordeaux varieties. The flagship wine, Trine, is a blend of the five Bordeaux varieties — Cabernet Sauvignon, Merlot, Cabernet Franc, Malbec, Petit Verdot — with the proportions changing by vintage. Pepperbridge also bottles varietally oriented wines, particularly Cabernet Sauvignon and Merlot. The latter has become one of the signature varieties of Walla Walla, with bursting fruits and savoury herbs followed by that crystalline acidity. Stop into the Pepperbridge tasting room for a flight of wines and views of the Blue Mountains. *www.pepperbridge.com; tel 509-525-6502; 1704 J B George Rd, Walla Walla; 10am–4pm daily; larger parties book ahead* ✕ 💲

05 GRAMERCY CELLARS

Master sommelier Greg Harrington spent his restaurant career overseeing some of the country's finest wine lists. 'Visiting Walla Walla, we realised that one could make earthy, balanced wines,' he says. 'We sold everything we owned in NYC and moved to Washington.' Harrington's Gramercy Cellars has become one of the most celebrated wineries in the state for making exactly those earthy, balanced wines from Rhone varieties such as Syrah and Grenache and Cabernet Sauvignon. Stop into the tasting room for its minimalist lounge feel and a flight of wines across the portfolio. Schedule in advance for a private tasting during the week, or drop by the winery on Saturdays. *gramercycellars.com; tel 509-876-2427; 625 N 13th Ave, Walla Walla; 11am–5pm Sat and by appt* ✕⑤

⑥ SEVEN HILLS WINERY

Do you want to taste different single-vineyard expressions of Cabernet and Merlot from different Washington AVAs side by side? Then this elegant tasting room is for you. Established in the late 1980s by the McClellan family, Seven Hills Winery works with some of the oldest Cabernet Sauvignon and Merlot vineyards in the Walla Walla Valley and beyond. Stop in to taste through a flight across the portfolio.

Or call ahead to schedule a more educational tasting accompanied by food. The tasting room is a converted warehouse, with high ceilings, natural wood floors, and tons of natural light. It's also right next door to one of the region's celebrated restaurants, Whitehouse Crawford. *www.sevenhillswinery.com; tel 509-529-7198; 212 N 3rd, Walla Walla; 10am–5pm daily* ✕⑤

⑦ A'MAURICE CELLARS

Three generations of the Schafer family work the slopes of the Blue Mountains while also sourcing fruit from some of the finest vineyards in the state. Then daughter Anna

Schafer gets to work in the cellar to create a'Maurice's award-winning wines with a mix of white and red Bordeaux varieties as well as Viognier and Syrah. Wines are bottled with changing art-focused labels; in the Artist Series wines, a Cabernet Sauvignon-based Bordeaux blend features a different painting as the image for each vintage. The tasting room is relaxed and welcoming with an eclectic feel inside the converted workspace (keep an eye on the schedule for some interesting happenings). There is also outside seating, weather permitting. *www.amaurice.com; tel 509-522-5444; 178 Vineyard Ln, Walla Walla; 10.30am–4.30pm Fri & Sat* ✕⑤

Courtesy of L'Ecole No 41 / Colby D Kuschatka; Leon Werdinger / Alamy Stock Photo

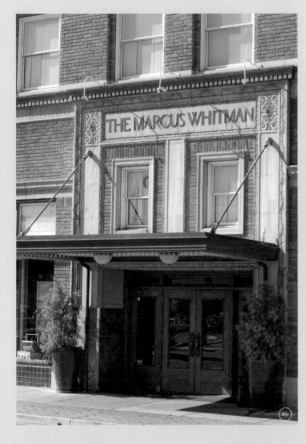

WHERE TO STAY

MARCUS WHITMAN HOTEL

A landmark in the middle of town, bringing together classic styling with contemporary upgrades and modern country comfort in a historic building. Downstairs the hotel includes the Marc Restaurant, one of the region's showpiece culinary experiences, as well as the Vineyard Lounge for drinks. *marcuswhitmanhotel. com; tel 866-826-9422; 6 W Rose St, Walla Walla*

GREEN GABLES INN

Walla Walla has come to be known for its B&Bs. The Green Gables Inn stands in one of the area's original homesteads, with rooms available in the main house or the carriage house in the grounds. Prix-fixe style seasonal dinners with wine pairings are available (reserve in advance). *www.greengablesinn. com; tel 509-876-4373*

WHERE TO EAT

WHITEHOUSE CRAWFORD

Whitehouse Crawford helped usher in high-end seasonal dining in the Walla Walla area when it opened in 2000. The building once operated as a planing mill and furniture company and the current owners retain its historic feel. In the restaurant, you'll enjoy seasonally revolving prix-fixe and à la carte menus relying on the best of the region's gardens and meats and an impressive list of Washington and international wines *whitehousecrawford. com; tel 509-525-2222 55 West Cherry St, Walla Walla; 5–9pm Wed–Mon*

PASSATEMPO TAVERNA

Passatempo Taverna is a firm Walla Walla favourite. The seasonal menu is inspired by the dishes of Italy, using local ingredients. That 'locavore' commitment carries into the cocktails, which are made fresh with seasonal garden ingredients. *passatempowallawalla.*

com; tel 509-876-8822; 215 W Main St, Walla Walla

ANDRAE'S KITCHEN

For a taste of Washington-Mexican cuisine seek out Andrae's Kitchen. It may be in a converted gas station but don't let that fool you. Chef Andrae uses all fresh, local ingredients and the food is delicious. Stop in and get some to-go for a picnic lunch. *andraeskitchen.com; tel 509-572-0728; 706 W Rose Street, Walla Walla*

WHAT TO DO

MCNARY NATIONAL WILDLIFE REFUGE

The McNary National Wildlife Refuge was formed to offset the impact of the McNary Dam. The Refuge has become home to a wealth of indigenous wildlife including a wide range of birds, otters, beavers, mule deer, and migrating animals, and has many walking trails. *www.fws.gov/refuge/ McNary; tel 509-546-8350; 311 Lake Rd, Burbank*

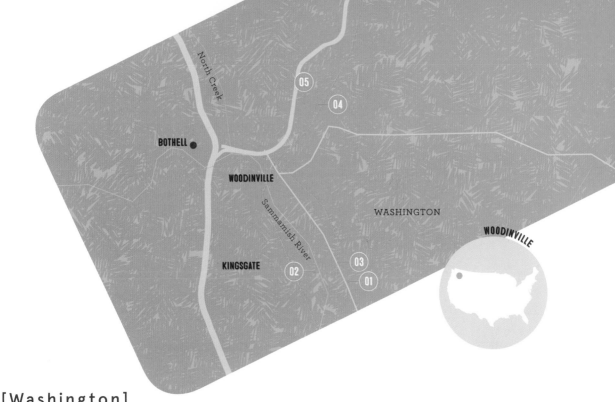

[Washington]

WOODINVILLE

Too pushed to get to the wines of Washington? Let them come to you in the 100 (and counting) tasting rooms of this bustling Seattle exurb.

For those in pursuit of the urban winery experience, Woodinville, on the outskirts of Seattle, is a dream come true. Within a five-mile radius more than 100 tasting rooms jostle for your attention alongside a plethora of breweries and distilleries, and plenty of places to eat. A rented bike is a good way to get around town (or even further afield on the excellent bike trails of greater Seattle). And for those who want to fully enjoy the advantages of the urban tasting rooms, there are plenty of driver services to get you from glass to glass safely.

Tasting rooms for wineries from all over the state of Washington can be found in Woodinville and the range of wines is extraordinary: everything from ultra-crisp dry whites and light bodied reds to dessert wines, via robust reds. Hundreds of varieties grow in the state of Washington. Keep an eye out for fun walk-up food trucks, art displays, and activities along the waterfront as well. For those wanting to venture a little further afield, Seattle proper lives up to its sky-high culinary repuation, particularly its seafood. Summer in western Washington is beautiful — it's generally warm without being hot but things can cool down at night, so pack layers. At this time of year plan for time beside the water, too. In the winter expect rain, not for nothing does this part of Washington have a soggy reputation. Pack appropriately. When the clouds do part, take a moment to drink in the setting: hills, pine forests, mountains, all within fine view from just about anywhere in Woodinville.

GET THERE
Just 19 miles east of downtown Seattle, drive to the north end of Lake Washington, then head east to reach Woodinville.

01 DELILLE CELLARS CARRIAGE HOUSE

Established in the 1990s by a group of friends, DeLille Cellars quickly became associated with premium wine from the state of Washington. Few other wineries have risen so swiftly. A boutique-sized producer, DeLille keeps the focus on smaller lots, and handcrafted wines. As winemaker Chris Upchurch says: 'We believe that Washington is a Grand Cru wine-growing region. The challenge for us is to create special wines from the expressive terroir Mother Nature gave us.' The wines are primarily blends of Bordeaux varieties, as well as a blend of vineyards. The winery works with some of the oldest, best-known vineyards in the state.

The tasting room is a nod to the smaller chateaux of Bordeaux, rustic and friendly. Stop into the tasting room for a flight across the DeLille portfolio and to learn more about the regions of Washington wine. *www.delillecellars.com; tel 425-489-0544; 14208 Woodinville-Redmond Rd NE, Redmond; 12–5pm daily* ✕ ⑤

02 CHATEAU STE MICHELLE

The biggest producer of wine in the state of Washington, this palatial winery is designed to offer visitors an impressive range of experiences, with multiple tasting areas, gardens, wooded walking trails and outdoor seating options. Though you can walk in to taste from a range of wines from

01 An arty interior at Long Shadows

02 Warming fire at Long Shadows

03 Long Shadows' vineyard in the valley

04 Harvest time at DeLille Cellars

multiple winery portfolios, it is worth considering a call ahead to learn more about the possibilities. Chateau Ste Michelle has its own range of wines, and collaborates with other winemakers to produce several other winery brands, including Eroica, a range of Washington Rieslings made in collaboration with Germany's Ernie Loosen; and Impetus, Washington state's very first winery. A range of private tasting experiences is available including multi-course seasonal meal options relying on ingredients from local gardens, seafood and meats, and in-depth educational tastings. Keep an eye out for an extensive range of events including world-class concerts, and even the occasional masquerade ball. *www.ste-michelle.com; tel 425-488-1133; 14111 NE 145th St, Woodinville; 10am–5pm daily* ✕ ⑤

⑬ LONG SHADOWS

In the early 2000s, Allen Shoup devised a showcase for the world-class potential of Washington wine. The result was five globally renowned winemakers from Germany, Bordeaux, Napa Valley, and the Barossa Valley who continue to work with Long Shadows resident winemaker Gilles Nicault to make a portfolio of wines designed to show off the excellence from Washington's largest AVA, the Columbia Valley. For Nicault, it's a dream come true. 'I am able to work with incredible, celebrated vintners from different wine regions around the world,' says Allen. 'They all come to Washington state. They give me their vision, and they share their techniques and practices.' Wines include Riesling by German winemaker Armin Diel, Cabernet Sauvignon from Napa winemaker Randy Dunn, Merlot from Bordeaux's Michel Rolland and more, each in their own packaging – it's designed to be an ultra-premium experience. Drop into the warm, den-like tasting room to sample across the portfolio (some wines are only available by the bottle). *www.longshadows.com; tel 425-408-1608; 14450 Woodinville-Redmond Rd, Woodinville; 12–5pm daily* ✕ ⑤

⑭ WILLIAM CHURCH WINERY

William Church helped bring attention to the burgeoning urban winery scene in Washington. A trip to Italy gave owners Rod & Leslie Balsley the idea that 'fine wine can fit into the fabric of life and be a part of creating lasting shared memories'. They started making wine at home as a hobby, eventually becoming one of the first to convert a warehouse in Woodinville

(04)

into an urban winery. Winemaker Noah Fox Reed keeps the focus on robust reds across a range of varieties and from vineyards all over the state. You're sure to find Syrah full of flavour, and Cabernet Sauvignon that's both spiced and juicy. Check out their attention-getting Viognier as well. The tasting room is casual, designed to be a fun hang out space to visit with friends or your family. *www.williamchurchwinery.com; tel 425-482-2510; 19495 144th Ave NE, Suite A100, Woodinville; 12–5pm Sat & Sun* ✕ ⑤

05 SAVAGE GRACE

The inspiration behind Michael Grace's winery was Cabernet

'The challenge for us is to create special wines from the expressive terroir that Mother Nature gave us'

– Chris Upchurch, DeLille Cellars

Franc. He fell in love with the lighter-bodied finesse of northern French winemaking. 'I like wines that are fruit and fermentation driven, rather than oak driven,' explains Michael. 'I also like lower-alcohol wines with freshness.' You can expect a sense of transparency, but still plenty of flavour from a range of varietal

wines. He has added Pinot Noir to the portfolio, and many of the wines are now from fruit sourced from the Columbia Gorge AVA along the Washington-Oregon border. The label now includes mouthwatering Riesling, crisp and aromatic Sauvignon Blanc, and even a hat-tip to old France with a bottling of Cot, or Malbec as it's known in the New World. The tasting room is a low-key friendly experience. You can walk in on weekends to taste across the portfolio, or call ahead for an appointment during the week. *savagegracewines.com; tel 206-920-4206; 19501 144th Ave NE, F-1100, Woodinville; 1–5pm Sat & Sun* ✕ ⑤

WHERE TO STAY

EASON ESTATES

The James Skirving House in Bothell is considered one of the historic homes of the region, with architecture from the turn of the century and beautiful gardens. Owners and proprietors Shaun Evans and Beth Rosenzweig restored the house and the result is an enviable combination of charm and comfort. *www.easonestates.com; tel 425-488-7923; 10425 East Riverside Dr, Bothell*

MCMENAMINS ANDERSON SCHOOL

In one of the more unusual finds of the region, the McMenamins Anderson School, the original junior high for the region, has been restored and converted into a multi-use space that includes a brewery, artist studios, eatery, poolside bar and comfortable lodgings. *www.mcmenamins. com/anderson-school; tel 425-398-0122; 18607 Bothell Way NE, Suite B, Bothell*

WHERE TO EAT

THE HERB FARM

The Herb Farm (below) creates rotating multi-course meals to showcase the best of the season. Each course is matched with wine from the state. It's one of Washington state's most praised restaurants, the epitome of casual fine dining, so book early. *theherbfarm.com; tel 425-485-5300; 14590 NE 145th St, Woodinville; 10am–7pm Mon–Sat, till 4.30pm Sun*

THE BARKING FROG

An upscale bistro experience relying entirely on locally grown ingredients, and wines of the Pacific Northwest. Expect low-key sophistication set around an indoor fire pit. *www.willowslodge. com/barking_frog; tel 1-425-424-2999; 14580 NE 145th St, Woodinville; 6–10.30 am, 11.30am– 2.30pm, 5–10pm Mon– Fri, 6am–2.30pm, 5–10pm Sat–Sun*

WHAT TO DO

21 ACRES

The Woodinville experience centres on food and wine. To dig deeper, visit 21 Acres, on the edge of Woodinville, which offers a day out at a working organic farm, as well as a farmer's market and a rotating schedule of cooking classes (recommended) on everything from ramen, to gnocchi, to fermentation and pickling. *21acres.org; tel 425-481-1500; 13701 NE 171st St, Woodinville; 9am– 4pm Tue–Thu and Sat, till 6pm Fri*

BOTHELL SKI & BIKE

Rent a bicycle to enjoy your wine tasting on two wheels, or go a little farther to enjoy a serene ride along Lake Washington. Rentals include a helmet in your size and a bicycle lock as well. *www.bikesale.com; tel 425-486-3747; 8020 Bothell Way NE, Kenmore; 10am– 7pm Mon–Fri, till 5pm Sat, 12–5pm Sun*

05

INDEX

INDEX

CONTRIBUTORS

Ashley Hausman is the first Colorado Master of Wine. Wine sales, writing and education fill her days. She sits on the Colorado Wine Industry Development Board.

Elaine Chukan Brown is the American Specialist for JancisRobinson.com and also runs her own website WakawakaWineReviews.com. Follow her on Instagram as @hawk_wakawaka.

Lorna Parkes is a travel writer/editor who developed a weakness for cellar doors while working for Lonely Planet in Melbourne. Follow her @Lorna_Explorer.

Christina Rasmussen is a London-based writer who unearths authentic and natural wines with stories to tell. See www. christinarasmussen.co. Twitter: @Christina _SvR

Eric Degerman has covered the Northwest's wine for 20 years. The co-founder of Wine Press Northwest magazine and co-owner of GreatNorthwestWine.com is found at @EricDegerman.

Paul Vigna is a writer and editor in Harrisburg who covers East Coast wines. Find him at the Wine Classroom at www.pennlive.com and on Twitter @pierrecarafe.

Dave McIntyre has been the weekly wine columnist for The Washington Post since 2008. He can be found on social media @dmwine and www. dmwineline.com.

James Tidwell, Master Sommelier, is a writer, speaker, consultant, and entrepreneur. He founded the TEXSOM Conference and owns/produces the TEXSOM International Wine Awards.

Todd Trzaskos is Northeast native, a wine writer, author of Wines of Vermont: A History of Pioneer Fermentation, and avid home winemaker. Follow @VTWineMedia.

Doug Frost is a Master of Wine, Master Sommelier, author and wine consultant based in Kansas City. See www.dougfrost.com and @winedogboy on Twitter.

Lenn Thompson writes and publishes thecorkreport. us where he focuses on the wines of the Eastern and Midwestern United States. Follow him on Twitter @lennthompson.

Treve Ring is a wine writer, judge, speaker, and perpetual traveller. She is based on Vancouver Island when not on a plane. Follow her on Instagram @trevering.

First Edition
Published in September 2018 by Lonely Planet Global Limited
CRN 54153
www.lonelyplanet.com
ISBN 978 1 7870 1770 2
© Lonely Planet 2018
Printed in China
10 9 8 7 6 5 4 3 2 1

Managing Director Piers Pickard
Associate Publisher and Commissioning Editor Robin Barton
Art Direction Daniel Di Paolo
Layout Katharine Van Itallie
Editors Isabella Noble, Mike Higgins
Image research Regina Wolek & Ceri James
Cartographer Rachel Imeson
Print Production Nigel Longuet
Cover image Courtesy of Ancient Peaks / Matt Wallace

Authors: Ashley Hausman (Colorado), Christina Rasmussen (Okanagan), Dave McIntyre (Maryland),
Doug Frost (Missouri), Elaine Chukan Brown (California, Oregon & Washington), Eric Degerman (Idaho),
James Tidwell (Texas), Lenn Thompson (New Jersey & New York), Lorna Parkes (Nova Scotia),
Paul Vigna (Pennsylvania), Todd Trzaskos (Vermont), Treve Ring (Ontario, Vancouver Island)

Lonely Planet offices

AUSTRALIA The Malt Store, Level 3, 551 Swanston St, Carlton, Victoria 3053 T: 03 8379 8000

IRELAND Unit E, Digital Court, The Digital Hub, Rainsford St, Dublin 8

USA 124 Linden St, Oakland, CA 94607 T: 510 250 6400

UK 240 Blackfriars Rd, London SE1 8NW T: 020 3771 5100

STAY IN TOUCH lonelyplanet.com/contact

Paper in this book is certified against the
Forest Stewardship Council™ standards.
FSC™ promotes environmentally responsible,
socially beneficial and economically viable
management of the world's forests.